Mileage Maniac

My Genius, Madness and A Touch of Evil to Amass *40 Million* Frequent Flyer Miles

Steve Belkin

ISBN 978-1-7366886-2-5

DISCLAIMERS

I am proud to represent that this book is based on indisputable facts and unvarnished truths, or at least I'm pretty damn sure it is. I mean, this mileage stuff primarily happened fifteen to twenty years ago, and I wasn't taking painstaking notes in anticipation of a best-selling book. Few, if any, people were made privy to my mileage exploits, so I can't lean on others to fill in the gaps of my fuzzy memory.

So, let's leave it at...this book is based on some hopefully accurate facts and some selective truths likely colored by my bias against the mileage program establishment.

ABOUT THE AUTHOR

Anything about me that would be relevant to the reader is in the book, so start reading.

ACKNOWLEDGEMENTS

I have always been a little cynical about the effusive praise heaped on editors in other books I have read. I mean, editors, have a job to do, they are paid reasonably for their efforts, so like any other contractor, they should be doing a great job as a matter of course. And as such, author appreciation should be expressed by paying editors on time, giving them a nice Yelp review, and maybe referring an aspiring writer their way down the line. But fawning public adulation wasting paper and the readers' time?

Well, my apologies to a 3/8ths of a tree and the readers' to-do lists.

Tiffany Hawk shattered my preconceptions about the routine role played by an editor. I'll spare you the gory details about how she transformed a dozen or so vignettes for a tiny hardcore mileage junkie niche into a bona fide novel with far broader appeal. Just know the takeaway here—no Tiffany, no book. Thanks, Tiffany.

As I was writing this book, I was contacted via Facebook by a lady who sent me a screenshot of her ninth-grade diary calendar from 1977 she found rummaging around her detritus in storage. Apparently, over a brief month or two, we played a little tennis together and got an ice cream before she unexpectedly moved to Arizona. And then she sent me a perplexing screenshot of a few letters I sent her. My hotness to the other gender was not remotely at its peak in ninth grade, so I distinctly remember the (very few) girls that I salivated over. This lady was not one of them. And not because she wasn't cute or cool. Lori Passov (Kavanaugh) was apparently my first platonic girl friend, not girlfriend. As we got caught up, the mileage book came up, and she asked if she could read a chapter. A couple of days later, she sent it back with some unsolicited notes, all of which really resonated. She morphed into my shadow editor and, for eighteen more chapters, contributed uncanny insights. Thanks, Lori.

There were a lot of folks in the frequent flyer world who were my brothers-in-arms. But time has passed, and connections have withered. And I figured that if I just used aliases in the book, no one would get mad at me (or sue me) if my rusty recollections didn't match their more clarity of the facts. While many of my mileage stories will seem like one-man-band performances, please know that although they were under the stage, like a Broadway orchestra at the theatre, their collective friendship, influence, and sharing of knowledge were crucial to my individual success. Thanks—you all know who you are.

Randy Petersen was my whack-a-mole. I was always desperately seeking him out for more than a decade, and I rarely found him … until he wanted to be found! And whatever I needed, he delivered. This book was no exception. I nicely hinted, then more frequently hinted, then nicely begged, and then frantically begged for him to oversee the content and then supply a foreword. For four months, it appeared that it just wasn't meant to be …until it was. Randy finally popped out of his hole at some remote ranch with a tequila stash. Before I could 'whack' him, he whacked me with a stunning offer to trumpet my book to his mileage junkie email list just short of a million people. Not to mention the priceless cache and credibility that his mileage guru status brings to the table. Thanks, Randy.

I am hopeless when it comes to original creative artistic visions, but once I actually see something, I know viscerally within five seconds if I love it or hate it. While in self-exile here in Cozumel, I was introduced to a graphic designer. While I was counseled to work with an established online book cover company, they mostly wanted me to have some direction to give them … and I just couldn't. Rosana Kancut met me in person, felt my passion and enthusiasm, and absorbed my longing for something extraordinary, even though I hadn't a clue what extraordinary I was seeking. On the very first try, she submitted a draft that was miraculously spot on. Rosana's book cover is truly an extension of who and what I am. Thanks, Rosana.

"A happy wife is a happy life" is a trite but incredibly true saying. You might think why the appreciation? She flies in business class, gets suite upgrades at hotels; hell, she should be thanking me. She is the primary beneficiary of my mileage largesse. But don't be fooled. She was totally there during the harrowing times when I was still earning the miles and contending with airline program fraud departments, booking thousands of reservations manually before online systems, and some uncomfortable financial maneuverings. But the mileage acrobatics are just a microcosm of my life, so my wife just took everything in her inimitable stride, like she always, somehow, does. Thanks, Julie.

FOREWORD

by Randy Petersen

Founder of *FlyerTalk* and BoardingArea

I started my own quest for the most frequent flyer miles in 1986 and have witnessed most every moment of their assent to become one of the world's most popular currencies and as well—the most gamified. During these years, I've known a variety of frequent flyers ranging from the man who flew too much (United Airlines flyer Tom Stuker with more than 22 million miles flown on a single airline) to the guy who helped popularize a creative way to earn miles, David Phillips, aka The Pudding Guy. Like scores of other frequent flyer miles fans across the world, I've always been enraptured by tales of a mile too far.

In this book, Steve Belkin lays bare that frequent flyer miles greatest innovation wasn't as a reward to the road warrior; it was as a behavior as old as time: #moreplease. When Steve set out to write Mileage Maniac, telling his story is all he was really trying to do. It is far more than that, though. Mileage Maniac is an almost anthropological examination of the attraction of frequent flyer miles. On one level, the gamification of frequent flyer miles is simply a great, rollicking tale which might be dismissed as too outrageous for non-fiction. But it's all too real. In fact, Belkin's ethical struggle of 'when is enough finally enough' became an ongoing dilemma for those travel hackers following his footsteps. While Belkin and his mileage scaling ilk reveled in rounding any earning scheme to the nearest million miles, it seemed as if the programs sensed that a measure of greed was making a mockery of their intended conventional ways to earn frequent flyer miles.

It's a story of a boy-next-door crushing the old world of loyalty program control based on the axiom that whoever has the gold makes the rules. Belkin didn't merely follow the rules. He deciphered, dissected and re-engineered them. By meticulously deconstructing promotional offers and their fine print, Belkin discovered whopping opportunities that the programs' army of marketing, legal and financial departments couldn't find...nor protect against. Belkin followed the rules and yet, ended up with gold!

Filled with unforgettable characters and capped by an astonishing number of schemes, "Mileage Maniac" is the behind-the-scenes, moment-by-moment account of how this hashtag was created #moremiles.

Every good book has "the chapter"—the one most often shared and bookmarked. This book doesn't disappoint. My favorite is the infamous Bhat Run (Chapter 6: Why Crunch The Numbers, When You Can Massage Them) in which Steve befriends a segment of the population in Thailand. You have my permission to skip ahead to this chapter.

It is impossible to read this book today, forty years after the advent of frequent flyer miles, and not wonder what other madcap frequent flyer miles schemes haven't we heard of. But the one thing that we do know once we finish reading this book—Steve Belkin is part of the forty years of that history.

PROLOGUE

This memoir was originally going to be called *Mileage Whore.* It seemed like a pretty provocative title for a book about my two decades of airline mileage exploits. It was edgy and politically incorrect, perfect for grabbing the attention of bookstore browsers. And just enough implied naughtiness and whiff of scandal to hopefully attract some equally negative, but free, media attention from the repressed Right and the outraged Left. From a marketing standpoint, the title was spot on.

I could take a hard look in the mirror and concur that the title seemed to accurately reflect that streetwalker sensibility... that I would do just about anything for a mile.

But my mom had some serious misgivings about the title *Mileage Whore.*

First off, she felt it would besmirch our otherwise well-regarded family name. Secondly, *Mileage Whore* also seemed to connote unsavory motives and murky ethical boundaries. My mom struggled to reconcile those traits with the clear and consistent moral code that I was raised with. She knew that I dabbled in frequent flyer miles, but until she read the first draft of my manuscript, she had no idea that I had earned over 40 million miles, nor any idea about the schemes that were involved to scale to such mileage heights. She felt a very uneasy sense of pride. The sheer volume must signal some kind of achievement. But, precisely because of this mass quantity, she couldn't conceive of how that was even possible…and was troubled by the dubious things I might have done to reach that number.

The manuscript seemed to be riddled with accusations, suspicions, and kangaroo court sessions about the airline Frequent Flyer Programs' (FFPs) unmitigated anger toward my uncanny knack for turning one simple promotion into millions of miles. They called it abuse; I called it scaling!

With all that in mind, my mom nixed the title *Mileage Whore*.

Maybe she was right; maybe the title would indeed have sent the wrong message. I mean, I wouldn't really do *anything* for a mile, just way (way!) more than anyone else. Maybe I was just an extreme hobbyist? After all, earning 40 million miles was an astonishing, maybe even a history-making achievement, so I maybe I should pivot my title search to a more heroic theme.

Mileage Magician
Mileage Wizard
Mileage Acrobat
Mileage Maven

Then I got to thinking about how much incredible complexity, creativity, and resourcefulness these mileage projects required. The motives and ethics notwithstanding, my mileage knowledge and expertise were pretty damn difficult to replicate. Maybe a title that reflected that I was at the bleeding edge of the mileage game.

Mileage Guru
Mileage Einstein
Mileage Genius
Mileage Mastermind

Those were upbeat, although admittedly a bit self-aggrandizing titles, but they were sorely lacking the friction, tension, and moral ambiguity that were actually involved in ramping up the dozen or so major mileage projects. While my hands weren't dirty, they weren't exactly squeaky clean, either. So maybe the title should have a fifth-column theme that while I wasn't actually dangerous … I certainly *could* be.

Mileage Menace
Mileage Fiend
Mileage Rogue
Mileage Guerrilla

Then I pondered if there might be some defensible middle ground between hero and zero. Maybe I was doing good things in a bad way. Or was I doing bad things in a good way?

Mileage Maverick
Mileage Mercenary
Mileage Outlaw
Mileage Rebel

Most people can't resist the cliched but always compelling David vs. Goliath motif. Maybe I should focus on titles that would reflect how I was outgunned by the airline programs, yet I still prevailed to outfox them.

Mileage Conquistador
Mileage Crusader
Mileage Vanquisher
Mileage Champ

While some people might think that 40 million miles would be a gonzo number beyond belief, others might perceive that amount as reflecting a borderline lack of control or discretion. Dare I say obsessive. Maybe the title should describe that my 'enough is enough' button was out of order.

Mileage Junkie
Mileage Addict
Mileage Frankenstein
Mileage Grabber

Maybe some folks would insist that I made very well-thought-out and rational decisions with my hyper-scaling. They might interpret my actions not as out of control but rather as outright and calculated pure greed.

Mileage Vulture
Mileage Scavenger
Mileage Gorger
Mileage Vampire

And then I got to thinking how I might have been perceived by the airlines. For the most of two decades, they were always one step, or more like one mile (!), behind my next mileage scheme. If not Public Enemy Number One, I was certainly in their top ten.

Mileage Raider
Mileage Snatcher
Mileage Marauder
Mileage Stalker

When I submitted this manuscript to my editor, it was a dozen or so self-contained short stories describing distinct mileage earning projects in chronological order. But my editor detected something far deeper than the raw numbers being tallied by my mileage accumulation. She connected the dots of the seemingly disparate short stories.

My original manuscript was about a scrappy mileage collector who continually bested the hapless, overmatched airlines. Everyone in the peanut gallery would be rooting for the lovable, if more than occasionally mischievous, prankster.

My editor, Tiffany, was suggesting a book trajectory that I wasn't sure that I wanted to reveal. Whereas I just wanted to brag about my accumulation of HOW I earned 40 million miles, she was suggesting that I take stock of the emotional, ethical, and moral baggage that was quietly accumulating as well … about WHY I was playing the mileage game. Inadvertently, Tiffany has forced me to get to know myself better. It was a painful, revealing, and I'll readily admit, not so cathartic process.

The final title *Mileage Maniac* straddles my wanting you, the reader, to be wowed by the bright lights of my mileage exploits, with Tiffany's wanting you to be perplexed about the dark shadows that lurked behind some of the motivations and ethics of my mileage earning conduct.

Good, bad, and ugly, I nonetheless nailed that 40 million miles number. My mom will hope that you, dear reader, will choose to focus on the good!

Chapter 1: GOBBLE-GOBBLE

Over the Thanksgiving holiday long weekend in 1988, I, Steve Belkin, flew on a United Airlines two-stop round-trip between Los Angeles and Cleveland via Denver and Chicago. The flight distance was about 4,200 miles for a $250 Economy airfare. Before the flight, I had about 10,000 frequent flyer miles from that year in my United Mileage Plus account and no elite status.

The following weekend when I checked my account, I had 1,035,000 miles and top-tier elite status of Premier Executive for Life.

It wasn't a data entry mishap. Yet, United's fraud department was mum.

I was an effortless instant mileage millionaire. Yet, there was no *Wall Street Journal* featuring me as a mileage guru. *The Johnny Carson* and *David Letterman* shows weren't fighting over exclusive interviews with such a mileage unicorn. My friends and family would be unaware of anything for four years.

Over 1 million miles in six days and absolutely no buzz? How was that possible? Well, that's what happens when you make airline frequent flyer program history *before* the history books had started being written about that topic. And that's what happens when you stumble into a destiny that no one in the world, let alone you, could have ever conceived.

Why I vaulted into the airline mileage stratosphere at the

tender age of twenty-six was perplexing. I didn't have an incurable sense of wanderlust to explore the four corners of the world. Mexico and Canada easily sated my zest for international travel locales. I had yet to contemplate the notion of basking in the luxury and exclusivity of sitting in front-of-the-curtain in Business Class. I wasn't a travel hacker (no such thing in '88 anyway!) waiting to pounce on a lucrative mileage scaling scheme.

Let's forget the esoteric *why* did I become a mileage millionaire in less than a week for the moment. Inquiring minds want to know—*HOW* the hell did I do it?!

It all started while I was waiting in line. I had ticket number sixty-seven, and the display monitor flashed number twenty-eight. I breathed deeply and savored the mouth-watering smell of hot pastrami sandwiches slathered with spicy mustard and coleslaw. The anticipation of winding my way to the front of the line to claim my 'bounty' was irresistible. After 45 minutes, my number was finally called, and I sauntered up to the counter where there was a familiar, smiling face. It was my bi-monthly ritual with Evy.

"Heyyyyyyyy, Steve. What'll you have today?" she chirped.

"The usual, please," I responded with a mix of politeness and mild annoyance. She knew exactly what I wanted. And yet, Evy looked at me with a puzzled expression. Then, she pondered a moment. And at last, a flash of recognition. She typed my order into the computer.

Thirty seconds later, she handed me my bounty with aplomb. "Is this right?" she said with a smirk.

I nodded with strained amusement, just barely playing along. She didn't serve up a mouth-watering sandwich. The bounty was my unemployment check that Evy handed over with a cheeky smile. That was her shtick to soften the blow of folks like me being on the dole.

Oh, and that delicious sandwich aroma, it always wafted over from the next-door deli.

I was no stranger to the unemployment office, having gotten fired three times in four years during my post-college foray to Los Angeles. In my hometown of Cleveland, the unemployment office was perceived as a den of humiliation and shame, full of ne'er-do-wells. But in LA, it was part of the cultural zeitgeist. The West Hollywood unemployment office was a cheerful and high-energy social gathering place for struggling actors, models, and waiters. The office was brightly colored with cool artwork and big windows with plenty of sunlight. The chairs even had cushions. It was like Starbucks without the joe … nor the ability to pay for the joe.

I had developed a casual social network of fellow jobless friends who would meet up at the office at the same time every payday. We would mimic Evy's heartfelt but ridiculous maternal shtick. We would encourage each other that the meager unemployment checks were more than enough to tide us over for another two weeks. But deep down, we all knew better.

In early October 1988, our bi-monthly rendezvous at the unemployment office took a troubling turn. Most of my friends' brave faces were starting to crack. They were stressing about how to get enough money to fly back East to spend Thanksgiving with their families.

Perchance, my daily copy of *USA Today* had an ad about a United Airlines triple-miles promotion. Had the first inklings of my inner mileage mad scientist started to stir? Was I connecting the dots that lots of people needed to fly coast-to-coast for the holidays, and lots of miles could be earned with the triple-miles promotion? And that I could end up in international Business Class for an unprecedented pennies on the dollar for years to come?

Uh, no.

The United triple-miles ad had not conjured up any mileage epiphany. In fact, the newspaper ad was summarily tossed in the garbage with nary a second, let alone first, thought.

But I would inadvertently connect a totally different set of dots over the next week.

My apartment building's lobby elevator had a bulletin board with the usual pizza, yoga, and used car flyers. A flyer advertising super-cheap airfares caught my attention as I was pondering my Thanksgiving travel plans. I called for more info. The guy explained that he had purchased a bunch of fares for Thanksgiving months ago when there was a big sale. The routings were terrible, with two zig-zaggy stops each way. But the upside was that even with his markup, he was still able to sell tickets well under what airfares currently cost.

There was one minor caveat that he explained.

The ticket would get me to Cleveland, but it wouldn't be under my name. I was confused, then suspicious. How was that possible? He claimed there was no rule that the passenger flying had to have the same name as the passenger on the ticket. And he said that neither the ticket agent nor security were checking that ticket names matched ID names. Still, it viscerally sounded dodgy, and I passed.

Later that week, I was at a party where there was some dude haranguing about corporate America greed. He seemed sincere, and some of his analysis sounded kind of legit. Still, most of the stuff about the military-industrial complex and genetic engineering went totally over my head. Then, he switched gears about some kind of conspiracy theory that the big airlines were colluding to crush smaller rivals right under the nose of the government. He warned that while big airlines couldn't use predatory pricing, they were using some crazy triple-miles promotion to bully the upstart airlines.

I pulled him aside later on to give me a more layman's understanding of this triple miles conspiracy.

He was exasperated. "How could the government let the airlines get away with a once-in-a-lifetime offer so lucrative that it will bleed the small guys to death?"

I was confused. 'Lucrative' and 'once-in-a-lifetime' seemed to have positive, not evil connotations to me. "It sounds like a great opportunity, especially if it's never gonna happen again," I meekly observed.

He was dismissive. "That's exactly what the big guys are hoping, that you'll look at them as mileage sugar daddies, while they starve the upstart airlines ... in a perfectly legal manner."

As he got more incensed about the triple miles cabal, I felt bad that I was intrigued, not outraged.

He dejectedly concluded, "I can't believe that the big airlines are gonna be able to bribe people's loyalty for 45,000 miles a pop from LA to New York." I went wide-eyed at that number, which prompted him to stomp away, sensing I was a traitor to his cause.

Actually, I had no clue what 45,000 miles represented, but if it had provoked such venom from that resident conspiracy theorist, who I dubbed "Mr. Area 51," then maybe it had some incredible value worth exploring.

The next day, I grabbed a United Mileage Plus booklet at a local ticket office. Sure enough, it appeared that Mr. Area 51 had an agenda. I was able to calculate quite easily that he had wildly exaggerated the big airline's triple-miles promotion bait. It wasn't 45,000—it was 15,000 miles.

Los Angeles-New York roundtrip
5,000 miles x 3 (triple miles) = 15,000.

The United Mileage Plus booklet was pint-sized, but it was packed with charts, strange vernacular, and tons of asterisks and fine print. At first, I was intimidated by it. But soon, I was absorbed in it. Then I became fascinated by it. And after six hours of exhaustive reading, I actually understood it ... really well. Really, really well. The booklet had a bunch of different stand-alone sections about mileage earning, redemption, elite status, partners, etc. But there was no overarching analysis about how to synchronize the different elements to optimize making the program work for a member.

I gathered all the compartmentalized information from each section and painstakingly tried to integrate them together. I realized that disparate information could be collated into powerful knowledge. Based on my newfound understanding of the program, maybe I had unearthed knowledge that even the authors of the program had not anticipated. The United Mileage Plus booklet revealed that there was math, and then there was frequent flyer program math.

My mileage awakening had officially commenced. I could now coalesce together my friends' yearning to travel home cheaply, Mr. Area 51's rants about the United triple-miles promotion, the sketchy dude's weird scheme to fly people under different names, and my newfound expertise about the quirks and idiosyncrasies of United Mileage Plus.

I was ready to build the perfect (mileage scaling!) beast.

Most of my friends wanted to fly back to the East Coast. LA to New York was a 5,000 miles round trip as the crow flies. But Mileage Plus actually calculated mileage earning per flight, and any flight under 1,000 miles still earned a minimum of 1,000 miles.

MINIMUM MILEAGE EARNING

	Actual Miles Flown	Earned Miles
New York-Pittsburgh	350	1,000
Pittsburgh-Chicago	400	1,000
Chicago-Los Angeles	1,750	1,750
2-Stop Total	= 2,500	**= 3,750**
New York-Los Angeles Nonstop Total	2,500	**2,500**

The dodgy dude who flew people under different names had explained his fares were so cheap because they were booked far in advance, had Saturday night stays, and two-stop routings.

He had warned against booking nonstop flights. Nonstop flights, though convenient, came with fares that were very high, and they got even worse with last-minute purchases and no Saturday night stays. My research confirmed he was spot on.

If someone had a lot of time but little money, United rewarded them with more miles than the person who had a lot of money but little time. It seemed like an odd system, but I liked it.

MORE STOPS / MORE FARE SAVINGS / MORE MILES

	Earned Miles	Airfare Cost
Advance Notice Airfare		
NY-LA 2-stop	**7,500**	**$250**
Last-Minute Airfare		
NY-LA nonstop	5,000	$950

Mr. Area 51 kept referencing that the triple-miles promotion would yield 45,000 miles, but initially, his math seemed way off.

TRIPLE MILES PROMOTION

2-Stop Earned miles	7,500
Triple Miles bonus	× 3
NEW Total Miles	= 22,500

But once I understood United's convoluted calculus, Mr. Area 51's seeming wildcat 45,000-mile reference was, in fact, precision in action. Once a Mileage Plus member earned 50,000 miles, they would qualify for Premier elite status that would shower them with perks. One of which was a 100% bonus for every mile flown.

ELITE STATUS BONUS

2-Stop Earned miles	7,500
Triple Miles bonus	× 3
Total Miles	= 22,500
Elite Bonus	× 100%
NEW Total Miles	**= 45,000**

Bingo. And Kudos to Mr. Area 51.

I had to admit that Mr. Area 51 had really unearthed the triple-miles promotion disparity that, in its most extreme form, would be devastating to the smaller airlines. A passenger flying LA to NYC with the triple-miles promotion could earn as much 45,000 miles with the big airlines vs. just 5,000 with the small airlines.

Mr. Area 51 had found the 45,000-mile treasure trove, and the dodgy dude had found cheap two-stop airfares for $250. But what were 45,000 miles costing $250 to generate even worth?

There were a few award options, but I focused on domestic Economy because I didn't really think anyone really needed First Class on relatively short flights. And I focused on international Business Class for the exact opposite reason: who would want to fly in Economy Class for 8-14-hour long-haul flights that had sleeper seats and amazing food?

MILEAGE REDEMPTION / ONE TRIPLE-MILES TRIP

	domestic Economy Class award	international Business Class award
No. of Triple Miles trips	1	1
Miles Earned	45,000	45,000
Award Redemption	25,000	80,000
No. of awards_per trip flown	1	0

Mr. Area 51 may have been impressed with a 45,000-mile stash, but upon closer inspection, I concluded that even that amount wasn't really enough. It was a terribly inefficient use of miles to redeem just one domestic Economy award and having another 20,000 miles that would only have value if more flights were flown in the future to top off to a second 25,000 Economy award. And the mileage shortfall for international Business Class would relegate that high-cost award as a pipedream.

I recalled Mr. Area 51 mentioning 45,000 miles 'a pop.' Apparently, the triple-miles promotion wasn't limited to one trip. I crunched the numbers for adding a *second* trip.

MILEAGE REDEMPTION / TWO TRIPLE-MILES TRIP

	domestic Economy Class award	international Business Class award
No. of Triple Miles trips	2	2
Miles Earned	90,000	90,000
Award Redemption	25,000	80,000
No. of awards per trip flown	3	1

Wow, the impact of one extra trip was compelling. Now it was possible to redeem triple the number of domestic Economy awards and leave fewer unused miles on the table. And the second trip would be the gateway to that seemingly unattainable award- international Business Class.

I was starting to understand why the airlines were calling themselves *frequent flyer* programs. The more someone flew, the more they were rewarded ... even if they paid a super cheap airfare. I would have thought that a more logical and sustainable business model would have focused on those members that spent more, not flew more.

But what the hell did a twenty-six-year-old newbie really know?

For about the same number of hours cooped up inside an airplane and for the same award redemption amount, redeeming for an international Business Class award instead of a domestic Economy award was a no-brainer: super comfortable sleeper seat, gourmet meals, huge video screens, private lounges, attentive service, no snaking lines to the bathroom, and arriving at your destination fresh, not jetlagged.

TIME SPENT IN ECONOMY VS. BUSINESS CLASS

	domestic Economy Class award	international Business Class award
Roundtrip flight duration	4-10 hrs.	16-30 hrs.
No. of awards per two Triple-Miles trips	3	1
TOTAL flight time	12-30 hrs.	16-30 hrs.

The second reason that international Business Class awards were a superior redemption option using the triple-miles promotion was the disparity in value versus a domestic Economy award. I could likely scrape enough money to purchase domestic Economy fares in the absence of access to airline miles. But I would never be able to afford international Business Class fares. *Only* being a very active Mileage Plus member in vigilant pursuit of earning the critical mass of miles would put me in the very front of the cabin.

ECONOMY VS. BUSINESS CLASS VALUE PROPOSITION

	domestic Economy Class award	international Business Class award
No. of awards per two Triple-Miles trips	3	1
equivalent cash airfare value of award	× $500	× $6,000
TOTAL award value	= $1,500	= $6,000
	vs.	vs.
cash spent earning miles	$500	$500

My debut mileage alchemy with the United triple-miles promotion had yielded undeniable paydirt:

$500 airfare spend = international Business Class award that would otherwise cost roughly $6,000

There were three perspectives on how to analyze those numbers.

Maximize Cash Savings

A $500 cost of miles vs. a $6,000 international Business Class cost of airfare. The cost of earning the necessary miles was 85-90% less expensive than the cost of airfare for one international Business Class trip.

Maximize Travel

A $6,000 outlay could purchase one paid international Business Class airfare vs. twelve with awards. Cash spent on earning mileage generated twelve times more Business Class trips than cash spent on airfare.

Maximize Inflight Experience

Mileage-earning costs for an international Business Class award was roughly similar to the cash-costs of airfare for international Economy Class. One could argue that I would never have been able to afford a $6,000 Business Class fare in the first place, so that the cost savings using miles was disingenuous. I would be happy to concede the point.

An international Economy airfare, on average, would cost $600 to $1,000. So, for a similar cash outlay to generate miles instead of paying for airfare, I would be guaranteed to fly in Business Class instead of Economy Class. Eight to fifteen hours each way with the amazing front-of-the-curtain perks would be accessible for a behind-the-curtain cost.

Mr. Area 51 had predicted that the triple-miles promotion would generate 45,000 miles. He was right. But I was about to become more right. Far more right.

Instead of building the perfect (mileage scaling) beast, I needed to pivot. I was now going to build the perfect *army* of beasts.

There would be a casting call of my informal social group of intermittently-employed actors. The meeting place was, of course, the friendly environs of 'Evy's Deli,' our snarky but affectionate nickname for the neighborhood unemployment office.

I kept things simple. I could offer everyone a *free* airline ticket back East for Thanksgiving. Initially, there was an air of relief and gratitude for my seeming generosity. But that quickly turned to suspicion. The group surmised that there had to be a catch.

And indeed there was.

Each person would have to agree to fly United on a circuitous two-stop route. There were a few muted groans. And then the group made the next inevitable follow-up question. Were there any more catches?

And indeed, there still was.

Each person would have to agree to fly using a ticket under a different name than their own. Now there were a lot of unmuted gasps.

But I wasn't quite finished with the laundry list of catches.

The kicker. Each person would be flying their free tickets under my name. Chaos ensued.

"That's gotta be illegal."

"I'm not going to jail over 250 bucks."

"What the hell is in it for you?"

"What if the plane crashes? No one will know that I died."

I was ready for all the incredulous objections, and I methodically assuaged their concerns.

There was no legal rule or airline policy at the time that

prohibited flying under a different name, and there were no ID checks at the ticket counter, security, or at the gate. I guess that dude from the elevator bulletin board and his business model weren't so dodgy after all!

I would solemnly contact surviving relatives if there was a crash. I would collect all of their next-of-kin phone numbers and pray that everyone would fly safe and sound.

Finally, I explained the mileage math behind the offer. It was more like mileage trigonometry when they heard it, and my brilliant project was met with a chorus of glazed eyes. Aggregating miles? Triple-miles promotion? United Mileage Plus?

To me, miles were becoming like a new type of currency. To the rest of the group, it was like Monopoly money. There was utter disinterest with what I would be doing with the miles.

As most of the group were actors, I anticipated the mental math they were all thinking. A lot of them had been offered get-your-foot-in-the-door roles that required some nudity. They had to ponder if showing skin was worth getting the gig. Now they had a new trade-off to ponder. Was portraying Steve Belkin as a passenger worth getting home for Thanksgiving for free?

While I was the ostensible director, I was starting to feel the judgment that was normally reserved for the actors. Would they reject being in my mileage requiem?

I knew it would be a challenge to convince these actors to be part of such an avant-garde and fringe production. Mileage production, that is. I would have been thrilled if just a handful would take the chance, so I could aggregate enough miles for a couple of once-in-a-lifetime international Business Class award tickets.

They slowly filed past with their decisions. No.

No.

Yes.

No.

Not off to a rollicking start.

Yes. Yes. No. No.

And then … a streak of twenty more Yes responses.

In my wildest dreams, I couldn't conceive of this overwhelming response … twenty-three flyers. I just wasn't sure if twenty-three airfares would overwhelm the modest budget I had saved up from the three jobs I had over the last four years.

My first job out of college in 1985 was on tour as the personal slave, I mean, the Continuity Coordinator for the soap-opera-star-turned-pop-rock-star Rick Springfield. On tour, the crew was a ward of the state. Springfield's management covered lodging, food, and per diem as well as a salary. So it was easy to sock away a lot of money over the course of a three-month tour.

I had parlayed that gig into being the Tour Sponsorship Road Manager for a big radio company that played matchmaker for company brands that wanted to hitch on the soaring popularity of '80's rock bands. I toured with the likes of Stevie Nicks, Bob Dylan/Tom Petty, and Genesis, among others, over the course of a year. Again, on the road, with no expenses.

Most recently, I was tethered to an office at a large Beverly Hills talent agency as a Soundtracks Agent. I was responsible for recruiting TV and film acting, soundtrack, and music scoring gigs for the agency's concert tour roster to keep them busy while not on the road. And to keep them from getting poached by rival agencies. I had worked with agency clients like Gregg Allman, Ozzy Osbourne, Bryan Adams, and .38 Special. I was making high-flying LA pay but still living a low-profile Cleveland (my hometown) lifestyle.

My job performance for what I was assigned to do delivered exemplary results at each job. But I got fired because I delivered those results in my own special way. I wasn't opposed to my former companies' existing systems. I just liked to tweak and tinker to make them better and maybe even more valuable. Kind of like how I was proposing to transform twenty-three unwitting Steve Belkin clones into a twenty-three-headed beast capable of churning out international Business Class awards for pennies on the dollar.

Back to the budget. Was paying for twenty-three airfares really worth amassing a mileage arsenal that I frankly hadn't anticipated nor desired and would likely take a decade to blow through?

STEVE BELKIN CLONE MILEAGE EARNING ANALYSIS

No. of flyers	23	23	No. of flyers
Triple-Miles earning	× 45,000	× $250	Triple-Miles airfare
TOTAL Miles	= 1,035,000	= $5,750	TOTAL Cost
Intl. Business Class award redemption	/ 80,000 #		
No. of awards	= 13	/ 13	No. of awards
		= $442	cost per award
		vs.	
		$6,000 ##	cost average per retail airfare

#- From 1988 to the mid-2000's, mileage award charts were incredibly stable. With awards to South America averaging 70,000 miles, Europe 80,000 miles, and Asia 90,000 miles, it seemed that 80,000 miles was a reasonable average to use for illustration purposes throughout the book.

##- Similarly, $6000 average Business Class airfare seemed like a conservative number that averaged fares to South America, Europe, and Asia. The average reflected a relatively high fare basis because there was negligible pressure from low-cost carriers.

I had enough money saved up. I had already flown earlier in 1988. Just one of the flyers' flights would qualify me for Premier elite status, so all of the subsequent flyers would earn the 100% elite bonus. An unexpected opportunity was that United rewarded its million-mile members with lifetime Premier elite status to access mileage bonuses, lounges, and priority treatment. I would receive a shiny gold card memorializing it all.

As I purchased twenty-three airfares and methodically entered my name and frequent flyer number into each reservation, I wasn't thinking about making mileage history, becoming a mileage millionaire, or picking out a wardrobe for the late-night talk show circuit. I wasn't thinking about exploring Bali or Paris or an African safari after a luxurious ride up front in Business Class.

I was thinking about how the hell to book the four women who had signed up as flyers.

Surely the names on the tickets didn't have to match up with the flyers, but names not matching the gender would be pushing it. I scrambled for a solution but came up empty-handed. Just as I was resigned to having to remove 20% of my mileage beast from active duty, a Fleetwood Mac song blared over the radio. The lead singer was the hugely popular Stevie Nicks, and despite her name, no one questioned her femininity. So, I would book the four women as "Stevie" Belkin … and hope for the best.

The week of Thanksgiving had finally arrived, and twenty-three flyers were happily on their free flights home, each doing their indiscernible but indispensable part to add 45,000 triple-miles promotion miles into my master kitty.

The triple-miles project went off without a hitch. No unexpected ID checks at the check-in counter or gate. No mileage posting issues into my account. And, of course, no crashes and premature demise of any of the other Steve Belkin clones.

There were twenty-three Steve Belkin clone flights to six different East Coast airports within a six-day period. It was statistically impossible for one person to do, and yet, completely within the United Terms and Conditions (T&C). The United Fraud Department was defenseless.

But there were some other close calls.

A couple of Steve Belkin clones decided to fly together on the same flights. Luckily, they checked in separately. And the flight crew apparently didn't eyeball the passenger list very carefully for the duplicate name.

One Steve Belkin clone became very friendly with a flight attendant, and she addressed him as 'Steve' throughout the flight. They walked together to baggage claim. There was apparently a surprise welcoming committee for that particular Steve Belkin clone, and they weren't aware of his incognito mission. They shouted "Jimmy, Jimmy, Jimmy" as that Steve exited baggage claim and as the very perplexed flight attendant tried to process this odd name discrepancy.

One Steve Belkin clone was provided a special Indian meal for dinner instead of the regular meal of spaghetti. He looked at the meal with disgust and pleaded that there must have been a mistake. The flight attendant was quite puzzled that Steve had such an abrupt change of culinary preference. She apologized to him, but she also showed him the passenger manifest that Steve (actually me!) had *always* ordered special Indian meals in his permanent account profile.

Those small oversights made for entertaining anecdotes when we all regrouped at the unemployment office in December. But I didn't really absorb them as cautionary tales for future mileage projects because I wasn't yet contemplating future mileage projects. I thought that this mileage project was just a one-and-done lark.

The only ongoing trace that the triple-miles project ever existed would be a playful wink-and-a-nod code between the people who participated. They would shake their elbows like a turkey and utter "gobble-gobble" when they would see each other, a subtle testament to their free Thanksgiving trip home as mileage mules. The Gobble-Gobble Run would be a cute nickname if future mileage archivists ever decided to dig back this far.

Mr. Area 51's conspiracy theory about the triple-miles promotion was ultimately wrong. The major airlines were unable to knock the upstarts out of the industry game. But he was right that the principle of mileage promotions by any airline could effectively influence consumer behavior. My one-million miles and lifetime elite status earned in six days was proof.

The Gobble-Gobble Run had happened so quickly that I didn't have a chance to accumulate a travel bucket-list to catch up with the miles I had just accumulated. I had miles, but didn't know where to go. All my friends worked nine-to-five, and some were getting married, and some already had kids. They were all pressed for time and/or money while I was single and unemployed with nothing but time. I had miles but no one to travel with.

And I had blown my meager nest egg on subsidizing the twenty-three Steve Belkin clones. I now had miles, but I couldn't afford to do anything once I landed in some exotic locale.

My million miles would need to sit in abeyance for a couple of years until I had a travel companion and budget. While I was out of the mileage game for the time being, my seeming obsession actually solidified while trolling the sidelines ...albeit in rather absurd ways.

When I married my wife, Julie, in 1990, she had a vague inkling that I had some convoluted past with airline mileage which she assumed was a phase that was now permanently in the past! Over the course of our first blissful year of marriage, I kept my mileage passion under wraps.

That facade of normalcy was shattered when she gushed about her newfound pregnancy. We agreed on most everything, and I couldn't wait for that trend to continue. I was hoping that this discussion would bond us as parents.

"What do you think of the name Miles?"

Julie knew that my name choice was not an ode to jazz legend Miles Davis. She slowly, but resolutely, nodded a silent no. Even my feeble attempt at softening the blow with the more regal 'Myles' was a non-starter.

My Plan B mileage naming strategy was a tad more subtle: Max.

Not Maxwell or Maximilian, just Max.

For Julie, the name Max conjured up the post-World War One immigrant experience of the Ellis Island officers changing their unpronounceable multisyllabic names to simple All-American ones. These folks would become the proud and hardworking backbone of the emerging middle class. She was in!

For me, Max was a simple literal term: his name would be short for Maximum, as in my scaling mileage programs to the Max! But I kept that naming methodology to myself for the time being.

The only uncertain detail left was ensuring that Julie would deliver a boy. She was convinced Max or Miles or Myles was a moot point because Baby Belkin #1 was going to be a Nikki or a Jacqui.

Well, it was indeed a boy. I wish I could say I was content with winning the naming game with Max, but I felt compelled to really pile on the mileage theme.

The birth announcement featured a couple looking outside a big window at an airport with storks holding babies in sacks. Upon opening the card, there was an Arrivals screen with listings of airlines, cities, and arrival times. In the middle of the listing was—Max P Belkin. October 6, 1992. 9 lbs. Arrival Time—Finally!

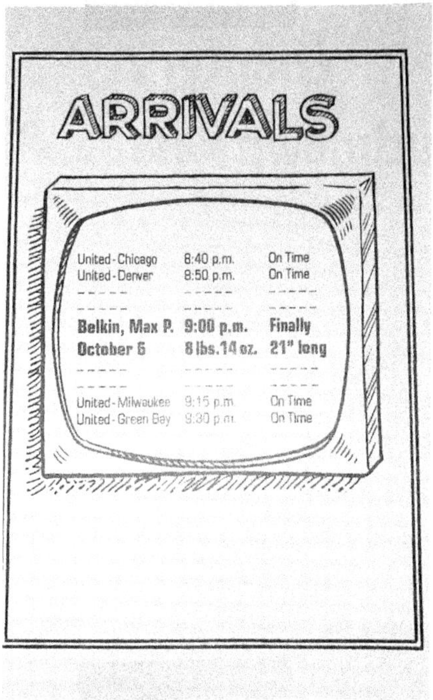

The mileage die had been cast. It would not take long to dry.

In 1991 United would dangle a seemingly innocuous mileage program in front of me. Sorry Julie, but it appeared that there might just be a sophomore project. An encore performance of my mileage alchemy skills, after all. Just the *one and only* Steve Belkin would be required. No clones necessary.

Chapter 2: Touchdown Pass . . . Plus

In 1991, United had approached me, as one of their few lifetime elite status members, about a new program called Pass Plus. It involved pre-purchasing a large bank of miles to fly otherwise expensive weekday or last-minute fares for a reasonable fixed price. At first blush Pass Plus seemed fairly innocuous just like the triple-miles promotion three years prior.

There were only two small details I had to tie up before committing.

One: ripping the guts out of the Pass Plus program to find a mileage-earning scaling sweet spot to justify the upfront expense of $15,000 for a 50,000 bank of miles to be flown over two years

Two: finding a job where travel would be a component.

Scratch that. Two: finding a job, period.

My wife Julie counseled me to do what I loved, and then the money would soon come. I was grateful for her unconditional support, especially since she was a medical resident bringing home actual greenbacks each week. But the truth was, I wasn't sure what the hell I wanted to do. Yet, my parents and in-laws were hoping I'd figure it out soon. They wanted to be reasonably sure that their first grandchild would be supported by a breadwinner, not breadsticks! As much as I was fascinated with the mileage game, I just didn't see any financially sustainable path with it.

It was time to cash in my family's 'get out of jail free' card equivalent of lifetime job security.

My dad and uncle had regularly assured their four offspring all during our childhood that there would "always be a place" for each of us in the family rock concert promotion business. And indeed, my sister and two cousins had found their places there in helping promote concerts like Pink Floyd, The Rolling Stones, Madonna, and U2 in our hometown Cleveland and throughout the Midwest.

I would be at the bottom of the family business totem pole as the family renegade who hightailed it out to LA and then returned to Cleveland jobless with no resume references with my tail between my legs. My joining the family biz was apparently met with quiet trepidation from the powers that be.

Before officially hiring me, my dad and uncle wanted me to meet with an industrial psychologist to take some tests to figure out how best I could "contribute to the company." It sounded pretty harmless, as I was a pretty good test taker. Instead of the expected battery of MENSA-level, mind-bending tests, I was given one sheet of unlined paper and a pen. I was given ten minutes to briefly describe two strengths and weaknesses of mine.

A pencil would have been appreciated to erase mistakes instead of the pen that required cross-outs. In the absence of lined paper, my sentences were closer to 165 degrees instead of 180 degrees across the paper. I was so focused on quality content that I neglected attention to margins and indentations. But I finally hit my rhythm and finished my essay in a winning eight minutes with two minutes to spare.

The eight-minute test apparently took more than two weeks to grade because it took that long for my dad to schedule our follow-up meeting. I supposedly had nothing to worry about as the test was ostensibly a formality. But the two-week delay had jangled my nerves. Then my dad scheduled the follow-up meeting at the house instead of his office. Not his normal MO.

The meeting started on the most terrible note possible when my dad uttered "Lemme ask you something…" To a casual observer, it would seem an offhanded lead-in. But my sister and I knew that lead-in telegraphed a very specific conversation. It was either about money, pending bad news, or both. He continued

"…what did you think about that testing?"

"I think they gave me the wrong test. I think it was meant for high school seniors. Yeah, I guess I pretty much aced it."

He looked down. "Uncle Mike and I finally were able to figure out your job situation…"

I was relieved but not really jubilant as the process was supposed to be just a formality before joining my rightful place in the family business. I failed to discern that what I thought was the end of his sentence was actually a pregnant pause. He slowly murmured the second part of the sentence: "…and we agreed that the timing to hire you right now isn't ideal. The industrial psychologist thinks your handwriting analysis signaled it might be prudent to wait a bit until we can figure a good situation for everyone. So, let's regroup in a few months and revisit working together."

Handwriting analysis? What about the important stuff, the content of the essay that demonstrated my analytical skills, my communication skills, and my problem-solving skills? My dad explained that my tangible job skills were self-evident—it was the intangibles that the handwriting analysis revealed.

The cross-outs showed that I was impulsive. The ignoring of margins and indentations showed that I would chafe under too much structure or authority. I wrote very small because I subconsciously had *so* much to say, I pre-emptively needed to preserve space to squeeze all my thoughts in. The company wasn't looking for boundless new ideas from me yet. They just wanted a solid worker bee.

Finally, my testing had demonstrated the inflection point that my dad and I had already known for years but never had to confront until now. My dad had a status quo personality: 'If it ain't broke, don't fix it.' I, in turn, had a restless and creative streak: 'Sure it ain't broken, but let's make it even better.' What seemed like reneging on a solemn family promise was actually a necessary evil to preserve the family financial engine.

I was sore for all of forty-eight hours. In the meantime, my dad tapped into his concert promoter Rolodex and snagged me a job selling radio time.

After a few months, my fundamental flaws that the handwriting analysis had revealed struck again. Too much thinking out of the box, too much questioning the status quo. I was fired by the station manager. Afterward, he advised me that I would also need to meet with the station owners. Great, I was going to getting fired *twice*. Why would the owners of a radio conglomerate and real estate holdings worth eight figures want to pile on another scathing indictment of my ongoing failed employment record?

The owners, Tom E. and Tom W. observed "We hear that you are the right guy just selling the wrong product." Tom E. wanted to propose that he had the right product for me to sell, but there was a caveat before he presented the idea. He wanted to make sure I wouldn't have a problem that the job would involve a decent amount of...

Air travel.

I was so enthralled with the prospect of being able to re-engage with the mileage world, however modestly, that I paid only cursory attention to the actual details of the actual job description. In fact after agreeing to the job proposal then and there, I actually had to sheepishly reapproach Tom E. to explain it again.

His radio company owned the media rights to the Cleveland Browns football team and was friendly with head coach Marty Schottenheimer. Marty's good friend was the head coach of the Green Bay Packers—Lindy Infante—and Lindy wanted out of the radio deal that the team management had apparently forced him to do: a one-hour call-in show. The show was at night, taking up his valuable time with family, and he hated taking questions from yahoos who were critical no matter how successful the team was.

Marty asked Tom E. a favor. Could he help Lindy get a different radio deal in the morning and not a call-in format. Whatever the money would be, it couldn't be any worse than what the team was apparently paying him. Tom E. had zero exposure or contacts in the Wisconsin media market. My job was to establish his company's presence there, from scratch, with no prior experience.

Tom E. knew about the twenty-three-flyer, million-mile-earning 'Gobble Gobble Run' because I included it prominently on my resume, which needed all the padding it could get. Tom suggested that if I could create amazing mileage results in LA, I could marshal my entrepreneurial skills to create equally impressive results in Green Bay.

I validated his instincts about me. I hustled a couple of decent radio deals that earned my credibility in the Wisconsin media market and some much-needed stable income. Coach Infante was pleased and indicated his interest in a deal extension with my company, even though the football season had barely started. I was ready to lay the groundwork to establish my media beachhead in Green Bay for the impending Infante deal renewal, which would require a lot more travel back and forth from Cleveland.

It was time to crunch some United Pass Plus numbers.

I was back in the mileage game, pencils sharpened.

At first, I was incredibly discouraged. It seemed like my mileage alchemy with Pass Plus was seriously hemmed in with some inflexible elements.

There was only one routing from Cleveland to Green Bay on United, and it was one stop. No wiggle room to add an extra stop and goose up the mileage earning. Pass Plus cost structure also denied me any creative fare finding or improvising, as each mile flown would cost three cents (50,000 mileage flown, bank/$15,000).

I would have to live with the following unchangeable formula.

PASS PLUS COST ANALYSIS

50,000	Pass Plus mileage to fly bank
/ 1,000	actual roundtrip flight miles Cleveland-Green Bay
= 50	TOTAL Pass Plus Trips
1,000	actual roundtrip flight miles Cleveland-Green Bay
× $0.03	cost per mile (50,000 miles/$15,000)
= $300	cost per Cleveland-Green Bay roundtrip

While Pass Plus did a masterful job in fixing my number of trips and cost per trip, the program authors apparently overlooked some of the moving parts on the mileage earning side of things. United rounded every flight distance under 1,000 miles to 1,000 earned miles.

PASS PLUS MINIMUM MILEAGE EARNING

Flown Miles	Earned Miles	
350	1,000	Cleveland-Chicago
150	1,000	Chicago-Wisconsin
150	1,000	Wisconsin-Chicago
+ 350	+ 1,000	Chicago-Cleveland
= 1,000	= 4,000	TOTAL MILES

So, right off the bat, for every mile I paid for, I would generate a 400% bonus, courtesy of United's existing policy.

The Pass Plus brochure touted its cost savings as that's what resonated with the business clientele that it targeted. Tucked away at the back of the brochure, almost as if it were a seeming afterthought, was the real mileage earning perk of the program. Every Pass Plus flight would earn a 100% bonus.

PASS PLUS BONUS

4,000	Cleveland-Wisconsin earned miles
+ 4,000	100% Pass Plus bonus miles
= 8,000	NEW Total Miles

Now, for every mile I paid for, the two bonuses would kick back 800% more miles.

If that wasn't enough…

The 'Gobble Gobble Run' had crested me over one million miles which qualified me for a new United elite status level called *Premier for Life*. There were a bunch of perks that I would get lifetime access to, but only one that impacted my mileage alchemy was a 100% elite bonus miles addition.

ELITE BONUS

8,000	Cleveland-Wisconsin earned miles and Pass Plus bonus
+ 8,000	100% elite status bonus
= 16,000	NEW Total Miles

These three bonuses—minimum miles per segment, Pass Plus bonus, and elite status bonus—aggregated into a 1,600% bonus per mile earned.

The Pass Plus formula had been mastered … right under United's nose using their published policies.

PASS PLUS VALUE PROPOSITION

No. of Pass Plus Cleve-GB trips	5	5	No. of Pass Plus Cleve-GB trips
Earned, Pass Plus and Elite bonus miles per trip	× 16,000	× $300	Cleve-GB airfare per trip
Intl. Business Class award redemption	= 80,000	= $1,500	cost of miles
		vs. $6,000	cost average to cost of retail airfare

I thought that I had meticulously covered every detail to ensure that I would be maximizing the Pass Plus deal. But I had overlooked my historical Achilles heel:

Job security.

At the end of the 1992 football season, I had to confront another firing. Not me, silly! Rather, Coach Infante's team had nosedived from the playoffs to last place in just one season, and he was dismissed. I had no client left in Green Bay and no reason to justify Pass Plus travel. I was devastated.

Until…

Before he departed, Infante spewed out all of his crazy Packer grievances about the team. He sounded like Mr. Area 51 from Los Angeles from the 'Gobble-Gobble Run' era. And like Mr. Area 51, amidst his rantings, Infante spouted an intriguing morsel of promising information that I latched onto.

He explained that the TV/radio deal was presented as a *fait accompli* to the head coach by the Packers management *after* the core contract was signed. The team plugged the coach's programming into their seventy-year-old network of generally low-rated stations that aired the coach's show in obscure, low-rated time slots. He groused that it was no wonder that Packer coaches were dead last in the NFL in media compensation.

Just like Mr. Area 51's nub of an idea sent me scouring United Mileage Plus for sweet spots for maximum mileage-earning impact, Infante's revelations sent me scouring the media landscape in Wisconsin. I was going to start an insurrection and recruit my own network A-list of media outlets with a totally new business model. And beat the Packers at their own game.

I would replace AM news-talk stations with top-rated FM rock stations, and the format would feature the morning drive DJs as treating the coach as a best buddy, not as a firing-line victim with the traditional call-in Q&A format.

For the TV show I accepted bartered commercial time, which the stations were far more generous in parting with, than the cash that the Packers demanded. Plus, I would feature the local station sportscasters, not some Packer shill as the host. My strategy vaulted the TV show from low-rated weekend afternoons that the Packers could muster into the best possible time slot immediately preceding the highest-rated TV show in America, *Monday Night Football.*

All that was left was to find an agent from one of the five Packer coaching prospects to accept my amazing media deal, better than any NFL market outside of New York and Los Angeles before the team could force them into their lousy media deal. Despite my unrivaled media deal, the only agent that agreed to work with me was representing San Francisco 49ers assistant coach Mike Holmgren.

After an excruciatingly long six-week wait, the Packers had finally found their man. MY man.

The team management was astounded when less than twenty-four hours after signing Holmgren, my TV and radio allies were already trumpeting their newfound on-air Packer presence. The Packers couldn't prevent what I had done, but they surely didn't like it. And United would be similarly astounded when they found out how my mileage calculus had subverted the original intent of the Pass Plus program.

It turned out United had targeted Pass Plus for business executives flying coast-to-coast on last-minute nonstop flights to protect against ultra-high airfares. The bank of flown miles would be depleted quickly after a few trips, thus capping any serious mileage bonus earning. Pass Plus was not targeted for ultra-short haul travel like my Cleveland-Wisconsin routing.

PASS PLUS LONG VS. SHORT HAUL TRIP ANALYSIS

	NY-LA nonstop	Cleve-GB 1 stop
Pass Plus Mileage bank	50,000	50,000
miles flown per trip	/ 5,000	/ 1,000
TOTAL Trips	= 10	= 50
earned miles Pass Plus/ elite bonus per trip	× 15,000	× 16,000
TOTAL miles earned	= 150,000	= 800,000
intl. Business Class award redemption	/ 80,000	/ $80,000
No. of awards earned using Pass Plus	= 1	= 10

My mileage earning was close to 700% more than United had anticipated when crafting the program. And 1,000% more award redemption power.

By 1994 I had expanded the company roster to include owning the media rights to Packer players Brett Favre and Reggie White as well as Milwaukee Bucks NBA head coach Mike Dunleavy. While my sweat equity had built the business, Tom E. provided the actual equity, and he had to sweat those early years, not knowing if his unproven partner would succeed in generating a return on his investment. Ultimately, Tom E. was a big fish/big pond player, and he had wandered inadvertently into the small fish/small pond as a political favor three years ago.

At the end of 1994, Tom E. called me into his office and gave me notice.

No, I wasn't being fired; I was being fired up to launch my own company. Tom E. was very (very) magnanimously offering that I could buy out his share of the company and launch my own independent sports media business. *That* was the kind of notice I had craved for years. My company would enjoy a fourteen-year history of success.

It would be flying on a Pass Plus flight that would be an actual history-making moment for me.

While Coach Holmgren was supposedly pretty pleased with my precedent-setting media compensation, effusive praise was not his strong suit. Nor was establishing a bona fide relationship. We spoke maybe a total of fifty minutes during our first three years. But I got it; he was an NFL coach with tons of everyday pressure and commitments. The media deal was basically an easy funding mechanism for his four daughters' college tuition.

In late November 1995, he broke his silence in a most peculiar way. It was a Thursday and I was in Cleveland sledding at a nearby park with my three-year-old son when my cell phone screen lit up with 'Coach.' I froze. Occasionally, on a Sunday or Monday, I would hear from him about a pressing issue like he was running ten minutes late for the show, or he was annoyed with a boisterous yahoo in the studio audience. During the offseason, I heard from him once about bumming some Bob Seger tickets off my dad. But in four years of working together, I had never gotten a late-in-the-week call out of the blue. I had a good early warning system in Green Bay between the coach's secretary, the Packers Marketing Department VP, and a local radio producer. Hmmm, no forewarning from any of them.

I had no reason to be concerned about anything, and yet

I was borderline terrified. My credibility in recruiting other Packer players was rooted in their firsthand evaluation of my media efforts and results for Coach Holmgren. My mind was racing through so many worst-case scenarios that I couldn't even answer the phone until the sixth ring.

The coach started with the brief pleasantry that was a statement, not a question waiting for an answer. "Hey Steve, how's the family." Like my Dad, the first few words from the coach set the tone. If he was pissed, he would go right for the jugular. So, that was an encouraging start.

"You're in Cleveland these days, right." Another statement, no answer was apparently expected again.

Before I could respond, he said, "Hey, I know you are swimming in all those airline miles, so this shouldn't be a problem for you at all."

Hmmm. Did the coach need some miles to take his wife on a surprise exotic vacation?

"Just hop on the next flight to Milwaukee and lemme know when you get there." This was clearly not a request. "And I mean the next flight. Gotta run, safe travels."

Click.

Cryptic. There were no explanations to the obvious burning questions as to where in Milwaukee was I going ... and WHY?

Upon arrival, I called his office. His assistant was apparently expecting me and told me to go to County Stadium, the home of the Milwaukee Brewers baseball team. As a matter of fact, the Packers also played three 'home' games there since Milwaukee was twenty-times the size of its northern cousin, Green Bay. Those games solidified the team's southern Wisconsin fan base.

Upon arrival at the stadium, I dutifully called the coach once again. This was starting to feel like a treasure hunt. This time his assistant answered and gave me a strange instruction. "Go to the box office and buy all of the available season tickets."

Click.

I must not have heard that right. There was a thirty-five-year waiting list of tens of thousands of fans for Packer season tickets. I reluctantly called her back for a much-needed clarification. But suddenly it was the coach's voice on the line and no more pleasantries, just a terse, "Steve, buy the damn tickets."

Click.

I gingerly approached the box office and was greeted by the manager, a sweet older lady named Marge. She was surprised to see me on a weekday. I knew her because the coach occasionally was able to sprinkle a few freebie tickets my way, and he left them with Marge at the box-office will call. The thick glass window was usually smudged with fingerprints on gamedays, so this was the first time I had such a clear vision of her. And the first time I hadn't seen her in her normal gameday frazzled and frenzied state.

"Hey there, Marge."

She knew my face well, but she still double-clutched before responding. "Steve? Steve. Steve!" The box office was desolate outside of game days since there were no tickets available to sell, which made my lone presence jarring to her. My line of questioning would only compound the jarring.

"Marge, I think I know the answer, but I still have to ask you a crazy question."

There was only one crazy question that Marge was ever asked, and she usually pre-empted it with her usual exasperated answer. She blurted out, "Of course, I don't." And she shook her head and pursed her lips dismissively, as if I, a Packer insider, should know better than to ask the impertinent crazy question, "Is there any chance any season tickets have shaken loose?"

I bid her adieu and slinked away.

There was no way I was going to call the coach back about the failed mission. What was I missing about this season ticket conundrum? I had two ingredients—the coach's command and Marge's empty ticket coffers. Unlike mileage alchemy, Packer ticket alchemy was not in my wheelhouse. I would have to conjure up a secret ingredient and fast as the coach demanded that I purchase the tickets today, and the box office was closing in ninety minutes.

In my Dad's concert promoting business, there were two types of tickets not available to the general public. The first were called 'comps,' short for complimentary tickets, that bands provided to the promoter to use for radio promotions and maybe spiff a few friends. The second were called 'kills,' tickets that could not be sold because the seats were obstructed by some part of the band's production set up, like behind the speakers or soundboard.

I wondered if Marge spoke rock'n'roll. I went back to her office and asked if she had any 'kills' expecting her to cock her head with a quizzical look.

Instead, she answered matter-of-factly, "Of course."

She explained that County Stadium had an upper deck supported by thick steel girders scattered across the lower deck. For half the game, people sitting in those seats wouldn't be able to see what was happening on the field because of the obstructing girders. So, of course they were kills, and of course they were never sold as season tickets. The sightlines were so terrible that even desperate fans wouldn't buy them on gameday.

She showed me the tickets with huge bright red stamps across them that read, "Obstructed View Seats."

Whoa! There was a big stack, 220 kills in all. The kills obviously had zero value because the stadium pillars killed their view, but they actually existed ...***and they were technically for sale.***

They cost the same $60 per game as the good seats, no discounting. If I bought all 220 for the three-game season ticket package, I would have 660 irredeemably crappy seats that would surely piss off my sponsors and media partners if I tried to pawn the tickets off on them. It would cost my company about $40,000 for these seemingly worthless season tickets. Buying beyond-lousy seats or questioning the almighty coach—it was classic lose-lose.

With time running out, I followed the coach's reckless order and prepared to purchase them.

Marge sternly warned me, "This purchase is non-refundable if you have a change of heart."

Great, no exit strategy.

Then she shifted tone. "I'm not sure what you are thinking or why you are here, but why don't you enjoy your evening in Milwaukee and come back in the morning with a fresh perspective."

Sounded like pretty sage advice.

And she chuckled. "I'm pretty sure no one will swoop in and snatch those awful seats between now and tomorrow."

That was helpful, if not obvious, reassurance.

I thought about walking away, but I stayed the course and bought the whole batch of obstructed-view season tickets as my company money disappeared into the ticket abyss.

I flew back to Cleveland in a catatonic state with waves of nausea. All that money down the drain. What was I thinking? And what was the coach drinking?

The following morning, the coach's assistant called me to advise that I check the headlines of ANY newspaper in the state of Wisconsin. The Packers announced that starting next season, **ALL** of their home games would be played in Green Bay's Lambeau Field. Milwaukee County Stadium season ticket holders would be seated in roughly equivalent locations at Lambeau. How could such a historic headline have been kept so hush-hush?

I had seat locations from the end zone to the fifty-yard line, about every fifteen yards at County Stadium in Milwaukee. Now, I would have 660 seats-worth of season tickets, with nary an obstruction at the historic stadium Lambeau Field in Green Bay! In an instant, I became the largest season ticket holder in Packer history, a carpetbagger from Cleveland, who was on the waiting list for all of two minutes while his credit card was being charged.

Why the coach decided to bequeath me with such incredible inside information, I'll never know. At the TV show taping the following week, I discreetly said "Thanks," and he slyly replied with a blank face, "For what?" as he continued to walk brusquely past me. And that was the start and the end of the matter.

My first mileage project discovery was in the newspaper, the second on a brochure. My next project would be unearthed via two missing pages of United's inflight magazine. Would the legions of Steve Belkin clones need to be dusted off for a mileage battle again?

Chapter 3: Vegas SKY High Rollers

My next mileage earning scheme had its roots in my adolescent love for comedy (and underage drinking)!

In 1980 in a desolate and dodgy part of downtown, the tiny 110-seat Cleveland Comedy Club opened up. The place was an irredeemable dump with low ceilings, a musty smell, and cramped tables. The room was literally twenty-five feet wide with no room for a proper straight aisle.

During my senior year in high school, eleven dollars was a lot of money to blow at a dinky comedy club with comedians that nobody had never heard of. But rumor had it that the club didn't check IDs and that a drink was included in the price. So, my buddies and I decided to become regulars there for the certainty of underage drinking. We were far less certain about the unfamiliar names on the marquis each week—Jay Leno, Jerry Seinfeld, Garry Shandling, Bob Saget, Steven Wright, Tim Allen, Paul Reiser, and Chris Rock, among others.

It was the golden age of stand-up comedy, but of course, no one realized it was the golden age as it was happening.

Still, there was nothing remotely golden about the Cleveland Comedy Club. After being introduced by the emcee, it easily took a minute and a half for the comedians to struggle through the dark and perilous labyrinth of sharp table corners, protruding elbows, and outstretched feet. By the time they got to the stage, the clapping had dissipated. It was awkward.

But once the comedians hit the stage, it was magical.

These guys hadn't bubbled up to their breakout appearances on the talk show circuit, let alone stared in sitcoms yet. My friends and I would stay after the shows and have drinks with these guys. They were deadly serious about their comedy. They would question us about their bits, take furious notes, and test out some new material on us. It never occurred to us to ask for photos or autographs. I mean, how could their autographs even be valuable if they were reduced to performing at the dingy Cleveland Comedy Club? We caught them as they were still earning their props. Too bad we didn't have a crystal ball so we could have name-dropped who we were hobnobbing with the next day at school. We didn't realize then that we had ringside seats to such looming comedic greatness.

Eleven years later in 1993, my enthusiasm for comedy remained unabated. I transitioned from being at ringside to throwing my hat in the ring. I was going to produce a national comedy competition TV show called *Kwik Witz*. It would turn out to be a harrowing eight-year odyssey, five years in development and three years on the air. *Kwik Witz* would also be the integral secret ingredient behind a mileage project that was so audacious it would require raising nearly *three-quarters of a million dollars* from investors. More on that in a moment.

Kwik Witz started from a simple premise. What if three stand-up comedians were given the same subject matter to prepare comedic material for objective side-by-side comparisons and judging. I tested the concept and it as a mixed bag. Onstage, the comedians were pretty funny, but offstage they hated being subjected to the hypercritical judging of a beauty pageant-like competition. I needed to pivot.

The improv world had an energetic and compelling stage presence by working in teams as opposed to comics passively standing in front of a microphone. Their improv training featured comedy exercises that fostered competition. These teams would be fearless and edgy, unlike the traditional anxious and static stand-ups. *Kwik Witz* would be a competition between improv teams instead of stand-up individuals.

I aligned with the Second City Comedy Troupe in Chicago, which was already the primary pipeline for the late-night comedy sketch show, *Saturday Night Live*. The management was enthralled with the idea of *Kwik Witz* being a proving ground to groom future *SNL* talent in a televised environment.

I produced a demo tape and pursued my dream of a Hollywood deal. It was a three-year nightmare of dozens of the same condescending pitch meetings. I was politely berated for having no experience, no name stars attached, and no deep pockets. And gasp, worst of all, I was from Cleveland.

But I actually had something that no Hollywood producer could muster: five top-rated ABC stations in Wisconsin.

During 1995, the Packers were having their best seasons in decades. I could have put the TV rights up for bid after two years, but I stuck by my initial choice of stations. My loyalty did not go unnoticed. The five TV stations around Wisconsin had followed my Hollywood travails with *Kwik Witz*. While big Hollywood producers could only test their shows in front of small focus groups, my TV allies offered me the chance to test my show on-air for thirteen weekly episodes. If the ratings were promising, instead of continuing to storm the gates of Hollywood, I could circumvent them by selling the show direct to the national TV marketplace.

But a thirteen-week on-air test would require producing thirteen episodes.

From scratch.

With no previous comedy experience.

With no funding partner.

With a breakneck three-month deadline before the Wisconsin stations' air dates.

Just as the Hollywood elite had mocked me, maybe they were right. Would my quantity of passion translate into a quality production? Could my access to only local resources achieve a national standard of success?

My station allies beckoned me to go to LA and find seasoned help. I lucked out in somehow finding Gary Shimokawa, the director of the popular and iconic "All In The Family," and Mark Maxwell-Smith, the hilarious producer of a bunch of game shows. To this day, I'm still not sure if either saw a spark of promise about me or were just gluttons for punishment. They both were fundamental to keeping my leaky and creaky production edifice afloat.

I had the wherewithal to fund some of the thirteen-episode test with cash from my sports marketing company, which was thankfully running on all cylinders. I also had the fresh infusion of six-hundred-and-sixty Packer tickets that were worth two to three times above face value. My wife, now with a second son in tow, had become a partner in her medical practice, so she kicked in a bit as well.

But there was still a bit of a funding shortfall. A chunk of my mileage stash that was intended for dreamy fantasy vacations would have to face a harsh reality. Trading flying to paradise for the mundane necessity of flying production staff to save from burning sparse cash.

With less than two weeks to spare, we were finally ready to cram thirteen episodes into a two-and-half-day period. While comedic improv performers feed on audience energy, we couldn't afford a bona fide audience recruiter. For evening shows, the audiences were packed with eager friends, family, and the curious Chicago comedy community. But for the unavoidably scheduled morning shows, the audiences ranged from special needs kids to hard-of-hearing retirement home field trippers to just the half-dozen strong studio maintenance crew.

The shows were dutifully sent off to the stations, and we anxiously awaited the ratings results.

For an established producer, the thirteen-episode test-market ratings would have been considered solid and promising. But as a rookie wildcatter from Cleveland, our ratings performance was considered astounding with great media word-of-mouth to boot.

Could some of my mileage alchemy skills rub off onto my ability to sell *Kwik Witz*? I had seen the offices of local program directors in Wisconsin with random black VHS tapes stacked everywhere and glossy presentations in the circular file. My presentation couldn't afford to be ignored—I only had one shot.

For starters, I not only spray-painted the demo tape an attention-getting bright purple, but I then packed it into a bright-red plastic lunch box and filled the rest with candy. I hand-wrote the show description and ratings on twenty-three oversized pages of an 18 x 36 sketch pad so it couldn't be filed nor easily fit in a small garbage can—which was the awful fate of most TV pitches to program directors.

And for my trademark secret ingredient: a combination lock.

The lock was fastened to the outside of the lunch box. The program director would have to read the entire sketch pad to get to the important stuff—the part where there was a phone number to call for the combination lock. What program director could resist the curiosity of a handmade oversized old school Power Point, a locked mystery package, and the whacko who must be behind it all? Most companies would be happy with two-percent responses on direct mail. I sent this pitch to twenty people at the five stations in the top-four markets—New York, Los Angeles, Chicago, and Philadelphia — and received calls and secured pitch meetings for the lock combination from *all twenty*.

There was lots of tire kicking and lots of "I can be the second station to commit to your show, but not the first." My narrative as the crazy underdog outsider was a mixed blessing as it generated admiration and inspiration from the stations but also skepticism about my lack of experience.

Kwik Witz was finally given its big break by the NBC station in Chicago committing to airing the show after *Saturday Night Live*, contingent on my convincing another eighty-five percent of the TV markets in the country to commit as well. I had six weeks to barnstorm the country meeting four station program directors per day.

Once again, my mileage stash would become a fundamental part of the business plan to make *Kwik Witz* an affordable reality, saving me tens of thousands of dollars but depleting the chances for the yet unrealized international Business Class sojourns.

All of the air travel to recruit a national network would be exclusively one-way, with no advance notice, and during the week, which normally require crazy high fares. I was spared the cost by using my United miles. But I was captive to United's routing system of always having to fly out-of-the-way one-stop routes via their hub airports instead of nonstops. It was a brutal trade-off of saving money by using miles. Routine one-and-a-half to two-hour nonstop trips were stretched to four to five-hour-circuitous routings like Washington DC to Atlanta via Chicago and Kansas City to Memphis via Denver.

Despite the overwhelming odds, this scrappy independent from Cleveland somehow cobbled together a ramshackle TV network representing 85% of the media markets in America, so *Kwik Witz* would debut on the national stage.

Kwik Witz aired for three years during late-night weekend time periods averaging 1.1 million viewers. *Kwik Witz* was recognized as a proving ground to help launch the careers of over thirty of today's truly gifted comedy performers including Steve Carell (*The Office*), Wayne Brady (*Whose Line Is It Anyway*), Nia Vardalos (*My Big Fat Greek Wedding*), and Jack McBrayer (*30 Rock*). Dozens of other *Kwik Witz* alums would migrate to acting or writing in network TV shows like *Mad TV, Politically Incorrect, Conan O'Brien, The Middle, The Goldbergs, The Drew Carey Show, Let's Make a Deal,* and plenty of movie roles.

After the final show taping in 1998, it was finally time to fly back to Cleveland and regroup with my family. Between juggling Green Bay Packers and *Kwik Witz* travel, I had been home less than seven months a year for the last few years. Most of the parents at my kids' school assumed that Julie and I were divorced because my kids always gushed to their friends that their dad was always out of town, but they got to fly to meet him every few months and do crazy cool stuff. While Julie had to juggle double duty with working and childrearing, she did so with aplomb. And it gave her a chuckle every time she flew out to the production set and have the crew look at her in awe as the 'producer's wife.' Julie was not easily impressed or ego-driven, so she was often embarrassed at the deference shown to her … and me.

After five breakneck years, could I really retreat back into a suburban lifestyle? Little league with my two pre-teen sons and diaper duty with my infant daughter? Even if we were able to travel together as much as we wanted to, could I bridge the gap between my wife's desire to lounge on a Cancun beach, margarita in hand, versus my desire to explore the jungles of Indonesia?

These conundrums would have to wait. My mileage-earning

radar was going berserk as I was leafing through United's in-flight magazine, *Hemispheres*, on my flight home from Los Angeles after the last taping of *Kwik Witz*.

There was a promotion that took up two-pages of the magazine. Fly a full-fare First Class (not Business Class) ticket during the month of May between any of the Star Alliance hub cities that were covered in a new magazine feature called 'Three Perfect Days,' then United would credit the member's Mileage Plus account with 25,000 bonus miles.

United was a charter member of the Star Alliance, a consortium of international airlines that banded together, ostensibly for marketing reasons, to offer customers one-stop-shopping airfares anywhere in the world. They probably were also a pretty effective means of colluding on key routes to keep airfares high.

In 1998 25,000 bonus miles were considered a substantial bonus as there were no such things as credit card sign-up bonuses or mileage-mall promotions to goose up mileage earning. So, yeah, 25,000 miles in front of me definitely got my attention.

The ingredients for this Three Perfect Days recipe weren't just scattered around the area; they were in cities and airlines scattered around the world.

United:	Los Angeles, Washington
Air Canada:	Toronto
Lufthansa:	Frankfurt, Munich
Scandinavian:	Copenhagen, Stockholm
Thai Airways:	Bangkok
Varig:	São Paolo
South African:	Johannesburg

Despite being cooped up on a plane for five hours before

the advent of wifi at 36,000 feet, I tapped into my encyclopedic knowledge of everything Star Alliance!

Right away, I eliminated Johannesburg, São Paulo, and Bangkok because they were so remote from each other and the other hub cities, so First Class airfares would easily exceed ten thousand dollars. No research was needed for that nonstarter scenario.

Next, I tried creating city pairs that were close by to one another in hopes of a more affordable fare. Frankfurt-Copenhagen and Toronto-New York were both short hops, but I knew they were only serviced with Business Class, not First Class, so they wouldn't qualify. The only city pair left was Washington-Los Angeles in First Class, which I recalled had clocked in at around a hefty $5,000.

At that point, I was out of options to join this promotion. It seemed like someone at United Corporate should be fired for conceiving this train wreck of a promotion. Why was United wasting ink on a two-page promotion that seemed to reward the .0001% of customers who had to be filthy rich and could care less about 25,000 miles? And considering that the promotion essentially required spending $5,000 for domestic airfares and $13,000 for international airfares, only offering 25,000 bonus miles was an embarrassing pittance. For the rest of us, this Three Perfect Days bonus promotion was totally irrelevant.

I was moving on.

I continued to leaf through the *Hemispheres* magazine. I noticed a couple of pages had been ripped out. After continuing to read, I realized that the missing torn-out pages were actually that month's Three Perfect Days feature. Oh well, so what?

On my connecting flight, I happened to open the in-flight magazine again, looking for an unused crossword puzzle. Lo and behold, I got a quick glimpse of the Three Perfect Days featured

Star Alliance hub city. There was a glossy photo with a lot of glitter and a lot of skin.

Huh?

Why was *Las Vegas* being featured as a bona fide Star Alliance hub when it paled in comparison to other United hubs like San Francisco and Chicago, which didn't make the cut in the article. But, more importantly, why was I obsessing about a seemingly irrelevant editorial decision by a magazine about the arcane nuances of Las Vegas in the Star Alliance hierarchy?

That would be the 25,000-mile question.

Las Vegas was only a forty-minute flight from Los Angeles. Was it possible that such a short puddle jump route would be serviced by a First Class aircraft? I wasn't optimistic. And even if there was a qualifying First Class cabin for the promotion, would it be a cost-effective fare? I still wasn't optimistic. The final 25,000-mile answer would have to wait until I deplaned in Cleveland and got home to research the intriguing LA-Vegas route.

The answer turned out to be a mixed bag. The good news was there was a First Class cabin, but the bad news was the fare cost $425 … normally a ridiculously high price.

But these were not normal times.

With Las Vegas as the secret ingredient, I could easily combine and whisk the other ingredients together to transform the otherwise backwater Three Perfect Days, 25,000-mile promotion into a scalable mileage earning project.

THREE PERFECT DAYS ANALYSIS

LA-Vegas earned miles	2,000	$425	LA-Vegas airfare
3 Perfect Days bonus	+ 25,000		
Total Miles	27,000		
No. of LA-Vegas trips	x 3	x 3	No. of LA-Vegas trips
intl. Business Class award redemption	= 81,000	= $1,275	cost of miles
		vs. $6,000	cost of retail airfare

My philosophy of converting cash toward earning mega-miles instead of mega-retail fares in international Business Class still worked with Three Perfect Days. To earn the 25,000-mile-promotion bounty simply required three roundtrips from LA to Vegas in First Class.

I discovered the LA-Vegas routing, but I still needed warm bodies to fill the seats to scale the mileage earning.

Cue the comedy improv actor pipeline from *Kwik Witz.*

Most of the improv comedy performers in *Kwik Witz* were your classic struggling actors. There were about fifty that cycled through our shows, and each of them were typically part of other improv groups. So, let's just say that I had theoretical access to several hundred struggling improv actors.

My game plan was to recruit improv actors to fly back and forth between LA-Vegas in First Class *twenty* times during the month of May under their own names, as airlines were now checking IDs.

No more Steve Belkin clones!

I chose twenty roundtrips as a big enough commitment to ensure only serious candidates would filter through. They would be paid a twenty-five-dollar stipend along with each free ticket.

THREE PERFECT DAYS FLYER COSTS/EARNING

No. of LA-Vegas trips per flyer	20	20	No. of LA-Vegas trips per flyer
LA-Vegas earned/ bonus miles	x 27,000	x $450	LA-Vegas airfare/ per diem
Total Miles per Flyer	= 540,000	= $9,000	Total Cost per Flyer
intl. Business Class award redemption	/ 80,000		
awards earned per flyer	= 7	$1285 $6000	Cost per award vs. Cost of retail airfare

I would open up new United accounts under each of their names and addresses. But I would create a separate phone number and email address that would be routed to me, so if United had any unexpected reason to communicate, I would be the contact on behalf of any given flyer. And I would create their account user name and password so only I could access their account. I would submit their account number on all of the tickets purchased.

While I would book specific flights and dates, First Class airfares were fully changeable without penalty and without notice. So, each person simply had to commit to flying twenty roundtrips *anytime* during the May qualifying window.

I decided to spread a wide net, hoping that out of 250 inquiries, I would get a handful confirmed. Maybe earn a couple of million miles or so to replenish my account from all the *Kwik Witz* redemptions and have enough for dream vacations for the next decade or so, like a retirement fund filled with miles as well as cash, stocks, and bonds.

Like The 'Gobble-Gobble Run', the initial response rate was not encouraging. But once the influential leader of a big improv group decided to pull the trigger, it was mayhem. In less than two days, four confirmed flyers became *eighty*.

First, I was flabbergasted, then I was jubilant. But when the initial buzz wore off, I was pensive, very pensive, very, very pensive. Eighty flyers were way beyond my expectations and my financial wherewithal to fund.

What if I could somehow actually afford to hire *every* one of them. They wouldn't be high rollers because most of them were close to broke, so maybe they would be playing the nickel slots. But they would be "SKY High Rollers" since they would be descending upon Vegas from 36,000 feet twenty times in a month.

SKY HIGH ROLLERS FLYERS ANALYSIS

flyers	80	80	flyers
LA-Vegas miles	27,000	$450	LA-Vegas airfare/ per diem
trips per flyer	x 20	x 20	trips per flyer
Total miles	= 43,000,000	= $720,000	Total Cost
Intl. Business Class award redemption	/ 80,000		
Total awards for partnership, split 4 ways	= 527		

Despite the audacity of the money and miles and logistics involved, I was mesmerized. Should I figure out how to give this promotion a go with *ten times* the flyers than I had planned?

To provide an appreciation of the scalable potential of the Three Perfect Days project, a comparison to the reigning mileage earning kingpin of the late 1990's 'The Pudding Guy' would be apt.

The Pudding Guy had catapulted the sleepy world of airline mileage earning into the collective consciousness with his history-making scheme. His methodology was far different than mine. While I earned miles through flying, he earned his through buying.

A food products company, Healthy Choice, offered a seemingly innocuous promotion that offered one hundred American Airline miles for each and every product purchase. Healthy Choice had dozens of products with the AA offer that all cost around three to five dollars. But he found the 'secret sauce,' a product that only cost twenty-five cents. A single-serve pudding cup. He found a way to save 95% on the cost of acquisition of the AA miles promotion. And he went to town!

Actually, he went to the grocery stores.

The Pudding Guy didn't just clean out his neighborhood grocery stores of twenty-five-cent individual pudding cups. He swept through over a dozen grocery stores amassing over twelve thousand pudding cups and banking over 1.2 million AA miles for just over $3,000. And he donated the pudding bounty to local food banks.

I don't know how he redeemed his 1.2 million miles, but I knew his options. He could redeem 15 international Business Class awards that each cost about $200 in mileage earning or 48 domestic economy awards costing about $65.

The Pudding Guy should have been my hero or my role model.

But he wasn't.

I was perplexed. Why did he stop at a million or so miles when his cost of earning miles was about 80% less than my two previous projects? If he was short on money, why not get partners or investors? If he was short on time, why not hire some college kids to fan out to more grocery stores? If he was short on pudding supply in his hometown, why not road trip to the next town?

I can't read his mind for what restricted his pudding escapades. But my sense was that he and I would have very different mindsets. He was collecting pudding and miles and having a blast doing it. One million miles was probably a perfectly satisfying and defensible big numeric marker to reference to the guys at the bowling alley or to amuse the grandkids.

One million or ten million miles, he still would have been The Pudding Guy, a media magnet for the novelty of his mileage accomplishment. He likely wasn't losing sleep about how many miles he left on the table because it likely hadn't occurred to him that there was even a table!

And here I was, with a cold, calculated understanding of not only how many miles were on the table, but their value to the nearest one one-hundredth of a cent. How many Business Class tickets could be redeemed? How to recruit and manage a large labor pool. How to strictly adhere to airline program terms and conditions. And over the horizon, how to raise three-quarters of a million dollars.

While The Pudding Guy was busy savoring his mileage recipe, I was busy monetizing, maximizing, and systematizing my mileage alchemy to lap him *forty-three* times. One-upping The Pudding Guy and making mileage history were admittedly vanity issues that in retrospect, I am not proud of. But my real overriding concern was about whether another scaling opportunity of this magnitude would ever happen again. If this was a once-in-a-lifetime chance to be mileage self-sufficient for life, I had to be ready.

I had to raise $750,000.

My parents and in-laws were approaching retirement age, and traveling the world would loom large for both of them. My pitch to them, in retrospect, was pretty naïve. I didn't explain the risks of airline programs going belly up in a recession or massive devaluations or extortionist taxes, fees, and fuel surcharges. Because I had no idea that they existed or even could exist. Instead, I focused on what I knew —that they could fly in Business Class for about 75-80% less by using mileage instead of cash as a currency. No stock or other investment could offer such a compelling value that would be fixed over time. And miles weren't taxable, which was always a welcome notion in their tax bracket.

My dad was suitably enough impressed that he brought a fellow promoter into the investment mix.

I had three partners, but they felt that since I found this inventive and obscure deal and had the herculean task of administering the *1,600* flights and managing the eighty mileage accounts that I should be a sweat equity partner instead of contributing my own cash. The mileage would be split four ways, but the costs would be split only three ways, excluding me. I was grateful for the validation.

Unlike The Pudding Guy, who treated his mileage earning like a lark, my role would be serious business overseeing a serious business earning 43 million miles with a $720,000 slush fund.

The investor partnership also let me use my United credit card to buy the airfares to earn another 1.4 million miles for my personal use.

I was so busy counting my good fortune for the 1.4 million-mile extra spiff that I failed to realize the consequences of using one credit card with a mere thirty-five-thousand-dollar credit limit and sixteen-day window to purchase 1,600 tickets within the qualifying promotion timeframe.

I contacted a Visa supervisor and explained that I could spend $720,000 in sixteen days with her company if she could help me allow pre-payments to avoid freezing the card due to maxing it out. She decisively said no.

Then, I decided on a Hail Mary. I actually explained to her this crazy mileage scheme and hoped that she would be totally impressed or at least dumbfounded enough to change her mind. She still said no. At the conclusion of the call, she oddly asked me to confirm my phone number and email address just to confirm that my account was updated.

Later that night, I received a call. From the Visa lady.

She apologized profusely for calling me after hours. She actually wanted to help and had an idea, but she could not share it during our call as it was being recorded by the company.

She told me I could send her twenty checks for $35,000 made out to Visa.

To her house. Each day when the account was about to max out, she would manually input the next check to clear the account in real-time so I would be able to charge airline tickets uninterrupted. For her trouble, she meekly inquired if it would be inappropriate to help her and her hubby get to Orlando for a much overdue vacation as I would soon have more than enough miles.

As you can imagine, I rejected that offer outright. There was no way I'd use my valuable miles for a domestic economy award. But I would gladly spring for the $175 airfare in cash to get her and her hubby to Tomorrowland! We sealed the deal, and the 1,600 tickets were processed as scheduled.

The tickets were sent to each flyer with a short set of instructions:

- Yes, you can drink liberally during the flights, but stay reasonably in control and well-behaved.
- If you intend on drinking on flights back to LA, please don't drive home. Instead, arrange alternate transport.
- Double check that your frequent flyer number is inputted in the system, even though we did so during the reservation process.
- You don't have to fly on the date and/or time on your ticket as First Class is fully changeable without penalty. Just make sure you complete your twenty roundtrips by May 30, a one-month window.
- We have invested roughly nine-thousand dollars in you and are reliant on your trust and sense of responsibility.
- Enjoy Vega$$$$.

During early May, I started auditing the flyer accounts. Most of the flyers were indeed flying but not on the flights we booked, as expected. I knew, and they knew that such travel flexibility was baked into our deal with them. By mid-May, about 10 million of 43 million miles were posted.

As the Three Perfect Days frenzy of mileage earning was on auto-pilot, I finally had a few moments to reminisce on some never-been-exposed *Kwik Witz* moments.

Steve Carell had signed a contract to do a second season of the show. He would be getting a raise from the TV-union minimum of $650 to $975 per show. He was that good! During the rehearsals for Season Two, he pulled me aside and begged that I keep this meeting in confidence.

He whispered, "ABC has offered me a holding deal."

I tentatively responded, "That is fantastic. Congrats. If anyone deserves that, it's you. And by the way, what the hell is a holding deal?"

Maybe the ABC top brass had seen Carell's comedy genius on *Kwik Witz*, and they wanted to call him up to the big leagues to star in a network show. Only they just didn't have a specific show yet, but they didn't want to risk one of the other networks to sign Carell in the interim. Hence, the holding deal. Steve was offered a hefty six-figure for ABC's right to exclusively do nothing with him for a year until if or when they found something … like *The Office*. Despite knowing that Carell had signed for Season Two with *Kwik Witz*, they wanted his exclusivity to start immediately. Steve could have easily just let his agent take care of the dirty work of wiggling out, or as they say in Cleveland, breaching his contract. But Steve was a mensch and insisted that he wanted to approach me directly for my blessing. I was grateful for his respectful gesture; he was grateful for the opportunity to get the ground-breaking exposure that led to the ABC deal.

Wayne Brady was cut from the same cloth. The producers of *Whose Line Is It Anyway* offered Wayne a lucrative offer, likely in the low five-figures. But like Carell, they wanted his services immediately and exclusively while he was still under contract to my show. Like Carell, he also kept his manager at bay and contacted me directly.

"Steve, I'm rejecting the offer from *Whose Line*. They can wait. It's just a power play."

I protested strongly. "But Wayne, it's huge money. Their show is a ratings hit. I'm thrilled to release you."

He was adamant. "You believed in me for two years when I

was knocking on *Whose Line's* door and was totally ignored. They found me because of you. They can wait."

And wait he did. His manager and I fretted as the amazing offer was indeed summarily pulled. Brady's power-play cost a lot of money down the line—*just not his*! After our contract with Wayne expired, *Whose Line* upped the ante to close to *double* the original offer per episode.

The first time I saw Tina Fey in Chicago, I immediately offered her a contract which she signed along with her teammate Rachel Dratch. A few days later, she called to tell me she had been offered a writing job. That required starting ASAP. In New York City. On a comedy show. *Saturday Night Live*. I never had the chance to announce that she was in our talent lineup, and since no one had heard of her anyway, no one would be impressed or crushed that she was a no-show. Dratch also followed Fey into *SNL* the following year.

Amy Poehler was an improv purist—all risk, no net. *Kwik Witz* was a TV show whereby comedy risk had to be balanced with the viewer possibly clicking-the-remote risk if a comedy bit fell short. Therefore, we gave teams their subject matter in advance to flesh out their material to *ensure* there was a critical mass of solid laughs in each bit. Not scripted, just sculpted.

Our short meeting backstage after one of her shows with the *Upright Citizens Brigade* ended with a vow instead of a contract. "I can't believe that your show bastardizes what I'm so passionate about. I would never come on your show. And, I would never do anything remotely scripted."

With that, she brusquely excused herself to remain toiling in the obscurity and poverty of pure improv … until she ended up with her 'never say never' stints on *SNL* and *Parks and Recreation*.

For the third year of the show, I moved production from Chicago to LA because, by that time, most of the talent was clustered there, and I could save huge money on flights, hotels, per diems, etc. But finding reasonable studio prices was a challenge. During my search, I found myself at an unassuming studio at the edge of suburbia. As I was waiting in the lobby, I noticed a steady flow of good-looking people traipsing around in robes.

During the obligatory studio tour, I asked to take a quick peek at the current production but was told it was a closed set. At that moment, a robed Adonis brushed by us and opened the door just wide enough to get a four-second glance at the proceedings.

There were people. There were robes. The robes were on top of the table. And the people were on top of each other.

The studio deal was tempting, alas a little too tempting.

Chapter 4:
Kangaroo Court On American Soil

My cell phone rang and 'United Airlines' glowed on the caller ID screen.

"Hi, there. I hope I'm catching you at a good time?" announced a pleasant female voice on the other end.

Actually, the timing was horrible. Not only was I on a porn set, but all eighty of the Vegas SKY High Rollers flyers' phone numbers were being re-directed to my phone. So, I needed time to stall so I could cross-reference all eighty accounts to decipher which member matched up with the phone line that United was calling. I hesitantly asked her to call back shortly.

In the meantime, worst-case scenarios raced through my brain. Had one of the flyers brought a stripper on the plane? Had someone absconded with the champagne served in First Class? Had Casino Security hauled somebody off the plane for counting cards?

After not answering her question for a clearly awkward amount of time, I finally responded, "Actually, I'm just on the tail-end of a meeting. Could we arrange a follow-up in the next hour or so?"

"Oh goodness, I'm sorry for the intrusion. Look forward to speaking, Thanks for your time, Jeff."

Ahhh, Jeff. Thanks for the clue. There were only two Jeffs on the flyer roster, and I was able to match it up in one minute instead of the expected one hour. I scanned the right Jeff's United account and his personal profile and was good to go for the next call.

An hour later, we resumed the call. She soothingly asked, "First and foremost, I hope everything is OK on your health front?"

Hmmm. I had no idea where this question was going to take us, so the answer had to be skillfully ambiguous.

"Oh, wow, I appreciate your asking. Thankfully, every day is a new day, and today is off to a great start."

She continued. "OK, I'm relieved to hear. We were just concerned about all of the no-shows last week for your flights to Las Vegas."

Ahhhhh, OK. I had advised the flyers that while they had to complete their twenty flights during May, their First-Class tickets were fully changeable, and they could fly anytime during that monthly window. Hence, the no-shows for the scheduled flights. I should have instructed them to call United if they weren't going to fly on a given scheduled flight on their ticket.

I split the difference between reconciling the health and no-show inquiries with the pleasant agent.

"Actually, I had some crazy workdays that precluded several of the trips, and then I was really exhausted from the workload a couple of days after. But I'm running on all cylinders now. My apologies for not giving you guys a ring with a heads-up about not using those tickets. I'll make sure it won't happen again."

She appreciated the reassurance. I thanked her for her time and was about to hang up. And then.

"By the way…" she rushed in. "Are you traveling with some friends or colleagues?"

I wasn't sure where this was going. When in doubt, stall.

"I'm sorry, I'm not sure I caught your question. Could you kindly repeat it? "

Luckily, she gave more details this time. "It seems like almost everyone who was booked on your flights last week were also no-shows, so we figured maybe you are all part of the same group."

Nothing wrong with group travel, so let's go with it.

"Yeah", I said with a chuckle, "We have a travel department that books flights now and asks questions about the staff schedules later." That response was actually rooted in truth. Because I had to book sixteen hundred flights in less than two weeks, I just didn't have the luxury of soliciting date preferences from each of the eighty flyers. I just seized every available seat on an equal rotation basis.

"Again, I'll make sure that any flights that are booked where there is a schedule conflict, we will alert United in advance." That was apparently exactly what she needed to hear.

It was a fair inquiry from United. If they had advance notice about a passenger schedule change, they could reopen that First-Class seat for sale. They were just seeking a bit of reasonable effort from us. I would call all eighty flyers with the new directive.

Just when I thought I had extinguished this no-show brush-fire, I received a call on my personal phone. It was someone from United Legal. I'm sure there was a name attached in the phone introduction, but in my shock, the only thing I could remember was that his first name was 'United' and his last name was 'Legal.' He never referenced his name again, nor did I have the guts to ask. It started well enough, but with a lawyer, it's usually down-hill from there.

"First of all, on behalf of United, I want to thank you for being such a loyal customer. We don't have too many members with eight years of consecutive elite status. And we were glad that somebody like you was willing to take the plunge on our Pass Plus product. And we hope you are enjoying your lifetime elite status for earning a million miles." He had my United resume down pat. And then the hammer.

"Mr. Belkin."

"Please call me Steve." Gulp.

He continued, "As I was saying, Mr. Belkin." Ouch.

"We need your cooperation to cease and desist this Las Vegas venture of yours." Although it was phrased as a strong request, his gruff and clipped tone suggested that it was a demand with an air of finality.

Venture. That word actually had a nice ring to it. *Cease and desist* not so much. But if whatever his concern was, why was he using such a neutral word like 'venture' when his underlying tone suggested words like scam or plot or perhaps a scheme or conspiracy?

He strangely didn't reference obvious buzzwords like illegal, fraudulent, against the Terms and Conditions. Apparently, he didn't use those more toxic words because he couldn't. The no-show issue was not a punishable offense either. I had paid all for sixteen hundred tickets with one credit card, so surely I wasn't trying to hide or scam anything. United had earned $720,000. So how could a good lawyer fail to explain their pretext for a cease-and-desist order in no uncertain terms.

I kept it simple. "What seems to be the *specific* problem?"

"We know what you are doing; and we don't like it; and you have really got to stop it immediately." Well, at least I was now clear about what United didn't like: "**it.**" The conversation then continued with the same circular references.

I asked, "Help me understand what you don't like about this 'venture' you keep referencing."

His reply: "You know what you are doing, and the airline doesn't like **it,** and it has to stop now."

In other words United wasn't exactly sure what the hell I was doing, but they were hoping that their strong-arm tactics would frighten me into unilaterally revealing my master plan. Since I was doing absolutely nothing wrong, I wasn't going to continue to be interrogated. If the lawyer had a specific grievance or accusation, then it was time to spit it out. Similarly, if United decided to define what **"it"** was that they "didn't like," I would address that as well.

Otherwise, this perplexing fishing expedition was over. I bid the lawyer adieu.

I reviewed the Three Perfect Days promotion. It stated clearly that there were "25,000 miles for *each* roundtrip." There were "*no* limitations or restrictions on the number of times the bonus could be earned." If United didn't like my scaling, why didn't they simply limit the bonus to one per customer? I would have had no interest in scaling if the maximum miles were capped at 27,000 miles per account, well below the 80,000-mile threshold for my sweet spot of international Business Class awards. They made the rules, so they would have to live with them … and maybe learn a lesson for future promotions.

The following day United Legal called me again. Damn, he didn't volunteer his name again. "We know what you are doing and we don't like it." Again, that cryptic **"it."** What's **"it"** for crying out loud?? He was so fixated on the word "it" that I started visualizing him looking like "Cousin Itt" from *The Addams Family*, his face totally obscured with long blond hair and glasses, which helped keep me calm.

And finally, the **"it"** that United didn't like, was revealed.

"Mr. Belkin, with tens of millions of miles being earned, it's clear that you will be brokering them, which is explicitly against our rules."

In other words, I hadn't done anything against their rules, but they were suspicious that I was going to be breaking their rules at some future point. They were going to punish me for something that had not happened, and, in fact, they couldn't prove that motivation for earning miles was to broker them.

Admittedly, the optics of the Vegas 'venture' didn't look good, but I knew that no brokering would ever transpire. Not to mention, there were no rules against bad optics. "Since you acknowledged that I have been such a good customer, you should feel comfortable knowing that I clearly understand and will continue to abide by the rules. And I appreciate your clarifying your concern, so there is no need to worry." I would not dignify his speculative accusation by even breathing the word 'brokering' in my response.

It was astounding that United could even think that I would be brazen or stupid enough to broker miles that had such a ridiculously transparent paper trail back to one person. And then, the Kangaroo Court commenced.

"Mr. Belkin, you can shut this down, or we can shut this down. If *you* shut it down, the miles earned up to this point will be honored and the unused tickets refunded. If *we* shut it down, the miles could very well be confiscated."

This should have been a shocking and arbitrary ultimatum to me. But it wasn't. His threat was enshrined in the Terms and Conditions (T&C) that I knew inside and out. Like every airline program, miles earned from United Mileage Plus were the property of the program, and they reserved the right to retrieve them at any time. And if that policy failed for any reason, United, like every other program, had the indisputable fallback position:

they reserved the right to change or cancel any aspect of the program or the program itself at their discretion at any time.

So, when United claimed "they didn't like it," that wasn't an opinion; it was a dictate. And because their T&C were published and my participation in the airline program constituted my implied agreement to it, there was nothing I could do. I had no legal redress since their program was outside the formal legal process. Their gold, their rules. But I had to protect the gold that my three partners had spent and ensure that their miles didn't disappear into thin air.

It was infuriating to know that I was right and that United knew I was right. But United was infuriated that someone could scale their program to earn miles for pennies on the dollar, using information that United had willingly provided in the public domain. My fury was principled and defensible, but United's fury could make the disposition of the ten million miles already earned go poof.

So, I blinked. Kind of. "I need United to consolidate the miles from all eighty accounts into my account since you can count on my being trustworthy. That way, the ten million would be totally safe from your fears of brokering. And I can save United the complex job of having to monitor eighty accounts for the future."

My eminently reasonable proposition was greeted with an eminently arbitrary and capricious rejection. "Mr. Belkin, you know quite well that our Terms and Conditions explicitly states that mileage cannot be transferred between accounts." In other words, United had the *ability* to consolidate all of the disparate mileage account balances into my account, but they simply had *no willingness*.

But this shutdown after only partial earning had some challenges that would impact my investor partners. I needed increments of eighty thousand miles for international Business

Class awards. The partial earning left all eighty accounts with far fewer miles than the anticipated 80,000-mile increment. Each account would require hundreds or thousands of dollars of expensive mileage purchases to top off. I had to be vigilant to protect my investors from such undue new costs, as it was bad enough that I would only be able to deliver on 25% of the expected miles earned.

I held my ground. "I will agree to wind down this down if you agree to the account consolidation."

He was insistent. "United doesn't permit this. Are you going to shut down this venture or not?"

If United confiscated the miles, my only recourse would be to fight them in the media. But even if I won the PR war and exposed United's dirty pool, I still would be out the 10 million miles that were still currently in play.

I stuck to my guns about the quid pro quo—the shutdown requires a consolidation. "You are asking me to do something that I ordinarily would not agree to, and I am simply asking the same of you."

"I am not *authorized* to allow these account transfers, I'm sorry." All of a sudden, I recognized the subtlety of his reply. **The account transfer policy morphed from being impossible to merely not authorizable** … yet! United had blinked, not sort of, but for real. They just didn't want to admit it … yet.

We both agreed to think things through and regroup the next day. Twenty minutes later, "Cousin Itt" from United Legal called back. It was like an *Invasion of the Body Snatchers* movie. I didn't recognize the soothing and friendly voice on the other side of the line.

"Hi, there, Steve."

Steve! He called me Steve!

He continued in earnestness. "It's a shame this situation got a bit messy. We never intended to question your trustworthiness. We appreciate your understanding our position and your cooperation for volunteering to wrap up things up. I was able to fight for you on the account consolidation front to get all ten million miles into your account."

What a cynical case of United-speak. It wasn't a 'situation;' it was an unfounded accusation. It wasn't 'understanding;' it was me being force-fed United's position under the threat of mileage confiscation. It wasn't my 'cooperation to volunteer;' it was my desperation to protect three partners who put their unwavering trust in me.

Suffice to say, we both agreed to the verbal quid pro quo. I wound down the project and explained to my partners that the bad news was that the targeted forty million miles weren't going to happen. But the good news was that I preserved the 10 million miles already earned, and that their money for the other 30 million miles would promptly be refunded.

But my shutdown arrangement with United was never in writing. I closed the venture in due time, and the miles were supposed to be consolidated. However, United never called back with a timetable to aggregate the ten million miles into my account. I checked my account daily. After two weeks, it looked grim, and I fretted. Had Cousin Itt reneged? I realized I didn't even know Cousin Itt from United Legal's real name. Doomsday scenarios swirled in my head as I imagined that those 10 million miles were sent back to the ether. No miles, pissed-off investors, my dad and father-in-law's trust in me shattered forever.

Seventeen days after the shutdown, the miles finally posted. Surely it shouldn't have taken so long for the routine number of computer keystrokes required for eighty electronic transfers.

10 million miles were earned, representing twenty-five percent of the SKY High Rollers project. The unused airfares

were refunded. While ten million miles were in my account, my three partners had access to their pro-rated shares. All the improv comedy flyers would have some fun bragging rights about flying in high style to Vegas.

In the aftermath, I couldn't stop deconstructing my every move. If I didn't have partners, would I have risked figuring out if United was bluffing or not by refusing to stop the SKYHigh Rollers flyers from continuing to fly? If the miles had been confiscated, would I have gained the necessary media attention to shame and force United to reinstate the miles and allow my bona fide ticket purchases to be honored? Was there any workaround to protect me from the arbitrary and capricious T&C and its kangaroo court? Was my mileage scaling for the Three Perfect Days promotion worth the aggravation?

The other thing I kept asking myself was—would The Pudding Guy even be pondering all of this crap I was saddled with? Maybe he was actually much smarter than me. Maxing out at one million miles and just enjoying the ride while United was enjoying making my life miserable on their firing line.

A few months later, I would stumble upon a place where my rhetorical question about The Pudding Guy could actually be asked to him directly.

Chapter 5: Mister Randy's Neighborhood

In late 1999 I had stumbled on a slim magazine at an airport lounge called *Inside Flyer*. I was surprised that its content was dedicated to FFP (frequent flyer program) news. Were there actually enough mileage geeks out there to support a monthly magazine? I thought I was the lone wolf. The magazine referenced something called *FlyerTalk*, an online bulletin board for the frequent flyer community. I was definitely a laggard in the internet era, so I was skeptical if *FlyerTalk* would resonate with me.

In fact the term "online community" seemed like was an oxymoron to me. How could you have a community when you couldn't see or talk to someone else? How could you possibly establish a sense of camaraderie or warmth or trust by posting online text messages? There were no emojis to give a dialogue some personality and context. And there wasn't enough bandwidth for video communication.

In the current era of social media hyperconnectivity via smartphones and Facebook, the *FlyerTalk* platform back in 1999 would be considered laughably primitive and archaic. But in 1999 it was cutting edge; it was like was the precursor of open-source e-learning. *FlyerTalk* had no classrooms, no teachers, no courses, no campus, just an astounding repository of raw information spanning sixty FFP and other travel-related forums.

My first challenge was to sift through the tens of thousands of posts to winnow scattered information into usable knowledge. I committed three to four hours daily for nearly four months to the endeavor.

My second challenge was to determine which members were the valuable sources of the raw info. I determined that there were three types of member posting profiles.

The *post-padders* were the majority of members who frequently commented so that their displayed post count beside their username would look impressive. But their actual post-content was basically agreeing or disagreeing with other members posts. By learning to identify and filter out the post-padding crowd, I could save a lot of time when scanning a thread.

The *reliables* were a small but visible group of members with good content to contribute on a consistent basis and were worth following. I jotted down names.

The *cameos* were members who posted infrequently and usually in the middle of a long thread with observations that were a bit technical or arcane. Occasionally, their post would gain traction with other members, but more often than not, their posts would remain unanalyzed, floating in anonymity. The best minds of every key *FlyerTalk* forum from the cameos group would ultimately constitute a virtual board of directors for my equally virtual mileage alchemy lab.

This board of directors would need a chairman of the board. There was only *one* candidate for the job, the ringleader behind *Inside Flyer* and *FlyerTalk*, who was widely acknowledged to be *the* FFP industry's mileage guru, Randy Petersen.

If he actually existed.

For three months, I tried calling him to set up an intro meeting but was unsuccessful. His secretary even had a hard time keeping up with his crisscrossing the globe. He met with upstart airlines that were launching new FFPs wanting his advice on how to one-up the competition. Next, he had to meet with the incumbent FFPs to help defend their programs against the newbies. And Randy was in demand with the corporate travel world about how to leverage the FPPs with coherent and strategic employee travel policies. Randy Petersen was the media darling since FFPs had finally resonated with the mainstream traveler.

With no meeting in sight, I was reduced to stalking. I flew from Cleveland to Washington DC, as I knew he had a speaking gig that day. I snuck into the hotel conference room unnoticed. I was underdressed and had no badge. I beelined it to a seat near the front of the room so that the suspicious hotel security guy wouldn't dare make a ruckus in front of so many people. There were several hundred people there to hear Randy's FFP presentation. He blew the room away so much so that the vast majority of them were staying afterward to shake him down for more information. This dude, Petersen, had his own coterie of groupies.

After my long-anticipated in-person exposure to Randy, I have to admit, I was an instant fanboy! He struck me as the "Colombo" of the frequent flyer world. While much taller than the actor Peter Falk, Randy had a self-effacing, "aw shucks" personality, and he spoke in a slow and deliberate manner with a mild drawl that sounded like a Mason-Dixon Line state, not a Deep South one. The mileage vernacular was fraught with obscure and head-scratching terminology, but Randy had a gift for transforming complex analysis into a homespun tale. But what ultimately sold me on Randy was how he expressed his passion for the mileage game. He was not a forceful advocate, a number cruncher, nor an arrogant braggard. Rather, he came across as being just a bit dazed and confused that anyone would really want to hear what he had to say; and yet, everyone jostled to get a piece of him.

Present company included.

I patiently waited for the line to thin, and two hours later, it was finally my turn. Randy noticed I didn't have a badge nor an expensive suit. His eyes narrowed. He played the "Sorry, I've got to get to the airport" card, which was impossible to argue against. I basically was left with a two-minute elevator pitch about the Gobble-Gobble Run, Pass Plus and the Vegas SKY High Rollers schemes, and, most importantly, my cumulative fourteen million mileage haul.

Randy had met his muse.

He checked his watch a second time. He opted for the red-eye instead, and he bequeathed me the treasured face time that I had been relentlessly pursuing. My mileage scaling intrigued him. I would ultimately be fast-tracked into his very tight inner circle.

Back in the day, he skirted the edges of FFPs with some type of discreet mileage brokering enterprise that was never officially referenced in his bio. So, we shared a mutually edgy past with the FFPs. The difference was, Randy was now a public figure in the mileage world, so he needed to be on his best behavior. I had no such constraints. Randy could vicariously root for my ongoing mileage earning exploits and brushes with airlines that I annoyed and beyond.

He would soon start offering me indispensable "smell tests" about my mileage projects. He was a fastidiously honest broker between FFPs and their members. So, if he advised against greenlighting a project, I would try and re-engineer it, and if that failed, I would ditch it. He also tried to give the FFPs the benefit of the doubt for being ignorant or greedy the first time, but if they chose not to learn their lesson, he did not begrudge me from pursuing unintended mileage opportunities that they should have caught.

Because of my voracious appetite for everything *FlyerTalk*, I posted regularly in the majority of forums and invested two to three hours a day to stay current. My username was "beaubo" after my second son Beau's actual name and its oft-misspelled alternative "Bo." It was an unusual username and would become was an unexpected, but effective branding vehicle for me down the line.

Before online matchmaking services like Tinder or eHarmony, there was the *FlyerTalk* Community Forum. Members traveling to another city would post their date window, and members from that city could arrange a casual meet-up to swap mileage war stories and flesh out otherwise virtual profiles. Participants would post how the meet-up went so future members would know who to engage and who to avoid.

The meet-up system wasn't working for me. There were no members in Green Bay and very few members visits to Cleveland for me to powwow with anyone in person. I still felt like a lone wolf. Maybe I could find a way to scale this emerging in-person social interaction on *FlyerTalk*.

A member from San Diego beat me to the punch.

She was going to have *FlyerTalk*'s first official community event (she called it a "Do," and the name stuck for future events) over a weekend in San Diego. The San Diego Do wasn't merely an informal get-together; it was a bona fide and exciting itinerary with meals, activities and, contests held at a cool downtown hotel. And everyone could use their miles to fly there for free. She optimistically planned for a capacity of one hundred guests. Was the thin reed of mileage commonality enough to motivate a bunch of perfect strangers to spend a few hundred dollars on the event price and hotel, plus burn twenty-five thousand miles to fly there?

Apparently not.

The event was posted about three months out, so there was plenty of time to try and juggle schedules. I was available and totally psyched, but I didn't want to be the first geek to sign up and be perceived as the eager beaver. Was I in good company, or was there just general apathy from other members? The first month rolled by with zero signups. The second month showed promising signs of life—a smattering of maybes, we'll sees, keep ya posteds, gotta clear it with work/spouse/etc., but nary a definitive green light.

With less than a month to go, some brave soul finally took the plunge with a "Yes," and two days later, the event was booked to capacity with a waiting list. There was definitely a shared hunger to give this community a human face. And there were thankfully a lot of familiar usernames on the guest list that I was psyched to meet.

The event organizer must have been a psychology major. She figured that everyone would want to be fashionably and nonchalantly late to the opening ceremony. So, whereas big raffles would normally be the climax of an event, she chose to draw it at the introduction. And everyone would want to be on time because the raffle grand prize was, drumroll ... a free award ticket, a sure crowd-pleaser.

Over the course of the event, guests were assigned seats at meals to avoid cliques and ensure we all met nearly every community member. There were human scavenger hunt contests where guests had to cull key info out of other guests to win prizes. Apparently, the airlines had caught wind of this ground-breaking mileage soiree, and they provided swag bags with airline-branded merchandise and a free domestic upgrade. The guests were treated like today's social influencers.

The group in attendance turned out to be the mixed bag that I kind of expected. A member who I thought was a young female turned out to be an old geezer. Another member who had perfect diction online was a total potty mouth in person. There were people who I perceived online as not so bright who turned out to be brilliant and vice versa. Beyond the superficial looks and personalities, what defined this group to a tee was their sense of empowerment. I don't mean like the way that word is used today as a political statement. I mean literally empowered. No matter how rich or poor, healthy or sick, old or young, each person in attendance knew that with just a few minutes' worth of tapping some keystrokes, they could redeem an award and be on a plane that day to anywhere. *Where* wasn't important. *When* wasn't important. *Wherewithal* wasn't important. What was important was that **they could.**

The power of possibility.

The most fascinating part of the event was the singular focus on the mileage game. I had assumed that at some point over the weekend, the mileage talk would dissipate, and there would just be awkward small talk to fill in the gaps. But it was ninety-seven percent miles, miles, miles. And yet, many of us left the event still feeling like we had far more questions than answers about the Almighty Mile.

The San Diego Do accomplished an incredible milestone that would have its own momentum as these Do events exploded over the next few months—Dusseldorf, Barcelona, Austin, and Vail, among others. Hundreds of people started attending, willing to spend hundreds of dollars to much farther locales to meet virtual strangers for jam-packed weekends of miles, meals, and mead. By putting real faces to e-names, tangible friendships were bonded, and trust was forged.

The Do events had revealed an organic and caring community. And Randy understood that any community, even virtual, needed a modicum of structure to nurture its health and growth. The Do events had provided Randy a recruiting base to establish a responsible group, including me, to serve as *FlyerTalk* forum moderators. We would protect newbies and their beginner questions from snarky veteran members. Extinguish flame wars between hot-headed members. Edit misinformation, disinformation, objectionable language, etc. It was basically an altruistic volunteer gig to keep the peace.

Unknown to the group, Randy had attributed far more value to the moderator volunteers. At his own expense, twice a year, Randy gathered us all together for a "thank you" weekend of fun and frolic at different locales around the country. Most of the moderators tended to be the experts in their forums and were already part of my mileage alchemy brain trust. Still, it was a huge plus to get to know these folks in person and reinforce the budding trust and friendship that would give us all the confidence to collaborate on future mileage projects.

FlyerTalk, as a whole, had developed into an informal brain trust that I had a symbiotic relationship with. I established contact with dozens of members who had far deeper expertise with dozens of programs with which I was unfamiliar. And in return, once these members ramped me up to their level of knowledge, I could offer my unique mileage scaling perspective to discover and coach them on becoming mileage self-sufficient.

While it had been fairly dispiriting and alienating having this mileage passion all these years with no peer group, this wolf finally had his pack as a social, not just a mileage plotting, outlet.

Thanks to Randy and *FlyerTalk*, I had networked a skillful

array of allies to go big or go home when the next mileage discovery was unearthed.

Less than a year later, I would be going big, but going as far away from home as I had ever been.

Chapter 6: Why Crunch the Numbers, When You Can Massage Them

I rarely contributed original ideas to *FlyerTalk*. Instead, I relentlessly looked for the non-intuitive angles to push forward mileage earning ideas that had been cooked up by others. Like any good chef, I could take others' raw materials and slice and dice until it was glazed and seasoned. My niche became turning chicken scratch into chicken salad.

But there was one time where another chef had actually created the chicken salad. So ostensibly, there were no additional ingredients to complete the recipe, and so no one else was looking.

But I figured out how to turn that chicken salad into Chicken Cordon Bleu.

My next mileage project, the 'Baht Run,' named after the currency of Thailand, was widely publicized and credited to me. But the original idea was hatched by an Australian member who was generous in his sharing his discovery with the *FlyerTalk* community. He found and mined the mileage gold. I just polished and set it. Thank you, 'Ozstamps.' You know who you are!

In early 2001 there was an eight-dollar, one-way airfare on Thai Air, a Star Alliance partner, between three cities in northern Thailand. Each flight was less than thirty minutes. The Aussie figured out how to leverage the cheap airfare with the United program. He knew that United awarded Premier Executive elite status after one hundred flight segments were flown. A key perk of that status was the issuance of six Systemwide Upgrades (SWUs). An SWU allowed elite members the benefit of purchasing the lowest possible Economy airfare and redeeming the SWU to upgrade into the Business Class cabin. The SWU was a valuable benefit, especially for members who did not have a sufficient mileage balance to redeem an outright international Business Class award.

The Baht Run strategy was predicated on accumulating those one hundred elite-qualifying flights in low-fare Thailand rather than other high-fare Star Alliance regions like the U.S., Germany, or Australia.

BAHT RUN SWU COMPARATIVE COSTS

	Thai-based airfares	US-based airfares
Flight segments to earn United elite status and 6 SWUs	100	100
average short-haul airfare	x $8	x $250
Total airfare	= $800	= $25,000
	/ 6	/ 6
Cost per SWU	= $135	= $4,200

Unlike the Aussie who was going to fly the one hundred segments himself, I didn't have three weeks of time, let alone patience, to travel to northern Thailand and slog through one hundred flights. Plus, he hadn't factored in the hard costs of flying from Australia, food, lodging, nor the cost of his time. So, his actual cost per SWU would really be nearly double from $135 to $270.

Plus, the SWUs were only available on United, not the other Star Alliance partners. And, of course, there was still the out-of-pocket cost of an Economy Class airfare to be eligible for the upgrade. Still, all in all, an amazing deal.

So, I had heightened interest, but I just didn't have the time. Maybe there was a ready labor pool of unemployed actors or improv comedians in Thailand that I could recruit! I couldn't recruit Steve Belkin clones anymore as the airlines now checked IDs to match tickets. I could, however, recruit folks to fly under their own names with me taking virtual control of their mileage accounts. Despite tangling with United over their distaste about my Vegas SKY High Rollers operatives, they had instituted no rule changes that would prevent me from trying it again. I would just have to implement smarter execution and order a 'smell test' from the mileage guru, Randy, for his expertise to mitigate the risk of another premature shutdown and the ensuing kangaroo court.

So, maybe I could hire a bunch of local Thais to fly the 100 segments. There would be no lodging costs or international travel costs, just wages and a modest food and ground transport stipend. The northern Thai minimum wage per day in 2001 was $3.20. Yes, you read that right, *per day*. If I could pay Thai flyers *five times* as much as the minimum wage, that would be $16 per day, which was a solid wage in that part of the world, especially for the unskilled worker who would simply need to show up on time each day and fly their one hundred segments.

The cumulative airfare and stipend would be a very affordable twelve dollars per flight. At that cost, I could afford to recruit a labor pool of twenty local Thais to fly one hundred short-haul flights to generate 120 SWUs. I could hire a local Thai administrator to keep a master list of the flyer accounts, and when the SWUs were delivered via mail, the administrator would then collect them and give to me when I returned to Thailand at the end of the Baht Run to pay the final balance of the labor pool wages.

The Baht Run strategy had no allowance for margin of error. Even at 99 segments, the elite status required to generate the SWUs would not be triggered. I needed firm guarantees that the labor pool would all fly one hundred flights and not conk out in the middle while I was back in the States, 9,000 miles away.

As a lark I briefly investigated the other dozen or so Star Alliance partner programs, just to see if they had any well-buried sweet spots that might exceed United's earning potential from the Baht Run.

I was zero-for-eleven in finding better options than leveraging the United programs, so when I got the last possible program, Air Canada Aeroplan, I was tempted to just pass over it altogether. Especially since in the Air Canada forum at *FlyerTalk*, the regular members had made a persuasive case that the program was only beneficial to members that specifically flew on Air Canada, not any other Star Alliance partners.

The pundits on *FlyerTalk* were predicting the labor pool size I would be recruiting to earn the United SWUs. They were close on predicting the labor pool quantity I would commit to, but they were dead wrong on the program I would leverage. Unbeknownst to the *FlyerTalk* peanut gallery, the conventional wisdom of my earning United SWUs was going to be supplanted by my crash course in all things *Air Canada Aeroplan*.

Mileage Earning

Despite each of the Bhat Run flights barely being one hundred miles, Aeroplan credited a minimum mile earning of 750 miles per flight.

Elite Bonus Miles

Every flight beyond one hundred flown earned 100% elite bonus.

Elite Bonus Vouchers

Upon earning 75,000 thousand miles, Aeroplan issued a complimentary voucher for one Business Class award anywhere in the world, but only on Air Canada aircraft. And at 150,000 miles, another of the same voucher was issued again.

Elite Qualification

200 flights were required for top-tier status called 'Super Elite.' This was double the number of flights that United required. The reason that this onerous policy was not a deal-breaker for me was because of Aeroplan's secret sauce.

Exclusive Elite Benefit That No Other Program in The World Offered:

No blackout dates for the low-redemption amount/saver award redemptions on Air Canada flights.

Saver awards were normally 'capacity-controlled,' an airline euphemism for 'almost never released.' There were opaque numbers of the attractive low-redemption amount Saver awards that were released on a given flight. Once that arbitrary allocation was exhausted, Aeroplan would black out access to any more inventory at that low-cost Saver award level. All subsequent awards were only redeemable at the 'Standard' award amount, between 250 and 400% more miles.

Even top-tier members of the other FFPs were captive to blackout policies.

Aeroplan Super Elites could redeem miles or vouchers year-round, anywhere in Air Canada's worldwide route system on their aircraft, with no blackout dates, at the low-cost award level. It was especially valuable during peak season vacation and holiday travel windows.

Compared to the one roundtrip for "The Gobble-Gobble Run" and twenty roundtrips for "Vegas SKY High Rollers," *100* roundtrips for the Baht Run flyers seemed like a daunting threshold. I would need to ensure I had an economic model that had incentives to motivate completion but also enforcement mechanisms to ensure that completion—especially since I had no margin of error. If anything less than 200 thirty-minute flights were flown, I'd lose one voucher and access to the critical no blackout perk.

I also needed to be mindful about the optics of the Baht Run. It wouldn't take Aeroplan long to catch wind of this scaling project, especially when they would have twenty new members with fifteen-syllable Thai names flying on routes that most Canadians would have never heard of. Not that I was doing anything remotely against their Terms and Conditions. But like United, Aeroplan management might just not like 'it!!!'

However, unlike United, the Aeroplan program had a surprisingly lenient policy about third-party access to primary account holders. A primary account holder simply needed to fax (yes, fax in 2001!) an authorization form giving permission to a specific third party (me) to access their account with the login and PIN. The third party (me again) could even book award travel for anyone of their choice. The authorization forms would be written in both Thai and English, to ensure there would be no issue of having the flyers signing documents they didn't understand.

The tally per Baht Run flyer traveling 200 segments:

BAHT RUN/AEROPLAN ANALYSIS

75,000	flights 1-100 earn 750 minimum miles
+ intl. Business Class voucher	threshold bonus at 75,000 earned miles
+ 75,000	flights 101-200 earn 750 minimum miles
+ 75,000	100% elite bonus
+ intl. Business Class voucher	threshold bonus at 150,000 earned miles
= 225,000	miles good for 3 intl. Business Class awards
+ 150,000	value of two international Business Class vouchers
= 375,000	TOTAL Miles
5	international Business Class awards per flyer

So, my discovery of a far more lucrative leveraging of the Baht Run was the reason that I received so much credit and publicity instead of the Aussie originator. I essentially put the Baht Run on Aeroplan steroids.

The only small detail that needed to be accomplished to greenlight the Baht Run was actually recruiting the local Thai labor pool that up until now, I had only been theorizing about. The truth is, I had absolutely no idea how, or even if, I could convince twenty local Thais to fly two hundred flights, no matter what the wage. I would need to fly to Chiang Mai in northern Thailand to complete the Baht Run mileage alchemy.

I had completed three mileage projects since 1988, yet thirteen years would elapse until I could *finally* redeem miles for their intended purpose!

My virgin experience in international Business Class with my 21-hour journey to Chiang Mai in northern Thailand was oddly anti-climactic. Don't get me wrong. It wasn't a letdown by any stretch. When the first gourmet meal was served, I was in awe. By the third meal, I was just quite pleased.

When the seat first fully reclined into a sleeper, I marveled at the technology and the comfort. After the third catnap, the sleeper felt like a fairly comfy couch, infinitely better than an upright economy seat, but not entirely luxurious. The first private airport lounge felt like I was being ushered into the Green Room like a special guest on a late-night talk show. There was a smashing smorgasbord, free-flowing booze, overstuffed couches, soothing music. To my unexpected pleasure, there were even showers and massages. By the third lounge visit, it just felt like a routine intermission between flights.

Consistent with my upbringing, it turned out that I wasn't overly impressed with the whole luxury, pampering, and exclusivity angle of Business Class. But flying Business Class was worth its weight in gold for a purely functional reason of avoiding the dreaded jet lag.

What did impress me, however, was that I could access Business Class for about a tenth of the price of the passengers next to me who paid full fare. I was equally smug that I was flying for nearly the same price as the passengers behind me in cramped Economy Class, eating mystery meat and having bladder contortions while waiting for the bathroom line to thin out.

I wasn't big on coupons or Groupon, but I did have a visceral distaste for spending money for something that didn't match its functionality. I didn't understand paying for brand names.

I needed shirts, not LaCoste. I didn't understand paying for expensive jewelry. I didn't understand buying a big house. Most rooms would go unused, and there was higher overhead with utilities, taxes, landscaping, etc.

But I understood fire sales. Most fire sales were astounding seventy-five to ninety percent-off deals with super short, grab-em-while-they-last bargains. My mileage alchemy could extend the life of a Business Class fire sale from days into decades. Having access to a steady supply of a fire-sale-priced product was an irresistible temptation for me.

When I arrived in Chiang Mai, I had just two contacts, if you could even call them that: my Dad's Marketing VP's wife's brother and a *FlyerTalker*'s ex-fiance's pottery class teacher. Neither of them seemed to know any local Thais who would want to fly eight short flights a day, five days a week, for six weeks. Incredibly, these expats, who had lived in Thailand for many years, hardly knew any local Thais, period. Each contact gave me one other contact, and I slowly expanded my network to over thirty people, all expats, but with no success in finding a pipeline to the locals.

All thirty people gently warned me about the same uniquely Thai cultural quality called *sanur*. It was more of an attitude than an actual means of behavior. It wasn't laziness or lack of responsibility. It was more like someone went down a path in good faith with an employer, discovered it wasn't the right path, and decided to backtrack and try something else with their life … irrespective of whatever commitment was made with the employer.

On one hand, I was really perplexed that five times the minimum wage wouldn't be a guarantee of a job well done. On the other hand, I guess I had a grudging respect for people who were not beholden to the Almighty Baht. What could I do beyond this generous financial incentive to ensure the two hundred flights, with *no* margin of error, were flown before the dreaded *sanur* kicked in? It was a perplexing and potentially risky situation I was grappling with.

Speaking of *sanur*, I was ready for a massage after the long trip. To avoid the 'happy ending' parlors, I needed to look for signs that said 'traditional massage' or, in the case of the parlor that I stumbled upon, a simple handwritten scrawl that said 'No Sex.' It was pretty spartan, no dividers, no soothing music, bright lights instead of candles. No Sex shouldn't mean no ambience.

Maybe it was best to keep looking.

A kind Thai lady purposely, but nicely, blocked my impending exit. She asked me to look more closely at my surroundings. I noticed a pair of crutches, a wheelchair, a walker, and a prosthetic leg (!) strewn about the premises. Then, I noticed that each device belonged to one of the masseuses.

This kind Thai lady was raring to give me a sense of place about her ramshackle parlor and its unusual staff profiles. She would have a rapt audience.

Her name was Katchikorn. She explained her shop was run-down not because she didn't have the money to pay for it, but because no local Thais were willing to repair it, even for premium wages. Furthermore, despite her expertly trained staff, no local Thais were willing to be customers.

Odd.

Then Katchikorn became forlorn. In Buddhism there was a belief in reincarnation, and that if someone came back handicapped, it meant they probably did something bad in a previous life, and this bad luck life was their cosmic karma. So, disabled people were marginalized and shunned, which made it difficult for them to make a living.

Her sad story was a stark contrast to the half-dozen or so staff who were all smiles and bundles of energy. If there was any bad karma amongst them, it was being drowned out by their joviality.

I had no idea if Katchikorn's sad narrative jibed with the upbeat staff energy in the parlor. It sounded plausible, but maybe business was slow because the place was just a mess, and maybe the massages were too. Maybe this parlor was empty because they were more interested in *sanur* than making a proper living.

Geez, was I letting the cynical warnings of the expats color my perspective? I snapped out of it and relented to have a massage there.

Afterward, each one of them introduced themselves to me and told me about themselves in halting English. I learned about their families, their social lives, their favorite food and music, their experience with other foreigners. Yet, I learned nothing about the origins of their disabilities, how difficult it was to be iced out of society, or how much pain they might be in. These people didn't seem to need the fleeting doses of *sanur* that I kept hearing about. I found genuinely happy, joyful people. It wasn't an act. It wasn't a ploy for tips. It was just their visceral sense of being poised to salvage whatever life would throw at them.

And life was going to throw them two hundred flights at five times minimum wage.

Epiphany.

I had found my labor pool—I could feel it. Katchikorn and the staff were electrified. She could supply ten staff altogether with varying degrees of mobility. It was critical mass. But damn, for traveling all that way, it would be ideal to caboose another ten flyers as projected.

Katchikorn was tapped out with supplying her staff, but she had an idea for the other ten. She made a quick call that was part animated, part exasperated, and mostly ecstatic. As we waited for the source of the other ten flyers to arrive, she explained to me the role of a chief in rural northern Thailand. He was the police, the judge, the mayor, the food distributor, the price-setter, the marriage arranger, the funeral director, the chauffeur. Sounded like the consummate multi-tasker or maybe enlightened despot.

As the impromptu sociology lesson ended, in walked a diminutive middle-aged man with a small frame but a big belly. Katchikorn introduced him as the chief of a nearby village who supplied her rice. She spoke to him briefly and slowly in Thai, and he seemed to repeat every word she said verbatim. Then, he turned to me and with visible struggle and determination on his face, he sputtered out in just barely understandable English:

"Two hundred flights, *not* 199. No *sanur* in my village. Pay some now, pay some later." Relief rushed across his face. He apparently had one more thing to say. Now his face transformed one more time, this time it was steely resolve:

"I am the Chief."

Like Katchikorn counseled, this chief would be a one-stop shopping labor pool source for the other ten flyers. Harvest season would be over, and work and money would be scarce, so this job was built-in motivation for his villagers. He would recruit the ten and be fully responsible for every aspect of their nailing the two hundred segments ... because he was the Chief!

My workforce would be secured based on the pleading eyes of Katchikorn and her motley crew of disabled masseuses. And the "oral contract" sputtered out by the village chief whose name

I didn't know from a place I'd never seen. No legal contracts, no binding co-signatures, no confirming notary stamps, no witnesses. No enforcement, no leverage, no accountability with tens of thousands of dollars at stake. The twenty folks would at least be flying on safe and secure airplanes, whereas I was about to be flying without a net.

Katchikorn, the chief, and I became fast friends over the next few days as we jumpstarted all the logistics, from ground transport to and from the airport, payment of a stipend on top of their wages, filling out the Aeroplan third-party authorization paperwork, ticket distribution, and a mechanism for making up missed flights due to weather, flyer illness, or excused absence.

The next order of business was the routine purchasing of four-thousand airline tickets (twenty flyers x two hundred flights). For some strange reason, the domestic tickets between Chiang Mai and the two other eight-dollar routes—Chiang Rai and Mae Hong Son—were only issued as paper tickets.

Not so routine.

All the travel agencies seemed to be small mom-and-pop shops. The shop that happened to be playing Bon Jovi instead of local Thai music broke the tie. The diminutive travel agent couldn't believe her good fortune. She asked me if I wanted regular or express service. Express cost an extra thirty cents per ticket. I nodded my approval as she seemed to be flipping through her day calendar pretty fast. She stopped, wrote my name on a calendar page, and proudly told me that my tickets would be ready in *only* three weeks!

Each ticket would take five minutes to manually process, and she will be doubling her staff capacity, from one to two, to handle the express request for four thousand tickets.

I asked if she could increase her staff to ten and finish in two days. She looked at me gravely about the cost involved to ramp up a makeshift staff. She wouldn't give me a revised quote. She just kept shaking her head no repeating "Too much baht" over and over. She was flustered. She apparently had never had an express service this large, and she was nervous the revised surcharge would price her out of my market. I finally coaxed the revised, ramped-up express price out of her. I owed her the consideration of sharing her pain at having to quote what she thought was such an extortionate price quote. So, I faux grimaced, and I looked coldly away from her. I skeptically punched some calculator buttons, and, in a grand flourish, I reluctantly agreed to … the *fifty-even cents* express price surcharge per ticket and the processing all to be done in two days.

We did a dry run with the airport transport. The ten rice farmers apparently weren't told by their chief that they were going to be surrounded by so much bad karma from the ten disabled masseuses. The rice farmers were visibly unhappy. They weren't the only ones.

Once at the airport, the ticket agents, security staff, retail shop staff, maintenance staff, taxi, and tuk-tuk drivers all seemed to have the same smoldering derision for our disabled group. But thankfully, the group was oblivious, or probably more like resigned, to such inhospitable conduct.

The airport staffs would be seeing a lot of these people over the next six weeks, so I had hoped the novelty of their bad karma presence would wear off soon enough.

I flipped the switch, and the Thai labor pool machinery had seamlessly roared to life. I headed back to work and family in Cleveland and slowly watched the mileage dribble, then cascade into the twenty Aeroplan accounts. And there were no spooky phone calls from Air Canada/Aeroplan Legal!

My Packer business was healthy, the stock market was on fire, and my wife was now a partner in her practice. Each of those sources would help fund the Baht Run. Having twenty Thai Flyers would more than restore the miles that had been pressed into service for five years of domestic Economy Class *Kwik Witz* travel.

No. of flyers on 200 flights	20	20	No. of flyers on 200 flights
Earned, voucher, elite bonus miles per flyer	x 375,000	x $2,400	airfare/per diem per flyer
Total miles	= 7,500,000	= $48,000	Total airfares
intl. Business Class award redemption	/ 80,000		
No. of awards	= 94	/ 94	No. of awards
		= $510	cost per award
		vs. $6,000	cost to purchase retail airfare

Unknown to me, besides the miles, there was something else cascading to a troubling crescendo.

Chapter 7: Suspicions, Superstitions, and Suspensions

There are some things that don't require any literary flourishes like foreshadowing.

Getting an unsolicited call from the United States Drug Enforcement Administration (DEA) is one of those.

The lady from the DEA sounded like an appointment secretary confirming a dental cleaning.

"Hi, Mr. Belkin. Can you let us know a convenient time that you can drop by our office for a quick chat?" Chatty was not a word that I usually associated with that particular government agency.

"Well, I'm not in your neighborhood at the moment." It was a colloquial statement that she took literally. I was actually nine thousand miles, not nine miles away.

"No problem. If today isn't convenient for you, anytime in the next couple of days would be fine." Convenient?! It would take me a couple of days just to make the four flight connections from Cleveland to Chiang Mai to arrive in her neighborhood.

We locked in a date just three days later, and she pleasantly said, "We look forward to meeting you."

"Likewise," I muttered to myself under my breath. I realized that I had neglected to ask her, nor had she offered, what precipitated this upcoming chat. What an oversight. I suppose that the prospect of being summoned by any U.S. government agency should be scary, but oddly, I wasn't actually gripped by fear but rather curiosity.

I booked an award ticket and was airborne just four hours later. I couldn't be sure if it was the altitude, the sugar rush of the decadent desserts, or the alcoholic haze of free-flowing booze, but I was definitely feeling high, thanks to Business Class perks.

The last leg of the flight to Chiang Mai ran late, and upon arrival, I had to hightail it directly to the DEA. The office was an unimposing building set back in a heavily wooded area. The security didn't strike me as unusually tight. The agent who greeted me was middle-aged with a faintly southern drawl, a white short-sleeved shirt, and a disheveled desk loaded with piles of paperwork. He had a disarming and charming persona like "Kenneth," the intern from *30 Rock*, as he was all smiles as we introduced ourselves. But as soon as he spotted my Business Class baggage tags, it became crystal clear that he was no intern; he was a grizzled and tough veteran. That warm and folksy smile faded quickly as he must have been wondering who else could afford a last-minute Business Class airfare that would cost nearly $8,500 … except for a drug lord! Dr. Jekyll had swiftly transformed into "Mr. DEA Hyde!"

He displayed a map of northern Thailand with three yellow pins stuck in it. It looked to me like an isosceles triangle. He actually called the pin-encompassed area "The Golden Triangle." Damn, I was good!!!

And then according Dr. DEA Hyde, apparently, I was very, very bad.

The agent explained the nickname was not a geographic term. It was a derogatory term for the world's largest region of opium drug smuggling. I was dumbfounded.

When I first went to Chiang Mai, I wasn't reading guide books to learn about its history or tourist dos and don'ts. I was on a singular mission to recruit a labor pool.

He asked why I had twenty people on various flights all on Golden Triangle routes multiple times per day and multiple times per week. To his credit, while the inquiry was clearly meant as an accusation, he verbalized it in an earnest manner. Was he hoping against hope that I actually had an answer that would preclude an impending jail term?! Was the agent actually on my side, poised to give me the benefit of the doubt, or was it some kind of trap? My Baht Run shouldn't have had a whiff of impropriety, yet I was suddenly feeling very defensive. I knew I wasn't guilty of drug smuggling. But maybe one of the flyers was? Maybe the travel agent or the airline got suspicious of my four-thousand-ticket purchases as a money-laundering operation? Maybe the chief was using slave labor as flyers?

Dr. DEA Hyde could see that I was getting rattled. But it wasn't from hiding guilt; it was from the uncertainty where this fishing expedition was headed. The agent was likely no stranger to the concept of overdosing, so it was time to inject him with mass quantities of facts to prove my innocence once and for all.

First, I showed him *my* two Golden Triangles. My first Golden Triangle was petite, spanning two hundred square miles. They were my flight routes to earn mileage. It so happened to mirror the three Northern Thailand cities that he showed as primary routes to earn drug money. My second Golden Triangle sprawled across two continents and consisted of the mileage-earning operations locales. Chiang Mai was my labor pool headquarters, Montreal was Aeroplan headquarters, and Cleveland was my mileage alchemy lab headquarters.

Then I brandished my mileage alchemy which was as sophisticated and byzantine as any drug lord worth his salt. I blitzed him with spreadsheets outlining the intricate methodology that interlocked twenty flyers, four thousand flights, $8.00 fares, 100% elite bonuses, 75,000-mile threshold vouchers, Aeroplan *Super Elite's* "no blackout perk," etc.

It was now Dr. DEA Hyde's turn to feel a little rattled. He was right that I was a kingpin—he just got the product wrong. I was in the Golden Triangle to harvest one hundred international Business Class awards anywhere in the world, not meth.

Once he saw how I could legally transform $8.00 airfares into Business Class awards worth up to $6000, he made a confession. He had actually thought I was the most idiotic drug smuggler in DEA history. Charging all the airfares on one credit card. Using disabled drug mules who didn't have the mobility to escape if pursued by cops. Using tribal rice farmers who didn't even speak the dialect of the various airport locales. And finally, my audacity as kingpin to show up at the airport to be captured on video.

We were both relieved that there was a perfectly illogical (!) explanation that would allow him to close my case. There was, however, one last administrative detail, which was a little fuzzy. "I have to slum it back to the States a couple of times a year in Economy, and boy, is it brutal." He was looking for my concurrence, but of course, I couldn't relate to flying in the back of the bus.

"Yeah, I can't imagine," with feigned empathy.

"I normally input my paperwork into our system before I take these meetings, but somehow yours got overlooked. There's no permanent record of this meeting … yet."

If there was something underlying his pregnant pause, I totally was totally clueless. I smiled weakly.

He continued, "You wouldn't happen to have any more of those rice farmers sitting in the bullpen?" I was clueless no more.

If I could help get him into Business Class, maybe the paperwork would not get inputted into the system, and our little rendezvous would not be part of my permanent file. We were able to conclude our business, and the Baht Run remained bulletproof.

I actually took a few days to enjoy and learn about Chiang Mai, savoring the delicious food, the gorgeous landscape, and the colorful history. My down-time would be short-lived.

I received an urgent call from the Thai Airways station manager in Chiang Mai. Thai Airways was the Star Alliance partner of Air Canada, and my flyers were using Thai Airways for their short flights.

Fortunately, I was still in Thailand. But I was confused. The tickets were paid for in full. The flyers had arrived at the airport every day in plenty of time, so they weren't causing any delays. They were all sitting next to each other, so they weren't disrupting other passengers. The mileage earning was with Air Canada, not Thai Air, so there shouldn't be any mileage earning questions or snafus.

The urgency of the message belied the serene tone of the meeting with the Thai Air station chief in Chiang Mai. The interior decorator of his office must have been the Marketing Department of Thai Air. It was like branding overload—every single item in the office was emblazoned with the Thai Air purple orchid and logo. I felt bad contaminating his pristine office with the beat-up Royal Jordanian tag on my backpack and my red t-shirt that decidedly clashed with his purple color scheme.

His name was Somchai, which is Thai for "man of worth." But as I was drowning in the purple overload of his office, I mentally nicknamed him "Purple Rain" to help keep me on an even keel. He was complimentary about me being such a valuable customer and trying to help with less-fortunate people. Ahhh, so he had done a little homework on me.

In Thailand, there seemed to be some kind of cultural norm

of deference when it came to foreigners. Which was odd because Thailand claimed it was one of the few countries in the world that never had an official colonial patron or occupation. It seemed like a nice trait to have in principle. But as a foreigner, it could serve as a velvet poker face. Indeed, it was.

Purple Rain reached for a file folder and handed me a check without any sense of cheer or celebration. It was a check for $12,000.

Huh?!

He explained that ten of my passengers had flown one hundred flights, but this check represented a refund for the other hundred that Thai Air would not be able to honor.

The news may have been terrible, but my thinking was, why were *only* ten flyers were being refunded when surely he must have known there were actually twenty flyers under my tutelage?

His initial explanation was alarming. My ten passengers had "disrupted flight operations." He was clearly zeroing on one of the groups of ten, but which group? The disabled masseuses or the rice farmers? Who among the seemingly timid, docile, and grateful flyers, was the rabble-rouser causing trouble? And why was there a need for collective punishment for the whole group?

It turned out that Somchai wasn't using the term "disrupting flight operations" euphemistically—he meant it literally. Thai Air was losing the literal capacity to operate the aircraft flying in the Golden Triangle.

He finally revealed that the problem was with the disabled flyers. Flyers plural, not flyer singular. His explanation infuriated me as a Westerner, but it made undeniably perfect sense as a local Thai.

I harkened back to the chilly reception the disabled group received the first few days by various airport-related staff. I remembered that Katchikorn, the massage parlor manager, had explained how Buddhism viewed disability as a possible result of karma or sins in a previous life—they must accept their suffering as part of their karma when reincarnated.

Purple Rain warned that all of the pilots and flight attendants on the Golden Triangle route were deadly serious about those beliefs. Some even believed that the disabled were cursed and dangerous even to be around.

The same Thai Air staff were scheduled to fly on the same aircraft for all eight of the Golden Triangle flights each day. The same eight flights as my ten apparently bad luck charms. It was one thing if the ten disabled flyers were on the same flights as a one-time-only happenstance. But being cooped up with them multiple times per day and then that rolling over into multiple times per week became unbearable for Thai Air crews.

The Thai Air staffs needed all the good karma they could get because Mae Hong Son, a Golden Triangle airport, had its short runway dead-end into a mountain! Every take-off and landing was already inherently stressful, and with my particular group, there was an added layer (OK, ten layers!) of bad karma.

In the initial three weeks that the handicapped gang had been flying, word spread like wildfire amongst pilots and flight attendants to avoid that newly-"cursed" route. Thai Air was literally running out of staff who would agree to work these flights. These routes were critical supply lines that could not risk operational interruption because of my flyers.

Hence, the refund.

I would be "made whole," and Thai Air could resume "blessed" instead of "cursed" Golden Triangle flights.

Except that while I was being made whole financially in Thai Air's eyes, I was still miles away (literally and figuratively) from the two hundred flights that were needed for my flyers earning Super Elite status, the slew of miles, the vouchers, and the no-blackout perk.

I was in panic mode. This check had already been cut, so a dialogue or negotiation was not likely. This was a *fait accompli* that had already been decided behind closed doors.

I ripped up the check.

I hoped that dramatic gesture would force renewed contact with the decision-makers, but Purple Rain was unmoved.

I needed a Plan B.

In the U.S. I might threaten to go to the press, but here in Thailand, that would surely be unpredictable. There was no Thai societal outrage about discrimination against disabled people. And my righteous indignation would be easily countered by the airline about their commitment to flying essential food and supplies to these Golden Triangle outposts. I would likely be perceived as a spoiled Westerner in the midst of a greedy scheme.

Plan C would be a long shot.

Instead of defending my position, I shifted to preserving his company's money … and I would make Somchai the hero. Those Golden Triangle flights held about one hundred people and typically flew at fifty percent capacity, approximately fifty people. So, my ten masseuses actually represented twenty percent of the revenue. Twelve thousand dollars wasn't chump change for them to walk away from on a route that charged eight-dollar fares.

It was time to channel my inner tenth-grade debater. I unleashed the holy grail of winning a debate: get your opponent to agree with you on something, anything … to be used later, when needed.

I briefly explained that these flyers were earning miles with another airline and were being paid to fly. I kept it simple, and he understood the concept. Then, I asked him if he were in my shoes, what would he have done differently. He laughed and initially said he would never use any disabled citizens, as there were plenty of other needy people who could use the work. Well, that seemed to shut me down right then and there.

But then Somchai reopened the door on his own.

He had relatives in America who told him how odd it was that Americans gave so much positive attention to their disabled people. So, he surmised that I was just trying to help these people, however misguided my efforts. I gingerly concurred. He sighed and paused.

He confided that if he was *forced* to use disabled people, he would put no more than two per flight and not more than twice a week so that it wouldn't be so easy for the flight attendants to recognize a disturbing pattern.

Two on a flight, twice a week … *his idea, his words*!

This theoretical change of frequency would take an additional three **months** instead of three **weeks** to generate the two hundred flights. But maybe the more leisurely travel pacing would be less exhausting and preserve the precious supply of flyers' *sanur*. I was getting ahead of myself, but I could live with his unwitting solution.

I asked him to repeat his handicapped scenario one more time so I could take notes … and sneak in the positive reinforcement of having him repeat it again.

Then, I asked if I could repeat it back to him again to make sure my notes were accurate. Now, his two passengers/twice a week suggestion had been cemented. Each succeeding time he heard it, he seemed more self-satisfied. He was feeling much smarter than the *farang* (a mildly derogatory term for foreigner) on the other side of the desk. And I was encouraging it.

I told him that it was a shame that Thai Air should be penalized $12,000 because of a problem I created. I wished I had adopted his great advice and counsel of *two-person/twice-a-*

week from the start and that my poor planning forced such an untenable situation.

Fourth time repeated.

It was time to unleash the premeditated debate tactic of convincing Somchai with his own words.

I told him I would be happy to cooperate and revise the disabled group's schedules based on HIS solution. HE could get credit for saving Thai Air $12,000.

With pride of authorship of the two-person/twice-a-week concept on the line, Purple Rain had painted himself into a corner … that he wasn't even aware of. All he knew was that he was my hero and the hero of Thai Air for solving this seemingly intractable situation.

This ended well. The tickets were rebooked, the schedule elongated, the Baht Run was back on track … again.

The next day, Purple Rain asked me back. Of course, it must be to take our victory lap together. So, I brought some Thai sweets and some nice pottery, an appropriate gift of gratitude. He refused both, but not of humility.

Apparently, he had another agenda.

He cautioned me in a respectful way but with a definite tone of gravity and suspicion. One of the airport routes, Mae Hong Son, was notorious for being part of an underage prostitution ring that snatched girls and shipped them to Singapore. Thai Air was concerned that my flyers might be scouts for this awful skin trade.

He wasn't actually accusing me, just warning me. Still, it was hard not to feel extremely offended. But, if I got too self-righteous, I risked piquing more suspicion as 'he doth protest too much.'

Instead of being defensive, I made the other mistaken reaction. I got snarky. I told him I would confiscate the binoculars from the two blind masseuses. I would snatch away the pens and paper from the illiterate rice farmers that might be used to pass secret messages.

He looked at me wide-eyed. Was I actually confessing to being caught red-handed? I spent the next hour frantically trying to bridge the cultural gap between American and Thai senses of humor. My sarcasm left Somchai with the very unfortunate impression that while I wasn't in the child prostitution racket, that I certainly *could* be.

Two months later, I flew back to Thailand to provide the final payment for the labor pool and to collect all of the Aeroplan Business Class vouchers. I surveyed my handiwork. Twenty flyers. Four thousand flights. No written contracts. No sicknesses. No loss of sanur. The twenty-four flying days represented the equivalent of 120 days' worth of wages with no backbreaking rice planting, harvesting, or muscle-fatiguing massages. That was my Western calculus—they did a good job, got paid well and the mileage mission was accomplished.

I took Katchikorn for a thank-you dinner before I departed Chiang Mai. It was a fancy waterfront restaurant full of tourists. She had never been to a restaurant with Western menu prices in her life. Katchikorn proceeded to give me some Thai context well beyond the money as to how the Baht Run impacted the lives of the flyers.

The rice farmers had never before ventured much beyond five miles from their village. They had never even dreamed of visiting the expensive and cosmopolitan city of Chiang Mai. Yet, these lucky tribes people got to see the big city, go inside an airport to see modern facilities, sophisticated equipment, shopping items, and food bounty that they had only witnessed on TV. They went thirty-six thousand feet in the air and saw the majesty of northern Thailand's gorgeous topography. On the plane, they were treated with (very grudging) respect, but respect nonetheless. They had to make minor, but independent, decisions and figure out new social interactions without the purview of their chief. Katchikorn concluded that their lives would be irrevocably changed. It was really touching to hear.

Until…

She continued. The village chief was sad. I was confused. The flyers were paid. The chief was paid his generous supervisor fee. No village work was sacrificed or disrupted. The flyers seemed quite excited about the whole experience.

Apparently, my Western rose-colored glasses needed to be discarded.

She concurred that all of what I was said was true. The entire village benefited from the financial windfall, but there were unintended consequences. The status of the chief had been diminished. Being out of the chief's long arm of authority for twenty-four days had made some of the farmers a bit more worldly, a bit more bold, a bit more self-confident, thus attracting a lot more attention, curiosity and respect from fellow villagers … possibly at the expense of the chief. The Baht Run had changed a status quo that had gone unchallenged for generations. Maybe it would revert back over time and the novelty of the Baht Run would wear off.

But she warned that maybe it couldn't revert back. And even more cryptically, maybe it shouldn't revert back.

On a lighter note, Katchikorn gave an exclusively upbeat assessment about the disabled masseuses. Other than tips, their meager massage wages were given directly to the families, so their existence was one hundred percent dependent on their families' discretion and financial situation. Katchikorn gave the equivalent wages to the families when the group flew but held back the difference for the flyers themselves. She gave each of them a small lockbox and key. The extra money wasn't just a financial reward—it gave them a sense of dignity, pride, and freedom.

I'm grateful that she shared these insights with me. Otherwise, this would have just been about entrepreneurship and risk-taking.

Instead, with the help of my newfound Thai rose-colored sunglasses, I could see beyond the miles … for once! I left Thailand wistfully, but with my newly refilled mileage coffers, I was excited to return soon.

About a month after the end of the Baht Run, the final miles trickled in and posted, and the vouchers were received and forwarded.

The End.

Oh, c'mon now!

About a month later, some members of the Aeroplan forum on *FlyerTalk* had heard some scuttlebutt that the Aeroplan fraud department had suspended some accounts pending investigation. My accounts had everything posted accurately, so I wasn't worried by the rumors. But that night, I did a routine login.

First account: I was unable to log in due to a 'technical error.' Maybe it was routine maintenance. Maybe it was too many logins overwhelming the system. Then I tried the second account. And so-on. Twenty accounts, twenty lock-outs.

It wasn't scuttlebutt, it was scuttle "baht!" My Thai accounts were the source of the murmurings; they were locked but not yet closed.

If there was actual fraud, what was there to investigate? The accounts should be closed and miles confiscated. If there was an ongoing investigation of fraud, it would be logical to query the likely source of the suspected fraud. Namely, the dude who paid by credit card and was on all of the third-party authorization faxes.

Unlike United Legal, who communicated with me firsthand regarding their disaffection with the Vegas SKY High Rollers project, Aeroplan was tight-lipped about why they "didn't like it." I waited for two weeks to see if the investigation would be complete and the accounts opened.

Nothing.

It was time to engage Aeroplan, but nobody there would return my calls or emails. I contacted my mileage guru, Randy, who put in a discreet inquiry.

The fraud department blinked, sort of.

They emailed Randy that the investigation wasn't my business, only the primary account holders.

I wrote back that all twenty account holders would be happy to communicate directly. As there were no provisions in the Aeroplan T&C about communicating only in English or French, all of my Thai flyer correspondence would be in Thai. Aeroplan would have to hire an interpreter to translate back and forth the responses, all of whom would have a totally different line of questioning.

OR…

Aeroplan could continue to let the one common authorized third party (me) communicate in one email and in English. They relented on communicating with me directly.

I volunteered to fly to Montreal at my expense on demand to help expedite the investigation. They stubbornly refused to let the one person who was the source of their scrutiny in the front door.

Aeroplan apparently "didn't like it" (sensing a trend here?!) that there were twenty Super Elite accounts with access to one hundred no-blackout international Business Class awards and vouchers floating out there. Like United, Aeroplan was grasping at crimes to fit the punishment, otherwise, this would have been an and open-and-shut case instead of an open-ended fishing expedition.

This time, I had no partners to constrain my problem-solving options. I was ready to match Aeroplan's kangaroo court with my court of public opinion.

I reached out to the travel editor of the Toronto *The Globe and Mail*, the country's largest newspaper, who apparently had some history with Air Canada and was happy to dig around.

Two weeks went by, and still nothing from Aeroplan. Randy and the Toronto daily newspaper travel editor gave me the green light to assess my credible threat. I contacted Aeroplan and advised that they had one week to reopen the accounts or provide definite proof of specific T/C violations. Otherwise, *Inside Flyer* and the Toronto *The Globe and Mail* intended on opening their own inquiries with Aeroplan that may be of eventual public and governmental regulatory interest.

There was no response to my barely-veiled threat for the entire week. At 11:50 p.m., ten minutes before the exposes would be filed, I checked one account and it was still locked, and the Aeroplan offices were long closed.

Wow, we all underestimated them. They were actually itching for a fight.

It was now 11:59 p.m. I logged into an account one last time, just for kicks.

It opened.

The miles were all there. At 11:59 p.m., 20 seconds. I logged into a second account. It opened. The miles were there. At 11:59 p.m., 50 seconds, same deal with a third account. By 12:15 a.m., I had logged into all twenty accounts successfully. Aeroplan had waited until literally the last possible second before they conceded.

Afterward, there was no apology, no explanation, no warnings that these accounts would continue to be under relentless surveillance (duh).

At the height of the hoopla for the TV show *Who Wants To Be A Millionaire,* the travel editor for the Toronto *Globe and Mail* wrote the story headline, "Who Wants to Be An Aeroplan Millionaire?" It created a minor sensation within the frequent-flyer community. Over time, a tangible influx of new members would flood the Aeroplan program in pursuit of the newly discovered *Super Elite* no-blackout perk, among others.

It thrust me into the spotlight without my knowledge. Since the situation had been resolved, there was no longer the need for the Toronto paper to run the story. But the editor claimed he couldn't let a story this novel stay in his inbox. The gist of the article was about the Baht Run with only passing mention of the dustup with Aeroplan.

But the article really pissed off the Aeroplan FlyerTalkers as the under-the-radar Super Elite status was now the talk of the town. Over the next three to four years, Aeroplan would slowly but inexorably shave that no-blackout perk down.

And the article would also position me into the crosshairs of every security and fraud department in the airline world. I was up to the challenge because I knew I was playing by the rules.

It was incumbent upon the programs to figure out a way to combat my scalable strategies, especially when they liked *more* business and revenues. But they liked their business from lots of people generating modest amounts of miles who redeemed them for cheap domestic economy awards. They "didn't like it" that one person was generating millions of miles and who knew how to redeem them for the best-valued overseas Business Class awards.

Thanks to Aeroplan, my family of five would trade the bunny hills of Cleveland skiing for the Swiss Alps, and I would catch my favorite band in the world, Steely Dan, onstage in Brussels. We would celebrate the Jewish New Year, Rosh Hashanah, at the Western Wall in Jerusalem.

While my contact with the Toronto travel editor was one and done, I knew that Randy Petersen would continue to loom large in my mileage pursuits. I was grateful to him. And a year later, I would demonstrate my gratitude to him in the most absolutely unconscionably *abhorrent* way possible.

Chapter 8: Friendly Fire

During the early 2000s, Starwood, the hotel holding company that managed Sheraton, Westin, and St. Regis, among others, issued one of the most sought-after travel currencies, which they named Starpoints. They were exceedingly difficult to earn and valuable to transfer into some very attractive airline programs that had no other transfer options at that time. And Starpoints offered a generous five-thousand-point transfer bonus for each twenty thousand points transferred.

FlyerTalk owner Randy Petersen announced a promotion involving his monthly print magazine, *Inside Flyer*. Purchase a subscription of his magazine for sixty dollars and receive 2,500 Starpoints.

Hmmm.

Twenty-five-hundred Starpoints wouldn't even redeem for a one-night award at Sheraton's most downscale properties that dotted freeway exits near truck stops. It seemed like an odd and certainly underwhelming offer for the mileage geek crowd. The *FlyerTalk* community was trying to grapple with the motivation behind the offer. Perhaps Randy needed to goose up his subscription base to be able to charge more for advertising. If so, we would all happily do our share to help move his needle.

One member inquired whether more than one subscription per person would be eligible for the promotion points. It hadn't really occurred to anyone to purchase more than one or two subscriptions, because it was such a niche publication.

That was, until Randy posted that there were no quantity limits.

We mileage scalers and monetizers sharpened our pencils. Starwood had a transfer option where hotel points could be converted into airline miles on a 1:1 basis and the five thousand-point transfer bonus for each twenty thousand points transferred. Was the mileage math compelling enough for earning and scaling to the gold standard—international Business Class awards?

INSIDE FLYER SCALING ANALYSIS

No. of subscriptions	26	26	No. of subscriptions
subscription bonus	x 2,500	x $60	subscription cost
points earned	= 65,000		
Starwood transfer bonus	+ 15,000		
intl. Business Class award redemption	= 80,000	= $1,560	cost
		vs. $6,000	cost to purchase retail international Business Class airfare

Scaling Randy's promotion was still above the savvy mileage-masters' current $900 to $1200 sweet spot for the cost of earning mileage.

Without the quantity cap, buying multiple subscriptions only seemed to make sense to redeem for hotel awards at Starwood's upscale properties like Westin or St. Regis for a couple of nights.

I personally budgeted for sixteen subscriptions to treat my wife for a long weekend in Miami at the upscale W property.

Just one day later, my budget would have to be amplified by *one hundred times.*

We all saw it dozens of times, but we never quite *looked* at it! QANTAS, the national airline of Australia, transferred *two* miles per Starpoint, which was 100% more than the one mile of all other airline transfers. The QANTAS forum on *FlyerTalk* was a backwater with very little posting activity. Although it was part of the *Oneworld* alliance, it was easily overlooked as we concentrated on dissecting partner airlines far closer to home and more relevant like American Airlines and British Airways.

Thankfully, the Aussie member that discovered the Baht Run, would not only alert us to his QANTAS discovery of double value point transfers, but he found an award on an aircraft that was double the speed of conventional planes.

Enter: The Concorde SST. Super Sonic Transport.

It was the sleekest-looking aircraft design in commercial aviation history. A narrow fuselage, downward-pointed nose and those signature curved wings. It was also the loudest in history, so its routes were restricted to between London/Paris and New York JFK. There was no denying the novelty of the sheer speed from New York to London: only three hours instead of seven. And flying so high that the curvature of the earth could be seen. This was definitely a vanity award, to be able to fly with passengers who paid the never-discounted rate of $10,000 while FlyerTalkers would be able to pay for just twenty magazine subscriptions!

FLY THE CONCORDE ANALYSIS

No. of subscriptions	20	20	No. of subscriptions
subscription bonus	x 5,000	x $60	subscription cost
points earned	100,000		
Starwood transfer bonus	+ 25,000		
Concorde award redemption	= 125,000	= $1,200	cost
		vs. $10,000	cost to purchase retail international Business Class airfare

Suddenly, instead of feeling like we were doing Randy a favor, it now felt like he was doing us a favor! The *FlyerTalk* community would be shelling out cash to support Randy, not with a token two or three subscriptions, but rather a hefty twenty subscriptions to get their Concorde fix. Many bought double, triple, or quadruple that number of subscriptions to allow for bringing friends and family in tow.

I didn't jump onboard the Concorde bandwagon so quickly. I did some research. My dad, the concert promoter, once had an urgent meeting with the manager of the rock band KISS and had to hightail it to Paris on the Concorde. I asked him about the experience. He related that indeed it was an unforgettable, once-in-a-lifetime experience.

But.

He conceded that the actual in-flight experience, once the

awe wore off, was a bit subpar. The Concorde was very narrow with low ceilings. It felt somewhat cramped, and the narrow seats had minimal recline and no personal video screens. The meal service was rushed because the flight was so short. And it was LOUD … for three straight hours.

I wasn't so dazzled about this shiny new object that mesmerized the rest of the *FlyerTalk* gang. While other FlyerTalkers were placing side bets as to how many Concorde awards I would scale up to, I disappointed them all when I revealed that I was going to pass on this supersonic airliner opportunity.

Just as I had discovered a better iteration of the already solid Baht Run, I wanted to skulk around the QANTAS program on the prowl for not-so-shiny objects that had been obscured by the blinding Concorde award.

The Concorde was one fixed route New York to London for 125,000 miles and $1,200 worth of magazine subscriptions. For just 80,000 miles and $780, I found an international Business Class award on *conventional* aircraft, with the flexibility of dozens of different routings on partners between anywhere in the USA to anywhere in Europe—and Israel, to boot. For 100,000 miles and $960, there was an award from anywhere in the USA to East Africa.

Basically, not flying the Concorde would allow me hundreds, not one, routing option for about 35% less cost and fewer miles. I would forge my own path.

Plus, there was actually a domestic Economy award that was a game-changer. Other programs charged a flat twenty-five thousand miles no matter the distance, while QANTAS had a distance-based award chart that was only twelve-thousand miles for short-haul trips under six-hundred miles, and they could be used on partner airlines, including American Airlines. My dad's company owned an apartment in New York due to frequently lobbying agents for concert tour dates for bands like Pink Floyd, The Who, Genesis, and Metallica. Continental had a stranglehold on this fifty-five-minute route where weekday and last-minute airfares routinely exceeded nine hundred dollars. I could clue my dad on locking in seventy-five percent savings by becoming *Inside Flyer* magazine's best customer.

For the *FlyerTalk* community, the Concorde award was a novelty one-and-done award. But my award finds using conventional aircraft were definitely worth stockpiling. I felt like Randy's offer to generate otherwise elusive Starpoints was a once-in-a-lifetime opportunity. I had the chance to lock in fixed-cost award travel to Africa, Israel, and Europe in top-notch British Airways Business Class for years to come. I geared up to scale.

Randy posted that although he hadn't initially noticed the Concorde angle before the promotion offer, he thought it was pretty cool. He could have capped the subscription purchase quantity, and that would have sufficed. He did not express any concerns with folks buying boundless subscriptions. We assumed that due to Randy's close ties with Starwood management, they were just assisting with his subscription situation. We assumed he had received an attractive discount price for the Starpoints.

I would not only be swelling Randy's subscription numbers, but creating a mileage nest egg that could last me for many years. I purchased *sixteen hundred* subscriptions to earn 1.6 million Starpoints, which transferred to four million QANTAS miles. I would generate a war chest of forty-five international Business Class awards and forty Cleveland-New York Economy awards for years to come.

My purchase single-handedly boosted '*Inside Flyer*' subscriptions by three percent. I sent subscriptions to hundreds of airport lounges around the country to increase Randy's exposure, hopefully generating new customers. The rest I donated to libraries and got a modest tax deduction.

I never publicly posted my sixteen hundred subscription purchase, but I did confide in several close *FlyerTalk* friends. But you know the drill. Each of those friends only told one other person in confidence. Nearly three weeks, later it was exposed and posted on the master Concorde thread. While I wasn't thrilled that people knew I had this kind of money to throw around, I was pleased they noticed I positively impacted our mileage guru, Randy.

One month later, I got a private message from a friend requesting a phone call. He was my mentor of the delicate art of trading miles, so let's call him *Trader Joe*!

Trader Joe shared distressing news. It was a massive punch in the gut.

My presumed win-win with Randy was apparently a win for me, but a ruinous loss for him. Randy had purchased points from Starwood but not at nearly the discount that we all *assumed*. His promotion was a "loss leader" to incentivize new subscriptions by accepting a short-term financial loss and hopefully retaining a customer with full price/no incentive annual renewals.

Apparently, Randy was prepared and budgeted to take a small loss. But he didn't expect so many of us to actually have the motivation, let alone the financial wherewithal, to purchase on average twenty to sixty subscriptions for the Concorde award, let alone my sixteen hundred subscriptions. I was confounded why Randy didn't say or do something once it was obvious that his innocent offer was super scalable.

Trader Joe didn't tell me how many subscriptions were sold, but implied it was an astounding number, and those expected small loss leader numbers had swelled to tens of thousands of dollars. And look who was inadvertently leading the charge.

Ugh.

I asked Trader Joe to divulge the shortfall per subscription, and I would write Randy a check to make him whole. He said don't bother. It would never get cashed. I told him to relay to Randy that I would set aside a portion of the miles for his usage to make him whole while. Trader Joe laughed and said, "If there was one person who needed more miles less than me, it was Randy!" He pleaded with me not to share this info with anyone or contact Randy direct.

Feeling awful for many months, I couldn't even face redeeming miles from that QANTAS account with Randy's blood all over it.

Two months later, there was another *FlyerTalk* get-together, the Vail Do that Randy was attending. The timing wasn't great, and it was expensive. But if Randy would agree to share a private meal with me at some point, I would come. He reluctantly agreed to squeeze me in.

I picked an epic Mexican restaurant because I knew he was a tequila connoisseur and collector. I myself was merely an enthusiastic partaker. We met, we ate, we drank, we swapped mileage war stories. This dinner was going to be my unspoken gratitude for his absorbing the hit from my QANTAS scaling.

But unbeknownst to me, he had preemptively given his credit card to the manager before I had arrived. So, my intended dinner of catharsis turned into Randy absorbing <u>another</u> loss leader … a three-hundred-dollar dinner tab. I was pissed and humiliated at the time. But then I understood. His gesture was telegraphing an important message—whatever the financial loss of the Starwood deal, he wanted to assure me that he could more than handle it. I still was still disappointed not being able to square up with him, but I was finally at peace.

Thankfully, in the years to come, *FlyerTalk* became such a

juggernaut that it was purchased by a huge company for reportedly millions of dollars. I apparently didn't bankrupt Randy after all. In fact, there would be occasions where he would actually be bankrolling me!

Randy decided to sponsor a pair of FlyerTalkers to represent his company in a travel competition called "The Global Scavenger Hunt," which was a twenty-three-day, four-continent romp featuring a mystery itinerary and surprise challenges while in hot pursuit of a ten-thousand-dollar grand prize. Randy was prepared to shell out the ten-thousand-dollar entry fee price tag per player. There were hundreds of eager applicants competing to make the cut to be on *Team FlyerTalk,* many with far more compelling and amazing credentials than me. Yet, Randy plucked me from the deep talent pool to be one half of his team. Regrettably, a SARS outbreak caused the travel competition to be canceled.

A few years later, I was poised to launch my own more modest *Amazing Race* for regular travelers called Competitours. It was far less ambitious than the Global Scavenger Hunt—smaller geographic area (Europe), smaller time commitment (nine days), smaller price (a couple of thousand dollars). I had kept Randy intermittently apprised of the project.

Out of the blue, he offered me a triple whammy. He wanted to reserve space for a team, and in year one, I could sure use the money. And what a privilege to have the Godfather of Miles on my trip. But Randy's gracing his presence was not his end game. Rather, like the Global Scavenger Hunt, Randy was going sponsor a *Team FlyerTalk* to compete on the inaugural tripod Competitours. And he was going to make an announcement on all sixty-plus *FlyerTalk* boards to generate a frenzy of exposure and excitement. His efforts spilled over beyond Team *FlyerTalk*; two other teams ended registering for the year one trip because of the impact of Randy's month-long drumbeat about how cool

Competitours sounded. Not to mention that Randy's credibility helped me immensely to attract mainstream travel media coverage from outlets that were otherwise skeptical of a new venture from an unknown quantity like me.

Randy's Starpoints-for-subscriptions promotion also had a profound impact on my view of the mileage game. He had proven that The Pudding Guy's buy instead of fly-to-earn mega-miles was not a unicorn occurrence. And there was an incredible sense of simplicity and elegance in just filling out a two-minute online order form and inputting your credit card number to trigger mileage earning. There were no labor pools, no clones, no scouring T&Cs, no kangaroo courts, no crazy flight routings.

Still, it seemed counter-intuitive to purchase a huge volume of utterly useless items. On the other hand, it was super-intuitive to accumulate mass miles so quickly, so conveniently, and so cheaply.

The buy-instead-of-fly strategy required investigating a potential new source of mileage treasure: online shopping portals that each frequent flyer program had half-heartedly recently rolled out. We called them "mileage malls." At first blush these mileage malls seemed to be full of overpriced and useless gadgetry with pathetic mileage bonuses offered as an incentive to purchase.

Second and third blushes were equally fruitless. But as 2003 came to a close, the fourth blush hit paydirt on the Delta mileage mall.

Some sales executive at 1-800-FLOWERS must have been trying to beef up their December numbers to qualify for a year-end bonus. That seemed to be the only logical explanation for an incredibly lucrative promotion lasting just a day-and-a-half.

On December 30, 1-800-FLOWERS offered three thousand Delta miles for thirty dollars in spend and one thousand miles for every ten dollars spent thereafter, with no quantity caps. In effect one cent in spending = one mile in earning. In my scaling vernacular, that meant

$800 in roses for the wife = 80,000 mile international Business Class award.

Sales goals apparently trumped any bean-counters' concerns. They should have been concerned because the cost of the flower company purchasing miles from Delta (we estimated approx. 1.3 cents) exceeded the value of the mileage offer (1 cent). Like my original rationalization with Randy's Starpoint promotion, I just assumed 1-800-FLOWERS had a method behind their madness. Maybe they made the loss back up with the overall markup of on flowers? This still seemed like a dubious business model ... but it wasn't my job to mindread this company's reason for a promotion. My job was to decide whether to buy ... and whether to scale.

It should have been an easy decision. I had United miles as a gateway to Star Alliance partners and with QANTAS to *Oneworld* partners. But I had no miles in the third major alliance, SkyTeam, of which Delta was a charter member. The flower deal would be a nice opportunity to diversify my mileage holdings.

My mileage scaling pattern had become somewhat predictable. I rounded to the nearest million.

But surprisingly, I would end up taking a hard pass on the flower promotion. Earning Delta miles was attractive, but redeeming them was not. So unappealing was their mileage redemption that *Trader Joe* had devised an informal derisive nickname—"SkyPesos"—that would continue to haunt the company's reputation to this day. Delta miles at any price were essentially worthless if you had to redeem at their extortionate Peak awards for 350-500% more miles.

My decision-making for the 1-800-FLOWERS promotion demonstrated that while I was ambitious, I wasn't reckless. Delta would be on my permanent blacklist, even when I had an unusual chance to earn Delta SkyPesos for *free*.

Logic would dictate that there would be no reason to visit a hair replacement center when you have a flowing mane of hair. However, *FlyerTalk* logic would dictate that a promotion for a FREE, one-time-only, ten-minute hair consultation at a Bosley Hair Transplant Center would be worth twenty thousand Delta bonus miles.

One per person. This deal wasn't scalable. Twenty thousand Delta miles had limited appeal: a one-way Economy award to North or Central America or the Caribbean. But free is free, right?

However, sometimes super cheap could be better than free. And sometimes, a one-per-person quantity cap could still be scalable.

Delta had a reasonable mileage transfer program between accounts for one cent per mile, plus a five-thousand-mile bonus for each twenty thousand transferred.

I could have recruited one of my famed and fabled labor pools! Send batches of three people to get free hair consultations and pay them twenty-five for their drive and consult time. Twenty-five thousand miles would post into each of their individual Delta accounts. Then, I could transfer and aggregate all three accounts into a master account, then top off with a five-thousand-mile purchase at one cent per mile to reach the 80,000-mile international Business Class threshold.

DELTA "HAIR"-BRAINED ANALYSIS

hair consult bonus miles (3 sessions x 20,000 bonus)	60,000	$675	Delta transfer ($.01 x 60,000) and per diem (3 x $25)
Delta transfer bonus (3 sessions x 5,000)	+ 15,000	+ $175	Delta miles top-off purchase (5000 x.035)
Delta miles top-off	+ 5,000		
	= 80,000	= **$850**	TOTAL mileage and cost of intl. Business Class award
		vs. $6,000	cost to purchase retail intl. Business Class airfare

Again, Delta's SkyPesos were a raw deal, so I passed. Had it been another program, I would have consulted Randy for one of his smell tests about the ethical tightrope of taking unneeded consultations even though there were no restrictions or eligibility requirements in the Bosley/Delta T&C such as balding hair or aggregating mileage transfers.

It would turn out that Randy and Delta weren't the only ones to roll out a promotion with unintended consequences.

A year later, not a rule, but rather the absence of a rule, would come to haunt a European airline program, making me a mileage millionaire with yet a third program.

An extra million or three would prove useful as my three kids would finally be old enough to fly to and appreciate the unique and exotic cultures of far-flung destinations like the mountains and sherpas of Nepal, the floating markets and war history of Vietnam, and the mythical Bali.

Chapter 9: Dutch Treat

National airlines have long been a source of a country's pride or even its national security. In Europe the successful national airlines had either a large domestic population to support a large domestic route network (Alitalia, Iberia, Scandinavian) or a substantial international network (Swiss, KLM). Or both (Lufthansa, Air France).

Sabena, Belgium's national airline, sadly had neither. Despite years of bleeding money and being propped up by the government, it finally met its demise in late 2001. The Belgian government chose not to honor or compensate the members of Sabena's program who had outstanding mileage balances, rendering them totally worthless.

Or seemingly so.

Sabena was a relatively small program, but Belgians were a high-value customer base, relatively well-traveled, and well-off. Surrounded by nearby airline programs, the Belgians could migrate to British Airways, Air France, Lufthansa, or Scandinavian. But their neighbor, KLM, the national airline of the Netherlands, offered a 'Dutch treat' too good to pass up.

KLM was going to resuscitate those left-for-dead Sabena miles.

KLM rolled out an offer (*presumably*) targeted to Sabena account holders to submit their mileage statements. And regardless of their balances and elite status, KLM would *match* in their Flying Dutchman frequent flyer program.

It seemed like a shrewd move since printing miles had no real hard cost to KLM. It just meant that all these new members and all their miles would now be chasing the same amount of award inventory and cramming the already crowded lounges.

KLM made this offer for a limited six-week time window. But for some strange reason, they missed a key limitation in the offer terms and conditions. In fact it wasn't just a key limitation that they missed; it was the linchpin of the offer.

Instead of specifying the mileage statement match exclusively for Sabena members, the offer language seemed to allow *any* program mileage statement to be eligible. Knowing the intent of the offer, it seemed to be an inadvertent omission that KLM would catch and correct in no time. Especially since a thread on *FlyerTalk* had opened about the unrestricted match access of the offer. Plus, it was widely presumed that every airline had a lurker checking the threads.

There were rumors that airline mileage statements could easily be easily doctored to show higher mileage balances and higher elite status, especially since KLM accepted fax copies that were fuzzy and wouldn't show slight texture and color differences from White-Out. It would seem a reasonable protection for KLM to require that an original statement be mailed to KLM to ensure no fraud. Surely, someone was minding the store at the Flying Dutchman program?

But weeks passed, and neither the language of the offer nor the statement submission process were revised. I had given KLM the benefit of the doubt for nearly the full six weeks that the offer would be revised to exclude non-Sabena applicants. With two days left I had to seize the opportunity. I still had 2.5 million miles in my United account from the Las Vegas SKY High

Rollers venture. With a more than sufficient mileage balance and bona fide top-tier elite status, I had no need to doctor my statement.

While KLM had announced a deadline date for statement submissions, they provided zero communication after that. Days turned into weeks and weeks into months. And still nothing emanating from KLM HQ in Amsterdam other than eerie silence.

Clearly, KLM had realized that their mileage match offer had gone awry. *FlyerTalk* members were hesitant to lead the charge to smoke out KLM management because our non-Sabena mileage match requests were likely the source of the delay. No one wanted to further provoke KLM, to poke the sleeping bear.

Thankfully, two months later, former Sabena members started receiving new account numbers with mileage and elite status match statements from KLM.

But non-Sabena members had no such luck.

In our minds, KLM had lost the high moral ground for not honoring the non-Sabena statement submissions. If there was a mistake, they should have fessed up in real-time when the offer was still live. They surely couldn't use the "it was an oversight" defense after ruminating for months.

And we were right.

KLM finally gave in. Several weeks later, KLM finally sent the non-Sabena mileage-match confirmations out. I was a newly minted Flying Dutchman Platinum member with 2.5 million miles at no cost.

The Platinum membership changed everything; it just took me some time to realize it.

I had coveted Air Canada Super Elite status for their no-blackout benefit, but the Baht Run flyers' status had since expired, so I lost access to that benefit. I was sure there was no other frequent flyer in the world with that no-blackout benefit.

I was never so happy to be wrong.

It turned out KLM offered the same super valuable no-blackout perk to its top-tier elite members, but it was an 'unpublished' benefit. And unlike the Aeroplan members on *FlyerTalk* who referenced the no- blackout perk in hushed tones, the KLM Platinum elites were truly observing mums the word.

I only stumbled upon the KLM no-blackout benefit when the award booking site crashed, and I was forced to contact the phone agents at the call center. Lucky for me that the website crashed, because I never made award bookings with phone agents, and yet with KLM, the only way to get access to the no-blackout inventory was via the time-consuming phone call to their call center. But the phone agents there were instructed to push members to use the website! Major catch-22.

"Hi there, I was hoping you could check award space for me—" Before I could finish, I was abruptly interrupted.

"Award bookings are only redeemable using the online site."

"Yes, I'm aware—"

Again, the agent cut in. "OK, since you are aware, then please follow the instructions. Thank you for calling Flying Dutchman."

Click.

Clearly, I needed to do a better job cutting to the chase. I called back. "Hi, there. The online booking site is down, and I'm a Platinum member."

"Oh, we're terribly sorry for the inconvenience. Please give me your award request." It was the same brusque agent who now turned into a solicitous servant as soon as she heard the word "Platinum." Apparently there weren't too many Platinums that were North American-based, and the KLM call center based near Toronto was ill-prepared for my Platinum ilk.

I asked for Chicago to Zurich in Business. "There is no award space I'm afraid. Oh, that's right you're Platinum. Let me see what I can do."

After being put on hold for almost thirty minutes, she returned. "I was able to release the space since you're a Platinum." Then, it took another fifteen minutes to spoon-feed all the reservation details. And then the kicker—after forty-five minutes of phone time, there was no e-ticket. A paper ticket would be mailed out versus a three-minute online award booking and e-ticket process with United. It was back to the 80's with my newfound preferred program.

But the no-blackout perk was worth the monumental hassle.

Ominously, just a year after the KLM match, my 2.5 million miles were under siege from a supposed friend, not foe, of KLM.

KLM had a very close partnership with Northwest, but their frequent flyer programs maintained their own operations and had totally different mileage earning, redeeming, and elite status methodologies. KLM's program *bested* Northwest's in every regard. A decision was made to fully integrate their mileage programs as the two airlines sought to officially evolve from a partnership into a bona fide joint venture.

KLM members were concerned because Northwest was the bigger company and likely more influential in shaping this integrated program into their own (subpar) image. There was a real fear that KLM would be compelled to dilute their program to match Northwest as it would be less costly to have a less generous program.

Since most indigenous Dutch KLM members were not as sophisticated and engaged about their program, it was unlikely there would unlikely be a hue and cry to lobby against such negative changes being made. The only protests would come from the American carpetbaggers who benefited from the Sabena mileage match like me, and our fifth column voices could be easily ignored. We braced for some kind of inevitable massive devaluation.

The integration planning seemed to drag out for months without any indications from KLM HQ in Amsterdam or Northwest HQ in Detroit. There were rumors that Northwest would convert KLM miles to a new mileage currency at the ratio of 1:75, meaning my 2.5 million miles could be devalued to 1.9 million miles in one fell swoop.

Just as KLM honored the Sabena miles on a 1:1 basis, we hoped against hope that KLM would hold the line with a 1:1 conversion to the new KLM//Northwest currency.

But our belief was not to be. It was announced that the 1:1 ratio was going to be scuttled. Yet, we would be kept in suspense another few weeks before the official announcement of the new currency and conversion rate for the KLM miles.

As the announcement drew near, the *FlyerTalk* crowd was morose. The depressing posts all had varying projections of how bad the mileage devaluation would be. It wasn't a question of if; it was just a question of how *bad*. And as expected, the final announcement was *BAD*.

As in Michael Jackson "BAD!" The "bad" conversion rate was 1.6:1. Every one KLM mile would be converted into 1.6 new program miles!!! Astounding, just astounding.

My 2.5 million balance would skyrocket to 4.6 million miles!

Normally, "free travel" was just a euphemism for redeeming an award ticket after earning enough miles from purchasing tens of thousands (or even hundreds of thousands) of dollars in airfares or credit card charges. In my case, the 4.6 million miles were literally free.

Dodging the Northwest bullet was a harrowing experience,

but another threat loomed over my newly expanded KLM mileage stash.

The era of airline consolidation was accelerating. American had swallowed TWA, USAir was taking over America West, Lufthansa was "merging" (in name only) with Swiss Airlines, and similar airline mergers were happening in Canada, New Zealand … and apparently in the Netherlands.

Air France had become an aggressive suitor to combine with KLM. Their Frequence Bleu program was far worse than Northwest. Since Air France was appreciably larger than KLM, it was unlikely the combined frequent flyer program would be based on a collegial approach; it would be an Air France diktat.

As the member with one of the largest mileage balances in the KLM program, I needed clarity on how bad things might get and how soon so I could put together an award redemption, maybe even a liquidation strategy.

The Flying Dutchman program was managed by a closely-held third party company, Cygnific. They spurned my entreaties for an in-person meeting for three months. It was company policy not to meet program members. The policy was specific about meetings during business hours. I suggested a weekend meeting that wasn't expressly prohibited. The manager in Amsterdam had noted that my frequent thirty-minute phone calls to the call center and my Sabena 'shenanigans' were notorious at HQ, so she was actually curious to meet me.

The meeting was arranged in Amsterdam during a long layover on a trip to Indonesia. To drive home the notion that this wasn't an *official* meeting that could get the manager in trouble, I arrived at her office incognito. I was wearing the Business Class-issued pajamas that looked vaguely like sweatpants and a sweatshirt. I was disheveled and unshowered from the eight-hour overnight flight. And I had my two tweener sons in tow.

Maybe I was too incognito? This Amsterdam manager refused to believe that their mileage millionaire Yankee could be a vagrant.

What should have been a leisurely two-hour dalliance was crammed into about thirty minutes. With all the distractions of my kids' raucous antics, she was still generous with freely sharing insights and predictions. She never used the terms 'off-the-record' or 'confidential' during our conversation. At the end of the meeting, she was clear that our meeting place was a secret, but no mention was specifically made about our meeting content, which didn't seem particularly valuable or classified.

And the meeting content was pretty much just an affirmation of what we were already predicting on *FlyerTalk*. KLM's awful online award booking site would not be upgraded anytime soon because they claimed it did not generate revenue. Air France intensely disliked the no-blackout perk, but the negotiations for the Air France-KLM merger were predicted to take a while. And once completed, the frequent flyer programs would be the last phase of the merger, many months later. So, there was likely a comfortable two-year window of protection.

I was relieved to have time to use the miles. How else would I have trips like the once-in-a-lifetime trip my sons and I had embarked on. We had so many Indonesian firsts: seeing a tribe in Papua New Guinea that had only been discovered fifty-five years ago and arriving at an airport so remote that they counted how many foreigners had traveled there that year—we were nine, ten and eleven from America. We frolicked with orangutans in their natural habitat, explored a cave that was taller and wider than a 747 with two million bats streaming out like a smokestack at each sunset. And learning everything from batik handicraft and poison arrow-making to blowgun shooting and biking down the rice-terraced path of an active volcano!

When I returned home a few weeks later, I dutifully shared my intel on *FlyerTalk*.

My post on *FlyerTalk* was short and sweet and pretty much verbatim from the Cygnific manager. A week later she emailed me that she had been fired. I was stunned. There was no proprietary or secret information that she had warned me not to share. And my post mentioned nothing about an in-person meeting. And during our conversation, she knew I was an active *FlyerTalk* poster. I fired off letters to the top brass of Cygnific and KLM, but to no avail. I found the manager's home phone to beg for her forgiveness, explaining that I had no idea I was breaching protocol.

She assured me her firing was not my fault. She had been lobbying KLM not to let the Flying Dutchman program be eviscerated by Air France. She was on a watch list well before our conversation. She was relieved and confided she was pregnant, so her departure was inevitable.

While I went from zero to 4.6 million totally free KLM miles—courtesy of Sabena and Northwest—there was yet another free miles opportunity that required quite a bit more heavy lifting.

Literally heavy lifting.

During the early 2000's, there was a strategy to buy stuff to earn mileage and then essentially have that stuff refunded, so the miles earned were free. Savings bonds and traveler's checks were purchased with credit cards to earn miles, and then those currency instruments would be deposited into checking accounts to pay off the next month's credit card bill. Rinse and repeat monthly. It was an early iteration of an earning strategy called "manufactured spending."

Over time the credit card companies got wise and eliminated savings bonds and travelers' checks for mileage earning.

FlyerTalkers didn't get mad. They got even.

The next big discovery was the ability to purchase dollar coins from the U.S. Mint, with no shipping cost, for Native American and Presidential coins.

I had no idea why the U.S. Mint would want to be in the retail sales business, especially since dollar coins had already been proven to be a flop vs. paper money, so what was the point in trying to recirculate them?

No matter, credit card companies treated these dollar coins as legitimate product purchases, eligible to earn miles. And until the *FlyerTalk* discovery, the U.S. Mint had no quantity limits. Frankly, business had admittedly been quite slow.

It wouldn't be slow for long.

People were ordering as many coins as the credit limits from their multiple credit cards could tolerate. Any given person could earn hundreds of thousands, if not millions, of free miles by buying, then immediately paying off, monthly U.S. Mint purchases. The U.S. Mint was probably initially ecstatic that their coins would now have a new lease on circulation life, pulsating through the financial system.

Their elation was premature. Those coins were actually pulsating back into the obscurity of local bank vaults!

FlyerTalkers wouldn't be spending and circulating the coins at Target or McDonalds. These coins were deposited immediately into their local checking accounts to cover their coming credit card bills … month after month.

There were a number of practical and theoretical risks here.

First off, most people were depositing huge sacks of coins every few days. The same UPS guy was delivering their coins. The same underpaid bank security guard monitoring their coins. The same dutiful banker collecting and counting their coins each day. These coin collectors had no personal bodyguards. They had a predictable deposit routine, month after month. Any of the above "observers" or co-conspirators could be tempted to fence their houses to burglarize their coins.

The second set of risks was with the government. Let's say someone had a relatively modest job and years of consistent deposit and withdrawal history, and all of a sudden, they were cycling tens of thousands of dollars per month or even per week (or if I would have gotten involved, maybe per day!!!!). Someone was going to get the attention of the SEC, the IRS, the DEA, or take your pick of any other three-letter-abbreviated government agency. Even if someone was totally innocent of money laundering, would they really want that kind of scrutiny? As one who knows, trust me, you don't!!

At some point it's unclear when, or if, the internal pressure at the U.S. Mint or from the credit card companies, the gravy train eventually stalled, but it didn't stop. Coin purchases were restricted to $1,000 per ten days. So, still a cool 36,000 miles per year if someone maxed out under their own name.

Once the cap restriction was in place, there still would have been a strategic work-around to allow scaling. Most credit card companies allowed a primary account holder to add secondary users. Secondary cardholders could spend, but the primary account holder would receive the monthly bill and would be solely responsible for paying any secondary user charges. So, coin orders could be placed for dozens of different people using their own names. Amex actually allowed up to *ninety-nine* secondary users per card.

I loved that math.

AMEX SECONDARY USERS U.S. MINT ANALYSIS

99	secondary card users
x 4	Amex cards
x 36,000	allowable annual coin purchase
= 14,000,000	coins and Miles

All within the rules. Jus' sayin'…

After the Mint deal was finally put to rest, once again, FlyerTalkers didn't get mad; they got even again. Savvy folks moved on to purchasing prepaid gift cards and preloaded credit cards, which also had a nice run as "manufactured-spending" items.

Make no *mistake*, *FlyerTalk* members started finding a slew of *unmistakably* amazing fares, and we would be woefully *mistaken* if we didn't purchase them with *unmistakable* vigor.

Chapter 10: Whoops or Whooooopy!

I needed to reach 75,000 miles worth of travel for ten years straight to get KLM Platinum for Life, a worthy goal since their program had that coveted perk of no-blackouts for award redemptions.

The first six years were a breeze. I was already spending budgeted money to journey back and forth to Green Bay for work on the company dime. When work ended after a fabled fourteen-year run, the next four years of earning Platinum status would be pulled from my personal piggybank.

Cringe!

That's when I started scrutinizing a forum on *FlyerTalk* called "Mileage Run." The concept was finding crazy low fares and strategic routing, to earn fast and cheap elite status. But I also discovered there were some controversial threads about something called "mistake fares."

Data entry could be a job full of mindless drudgery. So, it wouldn't be surprising if a low-level airline worker bee occasionally coded an incorrect fare into their online booking system. Maybe a zero was left out or a decimal point misplaced, or perhaps Business Class was inadvertently switched for Economy Class.

As a business owner, I would have much sympathy for the worker and the airlines, as we are all capable of making honest mistakes. There were two *FlyerTalk* schools of thought about the topic.

There were the *rationalizers*. They reasoned that there was no such thing as a mistake fare. There were just amazing short-term "promotional" deep-discount fares. The airlines actually did from time-to-time offer such promotional fares, but they were aggressively and publicly advertised on their websites. Yet, none of the crazy low fares identified by the *rationalizers* were ever found on the airlines' special deal websites. So, you be the judge!

Then there were the *ponderers*. They didn't want to unduly take advantage of an honest mistake. But they took it a step further. Their question was, "When was a mistake not a mistake anymore?" They postulated that if a bona fide mistake fare was posted on the Mileage Run forum, then the airline in question should find out about it quickly from their company lurker on *FlyerTalk*. Then, the airline would quickly correct or pull the fare and immediately contact anyone who purchased it to explain it was a mistake and expedite a refund.

FlyerTalk was absolutely well-known by every frequent flyer program, and there was no excuse for not having a lurker to take the pulse of their most rabid demographic ... and protecting their companies' interests.

But, what if a seemingly obvious mistake fare lingered on and it wasn't changed in the first twenty-four hours? Or forty-eight hours? Or even seventy-two hours? Was it still a mistake fare if it wasn't actually corrected in a timely manner or at all? This was a fascinating moral/ethical conundrum for the *ponderers.*

And then there was my take. I had been put through the ringer by United Mileage Plus and Air Canada Aeroplan. They blamed *me* for finding and exploiting vulnerabilities that they either didn't have the ability or the will to detect on their own. They had plenty of resources to protect their assets. They had huge administrative, IT, finance, and legal departments to thoroughly vet and ensure quality control of their operations.

So, if everyone at an airlines' corporate department were doing their jobs, there would be no reason to ever have to joust with the Steve Belkins' of the world. I was a *radical rationalizer.* My assessment: the airlines had twenty-four hours to identify and correct mistake fares once they were outed on *FlyerTalk*.

Both groups suffered through the 'countdown' process when an occasional mistake fare did bubble up, waiting and hoping for enough time to pass by without a dreaded post, email, or phone call from the airline advising they had discovered the mistake and would not be honoring the fare.

In general, most mistake fares were generally unattractive. If they were domestic-based, they were usually in Economy, so mileage earnings would be modest at best. If they were Business Class fares, they often usually required starting outside the U.S., so there were significant costs and time to get positioned at the originating airport.

For example, there was an attractive mistake fare that was available from Kuala Lumpur, Malaysia, to Boston round-trip for a few hundred instead of the normal few thousand dollars, but Boston to Kuala Lumpur round-trip was pricing at the normal fare.

So, the itinerary would be:

Boston-Kuala Lumpur: full fare or burn miles.
Kuala Lumpur-Boston-Kuala Lumpur: mistake fare.
Kuala Lumpur back to Boston: full fare or burn miles.

By the time you factored in the cash or mileage cost of the positioning flights to a far-flung place like Kuala Lumpur, not to mention the time required, the value of the mistake fare was pretty much obviated. The mistake fare had to start from the USA.

But Canada would suffice!

An apparent mistake fare popped up that checked all my boxes.

- International Business Class: Toronto to Larnaca, Cyprus
- My airline alliance: Alitalia (KLM partner)
- Killer fare: $37 fare plus another $200 in taxes and fuel surcharges.
- Platinum status fast: Toronto-Rome-Larnaca, Cyprus

MISTAKE FARE ANALYSIS

earned miles Toronto-Rome-Larnaca	11,000		
100% elite bonus miles	+ 11,000		
200% Class of service bonus	+ 22,000		
TOTAL miles	= 44,000	$237	mistake fare per trip including tax
2 annual trips	x 2	x 2	2 annual trips
need 75,000 for annual Platinum status	= 88,000	= $474	cost of qualifying for KLM Platinum status annually for 2 years

So, I was the first lunatic to actually scale mistake fares. I bought eighteen. Six for me to help me keep KLM Platinum status for another two years since Alitalia was a fellow Skyteam partner. And two for each of my four family members to lock in vacation travel to Switzerland and Israel.

I was the new guy on the Mileage Run forum block, and apparently, I hadn't made such a good first impression. I was confused. Hundreds of people were buying one or two fares. Were my eighteen fares really going to determine if the fare price was honored or not?

But it was perceived as a "pigs get fed, hogs get slaughtered" scenario. But worse, I was the hog that would be responsible for all the other innocent pigs getting slaughtered as well if the fare wasn't honored because of my scaled purchases.

After the first day of announcing the Toronto-Larnaca thirty-seven-dollar mistake fare, there was a decided air of gloom on the *FlyerTalk* forum. As the thread was exploding, Alitalia's booking site was imploding. Other travel forums were reposting the fare. Surely, Alitalia would catch this mistake fare carnage and eradicate it immediately. Plus, other Alitalia Business Class to Central Europe fares were suspiciously priced around $3,700. Surely, some type of fat-finger mishap was the culprit, and the Toronto-Larnaca fare would return to its rightful $3,700 price.

We expected the countdown to end in hours, not even days. But then again, it was Alitalia, which had a reputation for bare-bones competency when it did anything other than actually flying their airplanes! So, we lowered our expectations. At the stroke of midnight, seven days later, Alitalia remained silent.

Euphoria reigned.

There was actually a united front between the *rationalizers* and *ponderers* that the thirty-seven dollars was a legit fare.

People started making hotel, car rental, and onward travel

reservations, many of them nonrefundable. And why not? People booked the fare and paid for it. And despite the ruckus swirling around this Toronto-Larnaca fare, Alitalia was either blissfully ignorant, clueless, uncaring, or maybe it was *actually* the right fare. Whatever the case, no one, not even the venerable mileage guru Randy was concerned.

A few weeks later, there were some stirrings at Alitalia. Disturbingly, a post suddenly appeared on *FlyerTalk*. Alitalia was investigating a fare that may have been published inadvertently. They would keep us posted after a thorough analysis. Members were posting about filing class-action suits or going to *USA Today* for an expose or even urging the Department of Transportation to withdraw Alitalia's landing rights in America.

We needed cooler heads to prevail. Especially since Alitalia had not definitively said they wouldn't honor the fares. I felt that this was an opportune time to get my tarnished reputation on the Mileage Run forum restored.

While everyone else was throwing a tantrum and speculating terrible conspiracies of what was going on behind Alitalia closed doors, I beelined it for the belly of the beast. I picked up the phone and called the Alitalia New York office. I asked for the General Manager and was connected without even identifying myself.

Strange.

The General Manager picked up the call, and in his first few words of salutation, I could already detect a mix of weariness and defensiveness in his voice. I surmised that I wasn't the first FlyerTalker to call his office. He explained that previous callers had berated his poor receptionist so much that she demanded him to take the calls directly, without her screening.

I immediately took his side and apologized for the unbecoming conduct of my *FlyerTalk* peers. And I suggested that he was probably taking the heat for mistakes that were made five thousand miles away at Alitalia headquarters in Rome. Finally, I advised him that I wasn't calling to complain but calling to offer my help in being part of the solution.

My offer came at a good time. The GM was stuck between an angry mob of FlyerTalkers and a management insulated from the firestorm, concentrating only on crunching the numbers, not the tremendous negative fallout that was looming. The best news was that indeed no final decision had yet been made; he and I would have some wiggle room.

But not over the phone. I needed to put a human face on this *FlyerTalk* horde that felt so threatening to Alitalia. I asked if I could fly to New York the next day to brainstorm, and he readily agreed. I needed to find a solution where this New York General Manager of Alitalia could be the hero and save the day for his company like I did with Mr. Purple Rain at Thai Air.

Nothing makes a better first impression than food. With fresh-baked Italian pastry in hand, I arrived at his office, and we snacked together. That fifteen-minute cushion was crucial to get comfortable and establish rapport before diving into the mistake fare morass. His office was cramped like the hapless data input staffer who likely activated the thirty-seven-dollar mistake fare stampede. Plus, there were dozens of pink phone messages strewn about—all with similar themes: Larnaca, thirty-seven dollars, *FlyerTalk*, Business Class fare, going to the media, going to sue. The General Manager was named Antonio (not his real name), and he confided that Alitalia was in panic mode. Little did he know that despite their public blustering, the *FlyerTalk* gang was also privately in panic mode!

Our meeting focused on the key difference between *loss* of revenue and vs. *absen*ce of revenue.

I explained that there was no loss of revenue. Alitalia wasn't really losing $3,700 in actual airfares because *none* of the FlyerTalkers would have ever purchased a Business Class fare without the mistake fare rate. Toronto-Rome Business Class was rarely sold out anyway, so if a mistake-fare seat inventory was taken, and it wasn't displacing many, if any, prospective full-fare customers.

The actual impact of the thirty-seven-dollar mistake-fare was not a *loss* of revenue but rather an *absence* of revenue.

The plane was already flying with all of its normal overhead. The only actual hard cost to Alitalia would be food and alcohol consumed at the lounge and onboard ... which would be more or less covered by the thirty-seven dollars, actually paid.

There was a good analogy for HQ. When a flight wasn't sold out in Business Class, off-duty flight attendants and pilots who were on board were routinely allowed to travel standby in unsold Business Class seats. This was company policy. No one looked at that scenario as the airline taking a financial hit. Just treat the FlyerTalkers like "temporary" off-duty staff, and then it wouldn't hurt so much!!!

Antonio appreciated my logic, but he was concerned it was very "American" logic that might not resonate with Italian management thinking. I reminded him that the time for smart management thinking lapsed two months ago when Alitalia missed finding and correcting the mistake fare in the first place. I had him dry-run the pitch with me. After a half-a-dozen tries, his presentation was still very tentative. Maybe Antonio would exude confidence speaking in his native language? I wished him luck with pitching HQ in Rome.

I didn't expect that Alitalia would roll over and play dead. But one week had passed and there was still no decision. The natives on *FlyerTalk* were getting very, very restless. Where was

Antonio on all this? Had they fired him after sharing my heretical problem-solving?

Even Randy, who was the epitome of calm, was getting testy. And trust me, Alitalia didn't want Randy weighing in. He was considered a consumer advocate who also respected the need for the airline programs to be sustainable and profitable. He was the consummate honest broker, so if he decided to take sides, you wanted it to be yours!!

Antonio finally called me back after ten days.

Breaking news: Alitalia had finally conceded. They determined that the fare would be honored. But unlike the normal Business Class fares that allowed unlimited changes, this mistake fare had two new conditions.

The routing Toronto-Larnaca routing couldn't be changed, and flight dates could only be changed once.

Those conditions would likely cause some *FlyerTalk* grumbling, but they were a small price to pay to get the fare honored.

Antonio was jubilant about the wonderful news and would soon be posting this glorious decision on *FlyerTalk* in twenty-four hours. But I cautioned that "wonderful news" was Alitalia's opinion. There would likely be a bell curve of responses, and only very few of them would be abject gratitude or appreciation.

Ten percent or so would begrudgingly forgive and acknowledge.

Eighty percent or so would pull the entitlement card since they played by the rules yet were ignored and insulted for months.

The last ten percent or so, a disaffected minority, would maintain their resentment for Alitalia's incompetence and decision to accede only under tremendous pressure of lawsuits and negative media attention.

I just wanted to manage the GM and HQ expectations since they seemed to think their actions were so magnanimous. They felt that FlyerTalkers were the problem and that Alitalia was providing a paternal solution.

Everyone flew their Toronto-Larnaca thirty-seven-dollar fares. The reviews of the inflight experience followed a similar bell curve.

Ten percent or so thought the flight was pretty darn good.

Eighty percent or so were unimpressed but mostly satisfied.

Ten percent or so were disappointed and heavy on the criticism: spaghetti consistency, movie selection, towel temperature, lounge wine quality … you get the picture!

Welcome to the bell curve of the human condition. But it was better than legal trouble or a public relations fiasco.

The Toronto-Larnaca mistake fare had a short-term happy ending, but there were much more profound long-term implications.

The Toronto-Larnaca mistake fare was the first real mass mobilization of collective action of people spread out geographically but with a common locus of online connection—*FlyerTalk*. Everybody had the same access to the same information, and there was a central place into which to add your two cents. Based on the Alitalia outcome, FlyerTalkers understood that they had a newfound ability to organize. While we couldn't enforce any decrees on any travel program, a rough consensus coalesced between the *rationalizers* and *ponderers* after the Alitalia fiasco about mistake fares.

Airlines would have a finite amount of time—seventy-two hours, to be exact—to find and correct mistake fares before FlyerTalkers would pounce. Why seventy-two hours? After the Alitalia debacle, every airline was aware of the Mileage Run forum. They would now be responsible for monitoring it on a regular basis in order to protect themselves.

And although our community had hammered out this non-binding precedent that had no legal standing or any collaboration from the airlines, the seventy-two-hour "countdown" become became the unofficial standard. Only on very rare occasions in the future would an airline brazenly ignore it.

A couple of years later, KLM partner Aeroflot, Russia's national airline, had a similar mistake fare that I jumped on as they missed the seventy-two-hour catch-and-correct window, and the fare was honored. Business Class Dubai to Toronto via Moscow on Aeroflot for $567. My guess is that a pesky zero was inadvertently left off the correct $5,670 fare. Because I had children studying in Israel around that time, I would be visiting them, so Tel Aviv to Dubai positioning flight just a short hop … in theory.

I purchased fares that straddled two different calendar years, and with the mileage earning, I would qualify for the final two years of earning KLM Flying Dutchman Platinum status and finally achieve the coveted ten consecutive years to be bequeathed Platinum for Life.

A normal nonstop flight Tel Aviv to Dubai would be under three hours, but that would presume normalized relations between the two countries. Dubai had a policy of prohibiting anyone from Israel, or even those with Israeli passport stamps, into the country. Politics prevailed. In fact at the time, there was absolutely no booking engine that would even sell a published airfare, not even via legal routings such as Amman, Istanbul, or Athens.

However, that restriction was not enforceable with award tickets. I redeemed a short-haul Economy award on QANTAS's Oneworld alliance partner, Royal Jordanian. The QANTAS agent had no idea the firestorm she would be creating. The routing was Tel Aviv-Amman-Dubai.

I encountered surprises at every airport.

Tel Aviv airport security is the smartest and strictest in the world. But the airport wasn't crawling with armed soldiers. There were casually dressed, smiling staff asking pleasant and innocuous questions. But they were trained in interrogation techniques like detecting speech patterns, eye contact, body language, and subtle perspiration to do their threat assessments.

They didn't need any of those mental gymnastics techniques with me … they simply looked at my ticket! My ticket wasn't a red flag — it was a red searchlight beaming miles up into the sky!

Having Dubai on my plane ticket was apparently my ticket to the airport detention room. I was whisked without a word to a windowless office. In this office all of the pretenses of being Israeli airport security being friendly and easygoing were off the table. There were armed soldiers in full fatigues surrounding a very displeased-looking female agent.

The only thing scarier than being intensively grilled was not being grilled at all. There must have been two minutes of totally unnerving silence. Lots of sighs, shaking heads, looking at the soldiers, looking at my ticket, my passport, my backpack, everywhere but at my face.

The security lady was the epitome of the Israeli national fruit, the sabra. Sweet on the inside, hard on the outside. She started with the sweet.

"I see you have visited Israel a few times. You must be Jewish."

I nodded enthusiastically, hoping that would put a quick end to the interrogation.

Then at last, a cute smile. "You should come back more often. It is your homeland, after all." And then before I could even smile back, there was an abrupt end of her sweet persona.

Her eyes narrowed, her shoulders tensed, and maybe I even

heard a gun being cocked over my shoulder. She hissed, "Why is a Jewish man going to a country that supports terrorists against Israel? And why are you flying on a one-way ticket to an enemy country?"

I had two major concerns. First, answering her questions in a satisfactory manner. Second, extricating myself from this security cell in enough time to make to the flight into the Arab abyss, Dubai. I was afraid of being a no-show for the all-important Dubai-Toronto mistake fare flight and be stranded in Dubai with no onward ticket … and more importantly, no tens of thousands of miles being generated.

"It's not a one-way ticket. I have a departing flight from Dubai to Toronto four hours later, on Aeroflot. And then, after landing in Toronto, I have another flight back to Dubai five hours later. It's called a "mileage run." I'm just trying to earn a lot of airline miles on a crazy-low fare. It just so happens that the fare involves Dubai."

Her facial expression changed from steely to merely annoyed. She spoke in rapid-fire Hebrew to the guards. They laughed for two seconds before she gave them the evil eye.

She clearly knew what I was doing. This wasn't her first mileage-run rodeo. At this point she just half-heartedly went through the drill to cover her butt.

"You understand that if the Dubai government would want to put you in jail for violating that 'no-Israel' policy on your passport, neither Israel nor the U.S. could help you?" Empty threat, but I understood. I was released with twenty-one minutes to spare to make my flight to Amman.

So, in truth, Israeli security really was merely trying to protect me, not intimidate me. And after the fact I appreciated their efforts. But, at that point, they were simply my impediment to making the flight before check-in closed.

Once I arrived in Amman, there was an Orthodox Jewish guy in the lounge, and he was "bageling" me, meaning he was subtly trying to sniff out if I was Jewish since I didn't have any outward clothing or facial traits that instantly gave me away. First, he asked me where was I was going. When I told him I was going to Dubai, that's all he had to hear. I couldn't be Jewish. I got another thirty seconds of small talk out of him, and he went back to his group.

Out of the corner of my eye, I could see his whole group in deep conversation with plenty of surreptitious glances at me. When I approached the snack table for seconds, the outwardly Jewish man garbed in a black suit and long beard re-approached as well, ready for round two of bageling questions.

He asked if I visited *Yerushalayim* when I was in Israel. That is the Hebrew word for Jerusalem. No matter your stripe of Judaism, you know what that word means. My inherently snarky nature wanted to dismiss him a second time and shrug my shoulders with a look of extreme puzzlement … and I did!

So, that made ME feel good. But once my cynicism waned, I quickly said "*Hatzlacha*", which is Hebrew for "good luck" or "have a good trip." He turned back around beaming. You could see it on his face—*he knew it!!*

It didn't take long for every Jewish person in the lounge to hear about my destination.

Another bell curve: a few fellow Jews in the lounge were excited about this adventure. Most were nonplussed, as my trip was already a *fait accompli*, so there was nothing they could do about it. And a few were actually on the verge of physically restraining me from boarding a flight into enemy territory!

When I finally got to Dubai, it was strangely reminiscent of the Tel Aviv airport debacle. I was hauled into a small room with all armed guards sans the warm welcome to my second home.

"Who are you spying for?" That was the first question!

Considering I was leaving the airport in less than three hours, and Dubai airport was crammed with security staff and cameras, I would surely have to have possess Bond-esque spy skills to accomplish this seemingly impossible task.

I really wanted to just go into snark overdrive and answer, "For The Zionist entity, of course."

But I simply said, "I'm just a tourist."

It was anti-climactic from there. Filling out piles of paperwork, listening to the same awfully veiled threats about arrest, deportation, and no-fly lists.

Once I was finally released from security detention purgatory, there was a problem that neither security nor I could have anticipated.

There were no blank pages left on my passport. The immigration agent would have to hunt through my thirty-five passport pages to find space to squeeze in a United Arab Emirates stamp. But the Dubai stamp was larger than most other country stamps, so the only page space that had enough room for the UAE stamp without overlapping with other stamps was the page with an…

Israeli passport stamp.

Typically, it wasn't permissible to stamp over another existing stamp. This passport officer took *fifteen minutes* to thumb through all thirty-five passport pages to figure out the least amount of overlap of his stamp … just to avoid stamping on the same page as Israel.

A man of principle on the frontline of the Arab-Israeli conflict!

I finally had accumulated the ten consecutive years of Platinum for Life. But during my ten-year quest, the top-tier elite perks had been slowly diluted during the integration with Northwest, then diluted further during the integration with Air

France. And then, finally diluted to the point of no recognition when Air France actually commandeered the program and changed the name to Flying Blue.

My Lifetime Platinum status with KLM that I had invested ten years of time, money, and loyalty to was practically worthless. Then no-blackout perk had been eviscerated ... so had my trust in the KLM mileage program and in the mileage game in general.

Could I have possibly been wrong in assuming that my underlying assumption that mileage accumulation was a bulletproof investment? Mileage was unquestionably a fantastic short-term asset and a darn good medium-term asset for a few years. But it was not going to be that long-term mileage nest egg that I had envisioned a decade earlier. Instead of just amassing mileage whenever the opportunity arose, I would have to determine if I had a travel game plan to justify it.

The golden era of mistake fares was relatively short since airlines quickly became more vigilant about monitoring *FlyerTalk* and upgrading software to detect fare anomalies.

I had earned miles on a worldwide basis starting in Los Angeles, stopping in Cleveland and Green Bay, doubling back to Las Vegas, leapfrogging to northern Thailand, invading Randy's HQ in Colorado Springs, and literally freeloading twice in Holland.

My next earning opportunity would *not* take place in Cameroon.

Chapter 11: The Cameroon Swoon

By the late 2000s *FlyerTalk* had become more popular, and the regulars increasingly started using backchannels to communicate. Lurkers from the travel programs became the norm. And the membership had gotten so big that prospective deals were in jeopardy of being stampeded leading to quick shutdowns. While *FlyerTalk* private messaging became the norm, it was still terribly inefficient.

Reluctantly, the idea of invitation-only private bulletin boards for regulars to brainstorm more freely and protect newly discovered deals came to fruition. This private group was a new milestone. It operated like a virtual chop shop. A member would present an idea, and some white hats would try to improve on it, while some black hats would try to shoot it down. It was crowdsourcing before the term was invented.

The first idea to get green-lighted was so far-fetched, convoluted, and fraught with risk that while everyone agreed it could be done, *no one* wanted to be the test subject. I admonished the group. We can't really claim a project is green-lighted if no one is willing to drive through the intersection.

Cathay Pacific was a fantastic airline, but outside of earning miles via flying its expensive airfare structure, there were no creative alternatives for mileage scaling opportunities. I volunteered, but this project to earn Cathay Pacific miles required two to tango. Would I be able to find a second mileage kamikaze for this intriguing endeavor?

There were two completely unrelated and obscure promotions that our private group figured out how to marry together.

eBay, the auction site, had a relatively useless loyalty program called Anything Points. For a short window of time, eBay was offering a five-times Anything Points bonus for eBay purchases. In and of itself, a yawner.

Cathay Pacific Asia Miles was a transfer partner of Anything Points. There was a separate promotion where Anything Points that were transferred to Cathay would receive a two-times bonus. Again, who cared?

Well, our private group discovered that the two separate and unremarkable, but concurrent promotions were "stackable," which was mileage alchemy vernacular, meaning that they could be combined.

<u>Normal</u>

$1 eBay spend = 1 Anything Point = **1** Cathay mile

<u>Basic promotion</u>

$1 eBay spend X 5 Anything Point Bonus = **5** Cathay miles

<u>Stackable</u>

$1 eBay spend = 5 Anything Points bonus x 2x Cathay transfer bonus = **10** Cathay miles

The practical impact of that stackable promotion would be spending <u>ten times</u> less money on eBay purchases.

Normal

$90,000 eBay spend = 90,000 Cathay intl. Business Class award

Stackable (10X promotion bonus)

$9,000 eBay spend = 90,000 Cathay intl. Business Class award

Obviously, spending $9,000 in eBay purchases for an award instead of $90,000 was a huge improvement, but of course, still a non-starter as our sweet spot was about one thousand dollars in spend per award. There had to be another angle.

purchase product	purchase product
earn Anything Points	earn Anything Points
eBay deducts service/ credit card fees	eBay deducts service/ credit card fees
request refund from eBay	**request refund direct from seller**
service/credit card fees refunded	**service/credit card fees NOT refunded by eBay (approx. 3.5%)**
BUT Anything Points refunded as well	**BUT Anything Points stay in account**

There were no T&C on eBay that prohibited refunds outside of their system because eBay would have already received their

3.5% cut of the proceeds, and they weren't being asked to return it. So, a refund outside of their system would have no financial impact on them.

However, there would normally be no reason for a Buyer/ Seller to execute refunds outside of the eBay system because eBay's system was so fast, easy, and accountable, and besides, who would want to forfeit those transaction fees?

Here's who!

$9,000	eBay spend at 10 x bonus required to earn 90,000-mile Cathay Business Class award
x 3.50%	service fees NOT refunded by eBay because refund DIRECT with seller
= $310	cost of unrefunded eBay service fees to KEEP Anything Points for Cathay award

To earn a ton of very cheap Cathay Pacific miles, then simply process refunds outside the eBay system to retain the ten-times bonus Anything Points transfer to Cathay.

The strategy would require involving a Buyer and Seller *collaborating in advance* of executing the transaction on eBay. But for every step of the strategy, there was a risky challenge as well.

For example:

> Buyer: provides $200,000 cash to purchase designated eBay products to earn two million miles to be shared between Buyer and Seller (Challenge: who has that kind of cash liquidity sloshing around?)
>
> Seller: designates a product for sale for $200,000. (Challenge: what kind of ultra-expensive product could

be offered that eBay wouldn't flag as being fraudulent or extremely suspicious.)

Buyer: after the transaction, expect eBay to delay paying the Seller until an investigation clears the transaction

(Challenge: an investigation could take days, weeks, or even months with the $200,000 sitting in abeyance. Both Buyer and Seller could be subject to scrutiny as a potential money-laundering operation. The Buyer would have to be able to prove to eBay that its cash was traceable to a legit source. The Seller must then have to prove that the product being offered was bona fide and not a front to launder money.)

Seller: once eBay finally processed the order after the investigation would conclude, Seller would immediately refund the Buyer directly, not via eBay. The Seller would send the refund check to the Buyer:

$200,000 minus $7000 (the 3.5% service/credit card fee deducted by eBay) = $193,000.

(Challenge: Buyer must have incredible confidence, trust, and possibly other enforcement mechanisms to ensure refund of money from Seller.)

Buyer: transfer 200,000 Anything Points to new Cathay Pacific account to generate 2,000,000 miles with ten-times bonus. (Challenge: Seller would have lower stakesbut would be very reliant on Buyer providing log-in access to Cathay for their share of the miles.)

Cathay miles earned with 10X promotion	2,000,000	$7,000	cost of earning miles from not refunding eBay service fees
Cathay intl. Business Class award	/ 90,000		
Total awards	= 22	/ 22	total awards
		= $310	cost per award
		vs $6,000	retail international Business Class airfare

At this point, I realized that the only way this project would fly was if I was the Buyer, meaning I would have to somehow conjure up two-hundred thousand dollars to float for a few weeks (or months of the expected eBay investigation kicked in). More on that shortly. Just as important as the Buyer's money was the Seller's two-hundred thousand dollars worth of product, which had to have a bulletproof cover story to pass muster with eBay's inevitably prying eyes. The Seller who volunteered from the private group was one of the few *FlyerTalk* regulars that I had yet to meet in person. But he had the same crunch-the-numbers/cover-every-angle ethos that I did.

Keith (not his real name) and I huddled at his modest rental unit in a not-yet-gentrified part of Chicago. Looks weren't deceiving with him. He was a mileage geek cliché. Weird haircut, thick glasses, squeaky/tinny voice, and flood-length pants. However, his spreadsheet calculations contribution to the project research regarding the eBay/Cathay deal proved his acumen. He wasn't prepared to put up any money, but his value as a partner lay elsewhere, about seven-thousand miles east of Chicago.

Youande.

Cameroon.

Keith proposed a luxury travel package to Cameroon for *ten-thousand dollars* per person for twenty people. Forget the eBay snoops. Even I was incredulous at this suggestion. What was he thinking?

And then Keith methodically lobbied his case. Keith's family had a long history as successful and high-profile missionaries in Cameroon. Keith had lived there for many years, and his dad still had an impactful presence there and could most likely arrange a "priceless" trip with features like private meetings with politicians and business leaders. He knew all the expensive hotels, restaurants, and custom activities. Still, even Keith admitted that a week in Cameroon was a huge stretch as a high-end tourist destination. With all of the bells and whistles, we could glom onto the travel package, the stark reality was that costs were so low in Cameroon, that we were still far away from the ten-thousand-dollar cost per trip target. We couldn't believably extend the trip any longer. We pondered adding another West African nation to the mix. It would make sense from the Seller side. But I was worried about the Buyer side, my side. My family had taken many multi-generational trips with my dad at the helm, so we had a verifiable family history of group travel to obvious tourist destinations like Italy and Mexico. I didn't like the defensibility angle of two weeks in way-off-the-beaten-path-track Africa when I still wasn't sure that even one week would be defensible with eBay.

Fortunately, Keith's grasp of African history and language far exceeded my own, so he added, "*compartiments français d'outre-mer*," meaning French Overseas Compartments to the trip description.

Cameroon was a former French colony, or "compartment,"

so there was a thriving Cameroonian expat cultural scene in Paris, France, which Keith was sure would be a very believable (and helpfully expensive!!!) second part of the trip. In the French capital, it would *very easy* to add major expenses in very few days.

I was scratching my head. Why not ditch Cameroon and just structure a normal, high-end mainstream vacation?

Keith was far more involved with eBay than me, and he offered a brilliant observation.

eBay was not the go-to source for high-end travel, so any Seller offer would invite scrutiny. Because Cameroon was such an outlier location and such an outlier cost, it would be such a flagrantly obvious red flag that eBay would conclude that it couldn't be a red flag after all. Who would have the audacity to offer up such a blatant money laundering or other nefarious schemes?

Hide in plain sight.

Keith had me convinced. We now had a defensible trip for the Seller, because Keith could easily use his family's twenty-five-year history in Cameroon as to why that was the destination. And for me, the Buyer, the combo Cameroon/Paris fit well with my family's past travel history. We were confident both Buyer and Seller profiles and motivations would be very benignly perceived by eBay, and any investigation would be open-and-shut.

There was one small detail that Keith and I needed to hash out. The money, honey.

The biggest wildcard I had yet to contend with was eBay's valid concern about money laundering. The source of the Buyer's money had to be impeccable. That was my job.

And it turned out to be formidable.

First, we needed the money lightning-quick because the promotion window on the eBay/Cathay deal was closing in less than a month. After the close call with the Las Vegas SKY High Rollers project, my outside investor pipeline dried up. Margining stock would attract the dreaded "lemme ask you something" phone call from my dad. And although it was my money to steward, he would weigh in hard. I had siphoned some modest funds from my sports media business for past projects, but this time of year, I had to pay for my Packer season tickets in advance, so cash flow was unusually tight. Soliciting loan sharks was explored for all of eight minutes.

The obvious course of action was to simply kiss-off the eBay/Cathay project and wait for the next big fish. The private group was already brewing up new opportunities. Not one group member would have doubted my mileage earning prowess if I had decided to pass on this one. But I had boldly announced that I could conquer this project that no one else had the balls or wherewithal. There just *had* to be another path to those two hundred thousand dollars of cash flow. I was deep in thought as I was mindlessly beating a path around my house for the entire afternoon.

Rather, deep in thoughtlessness! Because had I been thinking clearly, I would have recognized that my financial solution was within walking distance that whole afternoon.

The house.

I would apply for a home equity loan to cover the two hundred thousand dollars for the twenty "phantom" Cameroon trips that I would purchase on eBay, then refund directly with Keith … all within eBay's T&C.

My wife Julie and I enjoyed a healthy marriage with the sturdy pillars of trust, family responsibility, and open communication in place. The problem with the eBay/Cathay project was that, frankly, I could barely explain it coherently to my mileage peers. I knew there was no way Julie could justify the risk of losing our biggest asset for a handful of Cathay Business Class awards, especially with a seemingly imprudent scheme. But there was no way that I could mentally extricate myself from the project without feeling like a failure or a coward.

It was the nadir of my questionable conduct in the mileage world. I took out that home equity loan without consulting Julie.

Forget GO BIG OR GO HOME. I had ratcheted up the stakes to GO BIG OR LOSE HOME (AND WIFE)! The foundations of my marriage could crumble if I couldn't pull this off.

My hope for success was based on an absolutely flawless execution on my end and an absolute minimum of flak from a security investigation team that might be flummoxed when confronted with a two hundred thousand eBay purchase for a trip to Cameroon. I was hoping that any potential investigation would be timely, so the eBay order would be processed and redeposited in less than a month—worst case, three months. If so, I could expedite paying off and closing the home equity line before any domestic disturbances would break out!

Keith and I structured what can only be called a "mutually assured destruction" pact to ensure that my money would be returned and his miles would be accessible. We swapped social security numbers, birth certificates, driver's licenses, bank accounts, and contact info for parents, siblings, accountants, lawyers. It was just for show, as we both knew that his cashing of a $193,000 check would be nearly impossible to hide. Plus, we had twenty other members monitoring both of us. We did our due diligence. We finally agreed upon the mileage split: my cash was worth seventy-five percent, and his Cameroon credibility and his trust to return the $193,000 were worth twenty-five percent!

The home equity loan was executed on my end, the Cameroon

listing was activated on eBay on Keith's end. The hardware was in place. We had accomplished the incredibly heavy lifting to make this project possible. The easy part was simply placing my forefinger on my computer mouse and clicking "Purchase." Yet, that one-second process would take me longer than the two exhausting days that Keith and I spent together in Chicago creating a bulletproof structure. I would take three days of soul-searching about the money, the secrecy, my marriage. Once it was clear that after much searching, I still couldn't find my soul, I clicked the eBay purchase button, and we were off to the races (but not Cameroon!).

It was a surreal experience waiting for eBay to react. Neither of us heard a peep from them. Keith knew something was up because the money had not transferred into his account. eBay was holding the money but not disclosing that fact, nor let alone why. What bothered me wasn't that they were holding the money. That was well expected. What was of concern to me was that, like Aeroplan, I was being left out of the investigation even though I was the primary suspect. After a month, there was still nothing but crickets from eBay. Keith joked that although we weren't being contacted by eBay, things must not be too bad, because we also weren't being contacted by governmental agencies like the DEA or SEC for RICO (racketeering) or money laundering suspicion.

Keith checked his eBay account hourly every day. After six weeks, the Cameroon trip purchases were finally processed, and Keith's eBay account posted $193,000. After thirty minutes Keith transferred the money to his checking account. After another thirty minutes, he hightailed it to his bank branch in Chicago and expedited the wire transfer to my bank in Cleveland, just as our "mutual assured destruction" agreement had required. Just twenty-four hours later, I paid off and closed the home equity account. The audit trail had disappeared without a trace.

While I was at the bank, I transferred the mortgage papers from joint account to individual ... in my wife's name. I trusted myself, but I trusted her considerably more. My leveraging the family nest egg would never happen again.

Despite our ultimately boring and routine success, no one else in the group was willing to give it a shot. The window on the 10X promotion closed, and then Anything Points was disbanded soon thereafter.

I was so looking forward to that Cameroon family vacation, such a damn shame we had to "cancel" the trip! But 1.5 million Cathay miles would be my cold comfort!

People often use the phrases "work the system," "play the system," "game the system," and "beat the system" interchangeably. I'm not sure if my mileage earning and scaling conduct neatly fits any characterization. Certainly, nothing I have ever done was illegal in the eyes of the government. And most certainly, I have never violated any program T&Cs. Nor have I ever acted in a furtive, opaque manner; I have always been transparent in using my real name, address, credit cards, etc.

I think that my ability to "dissect the system" is the most accurate characterization. It's like panning for gold. I could come up empty a few times and then quit because I didn't find any gold. But imagine that I actually *like* panning, and that finding gold is just a wonderful unintended consequence. That is what is probably so maddening to the Fraud and Security departments that have pursued me. I don't ever have a master plan. I'm just tinkering around their programs on an ongoing basis, waiting for a quick hit—a bonus offer or promotion that transforms their mundane program into a temporary goldmine.

I guess that I'm just a mileage 49er.

It was not my fault that one department at eBay decided to offer a five-times bonus promotion while a separate department responsible for Anything Points decided to offer a two-times bonus promotion to an airline program that I coveted. It wasn't my fault that the two promotions were running concurrently and were combinable. It wasn't my fault that eBay allowed refunds outside of their system so that points earned from those purchases could be retained by the Buyer for pennies on the dollar. And it's certainly not my fault that I choose to leverage my brainpower and that of twenty other experts into understanding a program maybe more thoroughly than the actual operators.

Everything that I have done involved information that was public. My edge was *aggregating* seemingly random and disparate information into cohesive and productive knowledge. The dots were out there for everyone. I just took the initiative to corral all the dots, sift through them, and cherry-pick the valuable ones, putting them in a strategic order, then use using tactics like labor pools or award sweet spots or home equity loans to connect those dots.

Sometimes, connecting the dots to scale a deal could be as simple as having a driver's license.

Jaguar, the luxury car company, logically tapped their home country airline, British Airways, to supply miles for a promotion to entice folks to test drive their new model Jaguar-X, which was supposedly their new entry-level, relatively affordable vehicle, for the not-quite-rich car buyer.

The promotion was straightforward.

Print out a form from Jaguar's website. Take it to any Jaguar dealership.

Do the ten-minute test drive.

Have form signed by a Jaguar rep.

Send form to British Airways to earn ten-thousand miles.

One per person limit.

At first glance, this promotion wouldn't earn a second glance for scaling. There was a quantity limit of one per person, and the value of ten-thousand BA miles was a yawner, yielding a one-way domestic Economy award.

But, for those of us in the know, British Airway's program had a quirk that no other program had replicated. It was a very quiet quirk, buried deep inside BA's T&C. If there were three other BA members that were part of your same household, then all four accounts could be aggregated into one master "household" account.

British Airways' definition of a household was an ambiguous one. The four accounts that could be merged didn't actually have to live in the same household together. BA wasn't checking utility bills for proof of residency! So basically, a "household" was any four names with BA accounts that could be arbitrarily grouped together.

By recruiting three other people to test drive the Jaguar (who didn't mind foregoing their "worthless" ten-thousand BA bonus miles), then those three drivers and their ten thousand BA miles from the test drive promotion could be merged into one household account of *forty-thousand* free BA miles... redeemable for a one-way Business Class award to/from Europe, easily worth $2,500 to $3,500. Now, that kind of payoff was not a yawner by any stretch.

Like the eBay rules that didn't require refunds through their system, the Jaguar rules didn't require the actual test drive to earn the BA miles, rather it was just the signed paperwork by the dealership. It made sense to ask the salespeople for signatures and save the time-consuming charade of the test drive since my labor pool wouldn't be hot prospects for Jaguars. They were just mileage prospectors.

It was possible to recruit groups of four people who would be given pre-registered BA accounts and go to the dealerships over a given time window. Each of the four BA accounts would be preemptively aggregated into a master household account earning forty thousand BA miles. Each person would be paid twenty-five dollars for their time to drive to and from the dealership to conduct the test drive (if dealer staff required it) and submit their BA forms. Once the forty thousand miles appeared in the household account, one of the four account names would be replaced by the name of the actual person who would redeem the miles (i.e., me), which was permissible per BA the T/C. Then, that actual designated person (me) could jump to another cluster of four accounts and replace one name with my name. Rinse and repeat through as many clusters as desired. There was no theoretical limit to how many clusters of four one-per-person test drives and forty thousand BA miles could be earned.

Furthermore, while looking at the legal loopholes in the Jaguar promotion, there was plenty of latitude for bad actors as well (NOT me). Jaguar had no idea if the customer names or dealership signatures were even authentic. A single customer could go to a dealership on different days and times, using a different name with a different dealer staff. Neither Jaguar nor BA did formal identity verification checks.

Curiously, Jaguar's partner, BA, likely wouldn't care about Jaguar's poor promotion oversight. BA would be paid by Jaguar for each submitted ten-thousand-mile promotion form, so the more, the merrier.

Jaguar might have well-exceeded their presumably limited BA mileage purchasing budget before they could turn off the engine for the promotion pipeline. I could only speculate, but frankly, it wasn't my problem.

Even though paying twenty-five dollars to a slew of Jaguar test drivers would have made only a minor dent in my mileage budget, I decided to show my wife that I possessed some restraint and financial responsibility.

It wasn't easy passing up earning a roundtrip Business Class award for the equivalent of recruiting eight Jaguar test drivers x twenty-five drivers = $200 per award! But with the British government charging the highest airport and security taxes in the world, combined with BA charging extortionate fuel surcharges, adding an extra $1,000 of cost, my enthusiasm was tempered, and I just participated on a token basis, so I could credibly include it in this book!

I considered myself a rather voracious reader. It was time to build a new bookshelf or maybe ten to house the thousands of magazine subscriptions I was about to sign up for.

Chapter 12: Getting Mauled at The Mileage Mall

As frequent flyer mileage programs gained traction in the mainstream pop culture, corporate America was poised to leverage miles to help market their products.

It was never gonna be a fair fight.

Big companies offering incremental promotions to stimulate incremental customer spending on incremental quantities of their products.

Versus.

The mileage geeks whose dictionaries didn't even have the word "incremental" in them.

Early on, these mammoth but clueless companies had no idea that folks like FlyerTalkers, even existed, nor that we would not rest until we could add two or three zeroes to an innocuous mileage earning offer.

As the *FlyerTalk* community slowly coalesced into a loosely organized force to be reckoned with by the airline and hotel programs, that sense of cohesiveness would be sorely tested. And I was inadvertently thrust into the forefront of that looming controversy thanks to the mileage malls.

Mileage Malls were online shopping outlets affiliated with travel programs. These mileage malls were known to be the worst possible value for redeeming miles. The only reason to ever enter their virtual doors was to redeem "orphan miles," a mileage balance too small to redeem awards for a flight or hotel night. Then fine, redeem for a toaster or gift card.

These mileage malls also offered the same worthless merchandise for cash with equally pathetic mileage bonuses as a purchase incentive. Every mileage mall had dozens of companies offering dozens of products, so it would be a time-consuming process to survey each mall for the very improbable chance of finding any hidden gem offers.

The Radisson hotel chain had their own online mall and currency called Goldpoints offering the usual crappy products for cash, at crappy prices, with crappy points incentive bonuses.

Until … holy crap!!!!

There was a new online company selling magazines called ValueMags. Whereas most Radisson mileage mall bonuses were a measly average ten-to-forty Goldpoints points per dollar spent, ValueMags was at a ridiculously high 450 points! It had to be a typo. It had to be a "mistake rate."

Like mistake fares, the *FlyerTalk* community consensus was to rush to purchase, as if the rate was correct. If the program (or vendor) identified and corrected the rate within seventy-two hours, then no harm, no foul refunds would be processed.

But unlike mistake fares, which were bookable on an open-ended basis up to a year in advance, the ValueMags offer was capped at two weeks. The last two weeks of December. That timing window suggested that this offer was indeed very purposeful. Maybe ValueMags needed holiday sales to trigger a management bonus.

Whatever ValueMags's motivation, it wasn't our responsibility to mindread their sales strategy.

Days before the promotion started, there was an unsettling post on *FlyerTalk* by a newbie.

"Hi everyone. There seems to be a lot of concern about whether the four hundred fifty-point bonus is a typo or not. ValueMags is based in my hometown, so I just gave them a call to find out. I talked to the president, who seemed quite nice. He told me he is well-aware of the Radisson Goldpoints/ValueMags promotion. It is totally correct, and he is excited to see the results."

Good news—no typo. Awful news—ValueMags could monitor the thread and easily cancel or prematurely pull the promotion once they fully understood the value proposition unearthed by the mileage savants. *FlyerTalk* regulars knew 450 Goldpoints was a crazy outlier of bonus miles.

Presumably, ValueMags had not anticipated three totally unrelated earning elements that our community had so deftly connected.

First, there were different portals to sign up for the Goldpoints program. For some inexplicable reason, signing up via the Goldpoints shopping site offered a ten-to-one points to airline mile transfer ratio, whereas the Radisson Hotel site offered a far better four-to-one transfer ratio. There was no rhyme nor reason for the same company to offer such different transfer ratios.

Second, point earning was based on per dollar spending, not per product, so it was irrelevant whether ValueMags products were a great deal or a rip-off.

$1 spend = 450 Goldpoints = transfer ratio 4:1 = 112.5 miles

Third, although the promotion had a very limited two-week time window restriction, there were no spending restrictions. That meant scaling was in the cards.

ValueMags was no doubt familiar with Radisson's well-publicized hotel award chart. They were hopeful that their promotion would incentivize people to buy enough magazines to generate enough points for maybe a handful of free hotel night awards. Radisson's airline transfer program was buried deep inside the site and offered no guidance on which airline program to transfer to and why.

FlyerTalkers didn't need such guidance—they *were* the guides.

Once again, the airline award grabbing all the attention was the Concorde's New York-London flight on British Airways. The sleek, supersonic jet was on its last legs, a victim of new noise-abatement laws, rising oil prices, and a declining demand for its five-figure airfare. So, besides the novelty of the inflight experience, there was the urgency of flying, as the opportunity was dying.

GOLDPOINTS/VALUEMAGS CONCORDE ANALYSIS

112.5	ValueMags point bonus per dollar spend
x $1,119	spending on ValueMags subscriptions required
= 125,000	Concorde NY-London award

Most ValueMags subscriptions were about $20, so sixty subscriptions of spending would cover the Concorde award. For most people, just a shade over one thousand dollars to fly the legendary, and soon to be just a legend, Concorde, was an unbelievable deal, but still steep after exhausting their holiday budgets.

Just as I felt during the Starwood/*Inside Flyer*/QANTAS promotion, I remained nonplussed about flying the deafening and cramped Concorde. Instead, I focused my efforts on the biggest bang per buck, not the biggest bang to my ears.

The Concorde award was only New York-London, while my

award discovery, using conventional aircraft, would be anywhere in the USA to anywhere in Europe or Israel. There was far more flexibility and less fear of awards going extinct … and for 40% less out of pocket magazine subscription.

112.5	ValueMags point bonus per dollar spend
x $711	spending on ValueMags subscriptions required
= 80,000	intl. Business Class award

I did all of my past scaling on a level inaccessible to most due to lots of moving parts, logistics, and complex program rules, as well as money. The ValueMags promotion was basically a creature of money and exposure; anyone with a credit card who read the *FlyerTalk* thread could participate.

Because of my psychology and experience with mistake fares, I knew that "buy now and think later" was critical. With no barriers to gain entry on this opportunity, there would surely be a stampede.

At 11:50 p.m. on December 15, I was awoken by the jarring sound of my alarm clock. My wife, Julie thought it was the daily 6:00 a.m. alarm, so she jumped out of bed and into the shower. She trudged downstairs and saw me on the computer. She knew something was amiss. I never got up with her at 6:00 a.m., and as I always hit the snooze 'til 8:30 a.m. Before she could start her morning coffee ritual, I pointed to the clock—12:01 a.m. on December 16. She decided to join me for what would turn into an impromptu all-nighter!

Julie knew I had amassed countless miles at a great rate, but since my purchases were from business, not personal funds, she didn't know any specifics. On this night Julie was going to be "Igor" in my mileage lab and see the Mad Mileage Scientist at work firsthand. Having a clean shot at earning international Business Class awards for the price of a cramped fifteen-hour flight in Economy Class was a far better rush for her than a shot of caffeine.

At 12:02 a.m. she and I started double-teaming ValueMags purchases opening with *fifteen hundred* magazine subscriptions at $20 (sorry Randy, *Inside Flyer* wasn't an option) to earn three million miles and roughly forty international Business Class awards.

But I wondered how many more scaled orders would actually be out there? Would the sheer volume of orders exhaust Value-Mags supply and force a shut-down?

My next-level scaling instincts kicked in with a twist. While the ValueMags deal was a sensation for our niche mileage-savvy community, maybe in the two short weeks of the promotion, *I could let the rest of the clueless world in on it.*

I was friendly with a FlyerTalker from London who not only claimed he knew how to build websites but, like me, had already made a mega-million purchase.

I pitched him on slapping together a website to offer newbies the chance to earn bulk miles with no effort. We would do all the work, and the clients would simply pay a markup for our insider knowledge.

This idea would need to pass Randy's "smell test." Randy was notorious for not returning calls for days at a time, and my friend and I lamented that the idea would likely be stillborn. Miraculously, Randy called back within the hour (a feat never to be repeated!). He approved the ValueMags re-marketing site, and he even volunteered the unexpected gesture to reference his name on the website for important credibility. I flew to London barely four hours later as there was not a minute to spare with such a short window of opportunity. Gotta love them miles!

I arrived at my friend's flat in the Canary Wharfs, a trendy part of London, on December 18. The clock was ticking with only thirteen days until the promotion ended. I had zero website knowledge, and my friend, it turned out, had only a few classes worth of Intro to Website Design and Programming.

Craig (not his real name) was a wiry Brit with Elvis Costello glasses and close-cropped black hair. Truthfully, I could never really wrap my arms around his professional life, but it seemed to involve a lot interfacing with big corporations who had big consulting budgets that allowed him to travel far and wide on other companies' dimes. It sounded cushy, and by the looks of his swanky address, it must have been. What Craig lacked in skills, he made up for in supreme confidence. Even though he had assured me that he could jerry-rig a proper website in a day, it seemed like he was doing a lot of phoning friends and consulting how-to textbooks. While I was a bit nervous if his end result would produce a credible website, I couldn't add any meaningful contributions to his efforts other than feeding and hydrating him. It was going to be a technical nightmare. But we hadn't anticipated the nightmare that preceded inputting the first letter of coding.

Optics.

A customer would see a brand-new website by a brand-new company with no track record.

The mileage offer would have to be opaque enough to prevent newbies from researching themselves, yet transparent enough to gain their confidence to spend hundreds or thousands of dollars with us. Having Randy onboard was a mixed blessing. He was assuredly credible, but if we referenced his *FlyerTalk* affiliation, we would be divulging a key reference for prospective customers' own research.

For three precious hours, we wrestled with this conundrum of keeping secret something that was actually public knowledge. We finally agreed on the plumber parable. Most folks could fix their toilets themselves using instruction booklets and online tutorials, but most are happy to pay a plumber for the convenience. And those who consider themselves capable should save the money and fix it themselves.

The Radisson promotion process was actually available on *FlyerTalk*, but spread out sporadically over hundreds if not thousands of posts. Maybe the entire process was summarized several hundred pages in. So, the ValueMags info was in the public domain, just not conveniently accessible. Our site would be simply offering a mileage "plumbing" service for those who wouldn't or couldn't figure out how to earn the ValueMags miles themselves.

After fourteen hours of grueling coding, designing, and assorted subpar Indian food deliveries, **www.MileSpy.com** was open for business. Instead of a one-off, we positioned the site as an ongoing, go-to source for future complex promotions that wouldn't otherwise see the light of day outside of *FlyerTalk*.

MileSpy set off a firestorm of controversy. How could two *FlyerTalk* regulars in good standing leverage the community intellectual property for personal gain? And also endanger the sustainability of the deal for the rest of the community? This was a conundrum that would remain forever unresolved within the community.

In our defense, it was firmly the *internet* era.

First off, no deal hatched by FlyerTalkers was self-contained anymore like in the early days. Within hours of any deal being fine-tuned for execution, it had been disseminated to at least eight other travel and discount hacker websites. None of whom were bound by our serious, but ultimately informal and unenforceable, codes of conduct.

Secondly, within days, there were dozens of eBay auctions brokering miles for purchase from existing accounts (against the airline's rules), whereas we were generating mileage into the end users' accounts, which was perfectly legal.

Thirdly, we did our ValueMags due diligence by confirming they could handle the volume, and with Randy's approval, we felt that commercializing the deal was acceptable.

And finally, no one was stopping anyone else from jumping on deals before MileSpy would be telegraphing to the broader world.

MileSpy had a thirteen-day sales window shrink to eight days when ValueMags unexpectedly changed, and by changed, I mean, severely devalued the offer. There were mutual recriminations about which party decimated the offer. ValueMags blamed Radisson and vice versa. It was frustrating that neither party accepted any accountability. The offer was published through December 31, and people had a fair expectation that they could participate anytime during that window. No one was thinking about the possibility of a promotion being prematurely shut down or altered for the worst.

MileSpy was stuck with a number of orders that were paid for *before* the offer change, but unfortunately, not processed in time. We scrambled for a solution to avoid having to disappoint our inaugural customers. Not being able to deliver on our debut would likely be fatal to our reputation.

It turned out an even more obscure hotel program, Baymont Inns, had a transfer partnership with American Airlines that per chance had an exceedingly generous transfer policy. As a courtesy to Randy, they allowed us a one-time exception to purchase their hotel currency direct, bypassing the need to purchase hundreds of rooms to generate the same miles to supply us the necessary miles to make our MileSpy clients whole.

Because Baymont was a low-cost property, it would typically take dozens of stays to accomplish what we did just by writing a check. We desperately tried to keep that steady supply of AA miles pipeline open. But Baymont countered that our one-time-only AA mileage make-good for MileSpy, was more than they had ordered from AA in three years!

While my London partner Craig and I were happy to clear nearly fifteen thousand dollars, we all donated our thousands of magazines to charity. The ValueMags promotion brought to the forefront the simmering issue about mileage scaling: when was enough, enough?

What was the magic limitation of future product purchases that FlyerTalkers would find acceptable? Could one limit really fit all situations and people? Was it fair to limit mileage earning to the same number for someone who could benefit because they traveled fifteen times a year to versus the same amount as someone who traveled just two times? What about families vs singles? What about the population who looked at mileage as a long-term investment, not just a short-term lark? And if, by chance, there was a community consensus on a self-imposed quantity cap, who would enforce it? And what would be the enforcement mechanism? There were people who got shut out. But why did they wait so long when the urgency to expedite purchasing was well-articulated?

I didn't have any answers, and realistically, no one could. Buyer behavior would be far too unwieldy to control. There were some definitive facts that I hoped would pivot the debate away from the buyers and instead focus on the sellers.

The airline and hotel programs were well-financed, publicly-held corporations with an obligation to protect their shareholders (and their own jobs). When a deal was rolled out, was it my responsibility to analyze the corporate motives behind the deal? How could I ever determine whether a given promotion was trying to make money, maybe just break even with a test market, or maybe even willingly accept a loss in order to expose a new product? Surely, all of these companies had a phalanx of marketing, accounting, and legal staff to structure and vet these deals. It would seem to be their responsibility, not mine, and definitely not the *FlyerTalk* community's.

For two weeks, ValueMags, Goldpoints, and their airline partners clearly witnessed the impact of their 450-point offer. They could have pulled it within hours, but they didn't. Only four days before the late December offer ending date did the ValueMags bonus change from 450 to 150. Instead of blaming the poor structure of the promotion, Goldpoints and Radisson blamed the buyers for such greedy and abusive conduct. It was a ridiculous double standard argument.

It was acceptable for a company to offer an unlimited supply of a product enabling them to maximize sales, but it was unacceptable for a consumer to have virtually unlimited demand to buy that product?

The offer was published as ending on December 31. While it was the prerogative of Radisson or ValueMags to pull the offer early, it was still perceived as a breach of trust. And it would have the unintended impact for future deals of spurring more people to buy greater quantities as early as possible before the barn door might prematurely close. It portended an ugly, free-for-all, panic-buying scenario.

And that scenario was not long in coming.

A few months later, a dairy company, Emmi Cheese, rolled out a promotion. On an array of cheese products ranging from

$2.50 to $5, there was a code (on each package) good for five-hundred American Airlines miles. There were no spending or time limit caps.

AA miles per Emmi product	500	$2.50	cost per product
number of Emmi products	x 160	x 160	number of Emmi products
intl. Business Class award	**= 80,000**	**= $400**	Award Cost
		vs. $6,000	cost retail intl. Business Class airfare

It would become The Pudding Guy on steroids as the Emmi Cheese deal was two-times more lucrative and two-hundred times more chaotic!

People were driving rental trucks to grocery stores within twenty-mile radiuses of their homes and not only purchasing every cheese product off the shelves but also those unpacked boxes still in inventory storage at the back of the stores. Some enterprising folks actually solicited huge food distribution companies to purchase bulk products on a one-stop-shop basis. Instead of waiting for the Emmi Cheese to be restocked, one impatient person did the unthinkable. They called Emmi Cheese headquarters and asked to purchase a huge quantity directly from the company. There's always one in every crowd!

The company had been perplexed but ultimately encouraged at the huge spike in recent sales. The American Airlines five-hundred mile promotion had no serious marketing push, so the company hadn't correlated the sales bump with the promotion …

until that fateful and baffling phone call from the misbehaving FlyerTalker newbie.

Soon, calls from grocery chains started streaming in about bare shelves and no stock.

The Emmi promotion was wildly successful for the handful of savvy and resourceful people who vacuumed their inventory clean … and for the grateful food banks who were recipients of their donations. On paper the promotion was exceedingly successful for Emmi with monstrous short-term sales. But the unforeseen carnage was far worse than they could have imagined. While waiting weeks for backlog restocking, grocery stores would fill the empty shelves allocated for Emmi Cheese with competitors' products compromising shopper buying patterns and loyalty.

Emmi tried to shut down the program immediately once they caught wind of the downstream damage, but there were still vast amounts of products that had been purchased but had not yet been redeemed for the AA miles. Emmi would face the wrath of their retailers for a major supply disruption along with the wrath of the mileage world for trying to renege on the offer.

Just like the mistake fare scenario, my expectation was that every other loyalty program on *FlyerTalk* would view the Radisson/Valuemags and Emmi/American deals. They would and learn their own lessons about the need for time and/or quantity caps.

I'm sorry. If a bunch of mileage geeks could outthink a big Goliath corporation, then congrats to David.

A smart program would have contacted a few key members of their forums on *FlyerTalk* to "white hat" their proposed promotions *before* ever being rolled out in public. Randy could have probably charged a consulting fee to do so. But to my knowledge, no program ever did that. I suppose programs never wanted to admit that their customers were smarter than their own management.

Actually, there was one occasion where I joined a small cabal of *FlyerTalk* members from the Air Canada Aeroplan forum to force the program to be more accountable to its members. Aeroplan had been steadily devaluing its Super Elite benefits, especially putting the squeeze on its precedent-setting no-blackout award availability perk. Worse yet, they were doing it stealthily. What little public communication the PR department churned out was purposefully meant to obfuscate their naughty deeds from their primarily less-engaged membership.

Aeroplan announced that their "enhancements" (read: devaluations) would be implemented in three months. Despite the outcry on the Aeroplan forum on *FlyerTalk*, the folks at HQ in Montreal were resolutely silent. They wouldn't even dignify our concerns with a formal acknowledgment, let alone a spirited debate.

In an era that pre-dated viral social media campaigns, our group had no choice but a boots-on-the-ground insurrection.

One of the Aeroplan forum members had derisively nicknamed Aeroplan as "Errorplan" when the devaluation was announced. The nickname would become a cornerstone in our campaign. One of the members was a brilliant graphic artist who created an exact replica of the Aeroplan corporate logo but with a subtle spelling change. We then collaborated on a subversive one-sheet that blared the headline "Great News For Super Elite Members" and then a couple of sentences of really upbeat content. And then the rest of the content was a brutal exposé on how Aeroplan was about to totally screw its top-tier members. The font size and style and the color palettes were spot on. We produced a masterful piece of propaganda that any casual member would breezily assume was an official Aeroplan publication piece.

The next phase was the all-important guerrilla distribution of the one-sheeter. We all knew that Super Elites were easy to find when they traveled … at the Maple Leaf lounges at the major Canadian airports like Toronto, Montreal and Vancouver. And all of us were Super Elites, so getting into lounges undetected would be easy. Once in the lounges, the one-sheeters would be discreetly slipped inside the newspapers and magazines on the display racks. There would be a morning and afternoon shift of members who would resupply one-sheeters inside the new batches of newspapers and magazines.

The final phase was attacking the popular business traveler routes where Super Elites likely flew. Some of us sacrificed some miles to redeem to fly on these routes and surreptitiously distribute the one-sheeter inside all of the Air Canada in-flight magazines. This required a lot of creativity, resourcefulness, and stealth.

But actually, some of the airline crews were unhappy that Air Canada's best customers might be chased away with these proposed program changes. These folks were happy to look the other way while we papered the cabin.

We figured that a sustained one week's worth of intensive distribution of about five thousand one-sheeters would get the word out. It took Aeroplan four days to even discover the one-sheeter and another three days to ramp up a security protocol to catch the offenders.

By that time, it was too late, and our work was done. We had generated solid media coverage about the mysterious "Errorplan" rascals and their agenda to protect Super Elites from their evil master-Aeroplan.

While our efforts defied imagination, what Aeroplan did

next defied the laws of physics. They invited a delegation of our choice of seven Aeroplan *FlyerTalk* members to HQ in Montreal to meet directly with management about the proposed changes in two weeks' time. And they offered complimentary airfare to each of the seven participants. We all had plenty of miles, and no one wanted to have any whiff of taint that we could be coopted by Aeroplan. So, while the meeting was accepted, the free flight was declined.

As the two weeks passed, the Errorplan delegation was frantically coordinating an epic set of debate points to vanquish the Aeroplan enemy. We were ready for a bloodbath, but we were convinced that we would prevail.

When we arrived at HQ, I had prepped everyone that Aeroplan was the master of playing head games (remember they waited until 11:59 p.m. to reactive my twenty Baht Run accounts). I told them to expect to be left cooling our heels for an hour after the scheduled meeting time. I advised everyone to bring their own drinks, that Aeroplan wouldn't extend the bare hospitality. Finally, I warned everyone that they would be likely be flagged on a secret Aeroplan blacklist, and there would be fraud department hacks lurking around taking names.

Well.

The meeting started late, just as I had predicted. But only two minutes late. They didn't serve water, just as I had predicted. But there was an appealing breakfast spread and an espresso machine. And the Security dude did pull me out of the meeting ... to express his admiration of how I pulled off the Baht Run. The Aeroplan staff had a dossier on each of us that they proceeded to use to shower us with compliments about being such loyal and long-term Super Elite members.

The meeting only got more pleasant from that point. The general manger preemptively conceded that the changes they were proposing were not well-thought-out. He promised at least for the next two years, Super Elite benefits would be untouchable. And then he congratulated us on the Errorplan campaign, that our passion for the program was laudable, and as such, couldn't be ignored. Our thick debate notebooks remained in our briefcases. Our righteous indignation was swallowed along with the amazing coffee.

We had won without firing a shot. And it felt very weird and anti-climatic not to have the expected war wounds of a hard-fought victory.

But a win was a win.

Other airlines and hotel programs took note over time and realized they didn't need to risk their own local insurrections. Company lurkers on the different *FlyerTalk* forums started outing themselves and became transparent and accountable assets for both their managements and memberships. Informal advisory boards of *FlyerTalk* members began to be proactive sounding boards for programs. Sometimes the forces of *FlyerTalk* could roll back a policy option; other times they could merely mitigate a devaluation or dilution. But at least there was finally a recognition that there was valuable brainpower outside the four walls of all the programs' corporate compounds.

While the Errorplan campaign demonstrated that there was strength in unity and organization and a bit of loyal opposition amongst its members, the ValueMags deal exposed a far more troubling portent of disunity over the horizon.

The ValueMags deal put the whole *FlyerTalk* community on a level playing field with each other and with those websites that re-posted the deal. As in any game there would always be stronger and weaker, faster and slower, as well as richer and poorer. The access to the opportunity would be fair, but the results might not be. Wealthy early birds could force companies to modify or shut down promotions or literally run out of product to sell well before the expected end date of the promotion.

The reaction to the ValueMags and Emmi deals in the *FlyerTalk* community was not exactly class warfare, but there would be an ongoing fracture.

I would also now have loads of new competition in the previously untouched mileage scaling arena. I would have to figure out how to stay one step ahead.

Instead of trying to operate in the glare and the competitiveness of the big leagues, maybe it was time to search for new opportunities in the hinterlands of the mileage minor leagues.

Chapter 13: Union Jack . . . Jackpot

In the mid-2000s, the major airline alliances were in mop-up mode, filling in niche gaps in their sprawling networks, often with decidedly second-tier airlines. The Star Alliance had one glaring liability: they didn't have a strong intra-Europe toehold in one of the largest and most lucrative airports in the world—London Heathrow.

The regional boutique airline, British Midland, otherwise known as bmi, had coveted slots at Heathrow and, as such, became slotted in as the news Star Alliance partner.

bmi was required to ramp up all their operational standards to meet the Star Alliance thresholds. But curiously, bmi's frequent flyer program, called Diamond Club, was allowed to remain intact. Although it would have never been said publicly, bmi would simply be a feeder airline for a handful of western European cities to merge and connect before dispersing among the twenty-strong alliance. The vast majority of Star Alliance members would never interact with bmi as an airline, so even fewer would have any exposure to its mileage program.

bmi's route network was so limited and flights so short that its Diamond Club program actually had to work harder to recruit members by tempting them with generous awards that no other Star Alliance airline could come close to offering. Compared to mainstream Star Alliance programs like United, Air Canada, and Lufthansa, bmi's "work harder" program ethic, would attract attention and enticement by the mileage scaling crowd.

	United	bmi	
Elite Status Threshold mileage requirement	100,000	55,000	
Elite Bonus %	50%	25%	
Class of Service Bonus %			
Business Class	100%	200%	
		400%	with elite status
First Class	200%	300%	
		600%	with elite status
Minimum miles per flight	actual flight distance	800 miles	

Because it was difficult to earn a critical mileage mass for their moderate flyers, bmi had a "Cash and Miles'" program where 50% fewer miles could be redeemed for awards offset by a reasonable cash component. Whereas United required 80,000 outright miles for an international Business Class award, bmi offered the *hybrid* 37,500 miles and a $400 co-pay, making the award much more attainable to those members with modest mileage balances.

There was only one formula to scale the bmi program:

- Find amazingly cheap ultra-long-haul (over twelve thousand miles each way) First Class airfares despite the fact that such airfares were almost never discounted.
- Earn 55,000 miles to qualify for Elite status as quickly and cheaply as possible to access the unprecedented 625% bonuses on all subsequent First-Class flights. (600% First Class bonus plus 25% elite bonus)
- Then cram as many First-Class domestic short-haul segments into international airfare as possible.

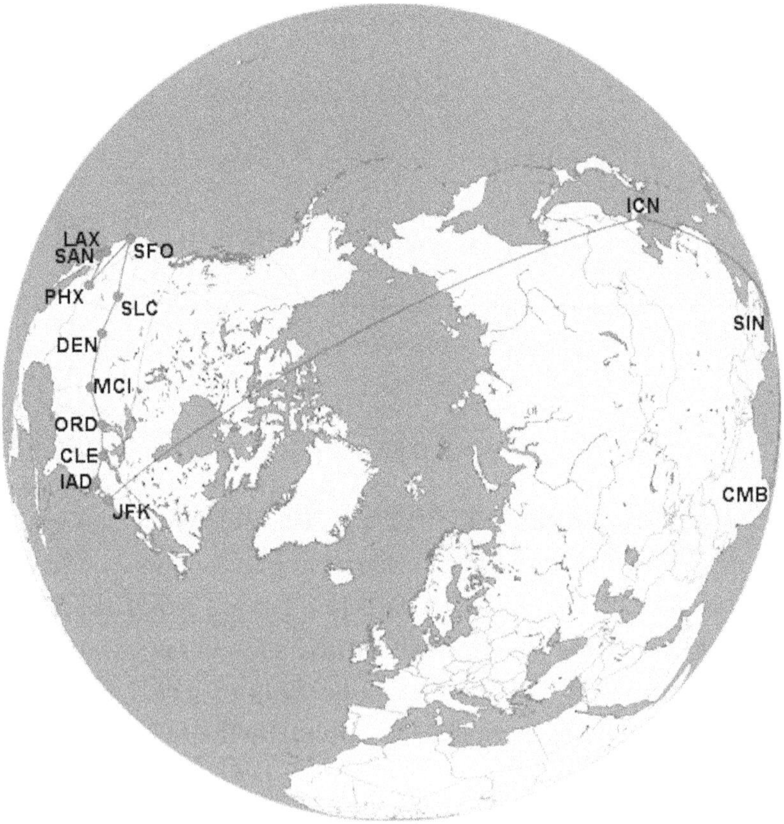

First roundtrip itinerary with no elite status:

Colombo→Bangkok 1,500 miles x 300% = 4,500 miles
Bangkok→Seoul 2,300 miles x 300% = 6,900 miles
Seoul→New York 7,000 miles x 300% = 21,000 miles
New York→Washington 800 miles x 300% = 2,400 miles
Washington→Cleveland 800 miles x 300% = 2,400 miles
Cleveland→Chicago 800 miles x 300% = 2,400 miles
Chicago→Kansas City 800 miles x 300% = 2,400 miles
Kansas City→Denver 800 miles x 300% = 2,400 miles
Denver→Salt Lake 800 miles x 300% = 2,400 miles
Salt Lake→San Francisco 800 miles x 300% = 2,400 miles
San Francisco→Santa Barbara 800 miles x 300% = 2,400 miles
Santa Barbara→Los Angeles 800 miles x 300% = 2,400 miles
Los Angeles→San Diego 2,400 miles x 300% = 2,400 miles

TOTAL = 56,400 miles one-way x 2 = 112,800 miles roundtrip

Second Roundtrip with elite status

Columbo→Bangkok 1,500 miles x 625% = 9,300 miles
Bangkok→Seoul 2,300 miles x 625% = 14,300 miles
Seoul→New York 7,000 miles x 625%= 43,700 miles
New York→Washington 800 miles x 625% = 5,000 miles
Washington→Cleveland 800 miles x 625% = 5,000 miles
Cleveland→Chicago 800 miles x 625% = 5,000 miles
Chicago→Kansas City 800 miles x 625% = 5,000 miles
Kansas City→Denver 800 miles x 625% = 5,000 miles
Denver→Salt Lake 800 miles x 625% = 5000 miles

Salt Lake→San Francisco 800 miles x 625% = 5,000 miles
San Francisco→Santa Barbara 800 miles x 625% = 5,000 miles
Santa Barbara→Los Angeles 800 miles x 625% = 5,000 miles
Los Angeles→San Diego 2,400 miles x 625% = 5,000 miles

TOTAL = 126,000 miles one way x 2 = 252,000 miles roundtrip

If there was a Guinness World Book of Records for the number of miles earned without any one-time bonuses or promotions, then the twenty-six flights First-Class Colombo-San Diego roundtrip routing would win! The mileage alchemy was a winner as well.

Earned miles from 26 flights Colombo-San Diego	40,300	$2500	airfare
First Class/elite bonus	x 625%		
TOTAL Miles	= 252,000		
First Class flights			
intl. Business Class Cash & Points award	/ 37,500	$2400	6 Cash and Points $400 co-pays
No. of awards	= 6	= $4900 / 6	Total cash outlay/no. awards
		= $815	cost per award
		vs. $6,000	cost retail intl. Business Class airfare

But a slew of disclaimers, fine print, and asterisks intruded on this too-good-to-be-true bmi mileage scaling strategy.

The $2,500 fare was only available from three locales: Colombo, Sri Lanka; Tripoli, Libya; and Cairo, Egypt. All three locales were suffering from various combinations of military, political, and economic strife. Besides the typically alarmist State Department travel warnings, even travel insurance companies were excluding these airports from coverage.

Further, the $2,500-fare only was available when originating *from* those cities. Starting from the U.S. would catapult the fare to about $12,000. So, either purchasing airfares or burning miles to get positioning flights both to and from these far-flung airports to commence travel diluted the opportunity.

Flying in First Class is normally unbeatable, but these routings took about *one hundred hours* of flying and airport connections, rendering your body (and maybe even your soul) beat to hell.

Still, I decided to do it for the novelty.

Entertainment systems were still pretty primitive with just a smattering of selections. I recall watching a Korean movie with no English subtitles just so I didn't have to watch *Mission Impossible* a fourth time. I had so many amenity kits and just a small backpack as carry-on that I implored the flight attendants to raffle mine off in Economy Class.

Cramming twenty-six segments into one itinerary could only be manually booked by a brave and supremely savvy travel agent in one of those three cities. Most agents were incredibly skeptical about why such itineraries had legitimate purposes.

Another occupational hazard of the bmi fare was the savvy and well-meaning gate agents once the routing hit the shores of America. We arrived in New York, mentally ready for the last eight domestic segments that would hopscotch across the country the next two days. A bright-eyed and bushy-tailed agent proudly presented us with a *revised* itinerary that streamlined the eight segments into two segments. She thought she was being incredibly helpful in rescuing us from a cruel travel manager. She was crestfallen when we rebuffed her spirit of generosity and concern and demanded our eight-flight segment marathon be reinstated.

I had an existing family trip to nearby Nepal and the following year to Malaysia, so I was able to sneak in a few First-Class trips without any positioning flights. Racking up a cool million miles.

One of my regrets about the Colombo, Sri Lanka project

was how little time I actually spent in such an exotic part of the world. Sometimes my zeal for the mileage earning strategies trumped my savoring the fruits of my labor. But there was one particular trip where my wife accompanied me into exploring Sri Lanka for all of sixty hours before taking an onward flight to southern India.

She endured a thirty-two-hour journey to meet me! Because she was using a mileage award ticket, the zigzag routing had several long layovers. Even comfy Business Class seats and airport lounge sofas couldn't compensate for overcoming the fatigue that comes with long-haul flights in a metal tube. She was spent when she finally landed at midnight. And apparently, midnight is the peak arrival time for Colombo airport, so toss in another two-and-a-half hours to get through customs and retrieve luggage. Unfortunately, I hadn't really factored her jet lag into the trip itinerary. So Julie had no idea I had crammed five days' worth of activities into three with 6:00 a.m. starts and 11:00 p.m. finishes.

On the third and final day, the climax of our trip was the annual Perahera. It was billed as a mesmerizing festival, celebrating the public viewing of a rare tooth from the Buddha. There would be 150 elephants tricked out in painted designs and strings of colored lights. They would be accompanied by colorfully costumed local dance troupes and bands from across the country. And no proper Sri Lankan celebration would be complete without firewalkers. It would be an unforgettable three hours of raucous and authentic fun that evening … if my wife could survive the daytime hours I had in store for her.

She had squeezed in a grand total of five hours of sleep for the two previous nights after my wildly overscheduled days. On the final day she had survived climbing a colossal mountain in 102-degree humid heat; visiting a pungent factory that made paper out of elephant dung in 103-degree sopping wet heat; missed eating lunch, as we were running behind; sampled many herbal remedies at a spice garden in 105-degree withering heat; and explored a secret deep cave adorned with Twelfth Century ornamental paintings … all in 104-degree sopping wet humidity.

Woefully, there was no time to go back to the hotel for a shower and dinner. We had to go straight to the Perahera. Our seats were in the middle of the bustling central square. But we would have to brave a crowd of tens of thousands of a tightly packed crowd, still in steam bath temperatures, just to get there! It was exciting to be swept up in the middle of the human swarm, but it also took an exhausting forty-five minutes to arrive at our seats that would have been a five-minute walk if not for the Perahera crowd.

Our pre-parade dinner box was presented by the company that got our seats. Spicy everything! I couldn't stop eating, but my wife couldn't even start.

The Perehera parade started, and it felt dreamlike to me. I had never seen anything remotely like it in my life. For my sleep-deprived, food-deprived, ice-deprived, downtime-deprived wife, the parade was a figurative dream. She was a trooper and soaked in the first three minutes before she joined Buddha, with his missing tooth, in the ether.

While that ultra-long-haul bmi mileage opportunity required flying half-way around the world, there was a new and limited-time bmi project that was simply a half-hour drive down the freeway from my house in Cleveland.

The airlines and their cousins, the hotel programs, started getting more sophisticated to prevent scaling, or what they liked to call "abuse." They couldn't actually call it "fraud" if you followed the rules, even if you earned millions of points instead of the tens of thousands as they probably intended.

Wyndham Hotels had a promotion: for every stay at *any* property brand during the slow season month of February, Wyndham offered a five-thousand-point bonus *per stay*, a seemingly innocuous term, but fraught with a complex and confusing definition, courtesy of Wyndham-speak. More on that soon.

Even though every hotel program has multiple redemption options with airline transfers and mileage mall products, the folks at corporate commonly assume members want to use their points for their intended purpose: free hotel nights. And because most members have busy lives and little leisure time to amass for more than several nights' worth of points, that becomes the default expectation of the programs. Corporate couldn't conceive of a member cohort occupied with underlining, highlighting, and dog-earing the program T&C and seeking out obscure earning and redemption strategies...

Like my unearthing that a Wyndham transfer partner was my fave, bmi, and the transfer ratio was a fabulous 1:1.

With opportunity came three challenges to overcome before actually greenlighting the promotion.

First, I needed to find a target hotel rate of about forty-five dollars. While Wyndham was an upscale hotel brand with high room rates, its portfolio included two downscale brands that met my affordable rate criteria: Days Inn and Knights Inn.

Secondly, I needed to figure out how to adhere to a recent rule that each room must actually have the guest check-in and check-out in person. Savvy FlyerTalkers had innovated something called a "mattress run." To earn points and status cheaply, they would find the absolute cheapest property anywhere in the U.S.A, book a month's worth of rooms, pay in advance, and then simply no-show. The local hotel itself was paid in full, so the local managers, who were typically franchisees with no skin in the game with the Wyndham loyalty program, didn't care about the no-show because they still got paid. They happily processed the members' hotel account numbers and stays.

But the hotel programs' corporate bosses didn't like the mattress run loophole, so they began requiring an in-person check-in/out policy. So, for my purposes, it was mandatory to find a property with not only a great rate but was also, in close proximity to where I lived. Fortunately for me, I found a Knights Inn about twenty minutes away from my house that met my forty-five-dollar budget threshold.

Lastly, I needed to understand Wyndham's convoluted definition of a "stay." A "stay" was defined as any number of consecutive nights. So, if someone stayed two nights or twenty nights consecutively, it was considered just *one stay.* So, the only way a hotel program could be scaled would require booking one-night reservations every other night for as long as you wanted. That was the strategy (or loophole) to comply with the Wyndham program policy, which was designed to protect from scaling and abuse. My strategy would be based on figuring out every-other-day check-in logistics. Pursuing the Wyndham/bmi deal looked solid on the surface.

Wyndham/bmi bonus	5000	$45	room rate
No. of nights, every other night	x 15	x 15	No. of nights, every other night
Total Bonus miles	= 75,000	= $675	Total Room Rates
intl. Business Class	/ 37,500 + $400		
No. of awards	= 2	/ 2	# awards
		= $337	cost per award
		+ $800	Cash & Miles co-pay ($400 x 2)
		= $1137	TOTAL cost per award

My gut feeling was to recruit two sets of labor pools to drive to the hotel on rotating days to check-in, then drive back the next day to check-out. Then, rinse and repeat for the duration of the promotion, which was the entire month of February. Each person would be assigned fifteen days of duty.

By the time I factored in the forty-to-fifty-minute roundtrip drive plus gas per stay, I realized it would generate too much labor cost. My famed and fabled labor pool strategy was out.

Was I actually on the brink of conceding that I had been thwarted by a travel program, especially one as small and not particularly savvy as Wyndham? I specialized in legal and logistical workarounds. Where the hell did my A-game go? I redoubled my scouring of the Wyndham T&C.

And then it hit me!

The rules required a check-in and check-out in person. But the rules didn't have the specific restriction that one person could only book one room. And there was no rule that the rooms had to be occupied between check-in and check-out, so we wouldn't have to physically stay overnight. Maybe, I could book a *bunch of rooms* under my name every other day, and I would check-in and check-out in person. And to be efficient, I would set up an account under my wife's name and book her on the alternate days that I wasn't booking. And she would check in and out in person. Obviously, I couldn't verify this with Wyndham corporate, but I sure could float a trial balloon run at the neighborhood Knights Inn.

This still seemed very edgy, so I contacted Randy, the mileage guru. I think he wanted to say "no," he was grasping to say "no", and his gut was probably hard "no". But he said everything I was doing was defensible, so I eeked past his smell test.

The Knights Inn was large, had two separate wings, and maybe three cars in the parking lot. The front desk staffer I met was the manager, Satish (not his real name). I noticed the last name on his name tag matched the certificate of franchisee accommodation from Wyndham. His family was actually the franchise owners of the property. I could be dealing with a potential decision-maker. He would have skin-in-the-game if he cooperated with my one person/multi-room check-in/check-out scenario.

Satish volunteered some key information before I even broached the subject of booking three hundred room stays during his dead February season. He lamented that business was so slow that the twenty-five rooms of the second wing of the hotel was closed off—no electricity, no housekeeping, but no cost. He also whined about the cold and wished he was back in India with his family.

I could potentially help him on two fronts—filling his rooms and fulfilling his travel wish to fly to India.

It was time to talk business.

"Satish, can you check availability for twenty-five rooms for any two-week window in February?" We both knew my question and his answer would be a charade, but a matter of politeness. It appeared that he just typed random keys on his computer keyboard, squinted for a few seconds, paused, and then gave me the good news.

"Yes, at the moment we can accommodate that group size."

I humored him back with visible relief. "Thanks for checking."

His eyes narrowed. "Two weeks is a long time for a wedding party or a business conference." He was ready for the "what's-the-catch'" moment, and I didn't disappoint.

"First off, I am happy to pay you upfront." Soften the blow. "I will need twenty-five rooms booked under my name Monday, Wednesday, and Friday for two weeks, and twenty-five rooms booked under my wife's name, Tuesday, Thursday, and Sunday for two weeks." As he struggled with the math, I chimed in, "Yes, that's *three hundred* rooms during that two-week window. We will be responsible for checking in and checking out of all the rooms each day."

To my relief he didn't object nor did not ask any follow-up questions. He was inches away from his guaranteed-in-advance, $13,500 windfall during his empty hotel being covered in snowfall. But I could tell that he sensed I wasn't telling him something, so I spilled the bmi/Wyndham beans by specifically tying it to his India travel yearning.

room stays	4	4	room stays
Bonus miles	x 5,000	x $40	room rate
Total miles	= 20,000	= $160	TOTAL room cost
		+ $105	bmi Cash & points co-pay
India Economy Cash & Points award	**= 20,000**	**= $265**	**bmi Economy Class award and cost to India**
		vs $900	paid Economy airfare to India

Satish would not only cooperate with the check-in/check-out strategy, but he would also be a beneficiary.

Success story? Not quite.

We were about to shake hands when he abruptly pulled his hand away. I could tell he was having an ah-ha moment, but it wasn't a pleasant one.

Whatever was next, I knew I was going to have to snatch victory from the impending jaws of defeat.

He wanted to be paid in cash.

He was afraid that I would use my credit card, get the Wyndham points, transfer them to bmi and then dispute the charges, claim that no-one stayed at the hotel, and demand a refund. It was a silly and implausible argument. But like the Thai Air station chief, I needed to assuage him, not get defensive, and try and abate his paranoid conspiracy.

Of course, I would pre-pay in cash, but I would have to pay in three equal installments: before, during, and after our stays, so that I also wasn't at risk of giving him all the cash and having him cancel all the reservations, which was equally implausible. The cash arrangement was acceptable to both parties.

Once we started the operation, it really did have a money laundering/drug smuggling feel to it.

I waited in the parking lot until there were no guests or staff in the lobby. The money was in a Starbucks paper bag, and it looked like I was just bringing a couple of cups of Joe to share between two friends.

When he came out from the office after counting the money, if he gave me an apple, the count was fine. If he gave me an orange, we had a problem. Suffice to say, I enjoyed three straight weeks of fresh from the Knights Inn signature breakfast apples.

And the best part was that Satish eventually volunteered to make our lives much easier. Instead of us driving to check in and out each day, he had two of his employees wear hats and wigs to check in and check out for us in front of the security cameras. Cloak and dagger stuff for sure, but certainly not necessary as we were already playing by the rules.

He whispered to me that he checked in with Franchise Relations. My heart stopped. What possible good could come out of that? Well, to his credit, Satish surprised me with his own sleuthing. He confirmed if there was a second person on the reservation as a roommate, they could check in as well. He simply added his staff names to my (and my wife's) Knights Inn reservations.

As long as someone with a pulse was checking in and out each day on-camera, we were all within the rules. Simply brilliant. Maybe Satish was destined to be the next Steve Belkin?

And maybe, I could use someone like Satish because my magic with bmi was in peril.

While Colombo was the default city to originate inexpensive

First-Class airfares with lots of stops to earn bmi miles, I was made aware of another option by a New Zealand FlyerTalker.

Auckland to Madrid for nearly the same $2,500 fare as Colombo to the USA. He suggested that I come to New Zealand (never been) to recruit a labor pool of college students who would kill to fly to Europe in First-Class three to four times during their school breaks.

It sounded good because there was a rule of law in New Zealand where I could have proper contracts signed with the students regarding their commitment to fly the full number of flights booked, my access to their accounts, etc.

The timing was perfect. My wife and I were in the nearby Cook Islands taking advantage of a $1,000 business class airfare on Air New Zealand from Los Angeles to Auckland instead of the regular $10,000 fare. It wasn't clear whether the fare was just an unusually short-term discount 'promotional' fare as sometimes airlines were known to do or if it was a mistake fare where a zero was inadvertently left off? After much anticipation, the airline decided to honor it. But, unlike most Business Class fares, the airline restricted any changes.

Unfortunately, it turned out I booked for July, which in my mindless zeal to grab the fare before it was pulled, I hadn't realized it was actually wintertime in New Zealand. The nearest warm-weather respite was the Cook Islands, a four-hour and forty thousand=mile award flight away. All the mileage earning from the mistake fare would barely cover my mistaken understanding of southern hemisphere weather patterns.

So, after the Cooks, my wife headed eastward home and I beelined west, for "Operation Lambchop" (as there are more sheep than people in New Zealand). Flying college students from Auckland to Europe in Business Class for free would be an instant red flag, as it should be. So, I decided to take the establishment approach for a change.

I met with the Job Placement Services staff at five universities scattered around the country to earn their approval to post this most unusual summer job!

Apparently, a New Zealand parent of a prospective student flyer scoured the internet to learn more about me and stumbled on an article that referenced the DEA during the Baht Run project. Once it was exposed that the DEA was in the same article as Steve Belkin, I was kryptonite, and my mileage mule offer was instantly exiled from the Job Placement listing.

I guess it made sense. As a parent of three kids, I would have done the same due diligence and probably drawn the same conclusion. But the aborted mission still stung, and it got worse when an article about a "Yankee snake-oil salesman" was printed in the college paper by a local parent. The paper never contacted me, and I came across as a mileage predator who would send innocent Kiwi kids to Spain unaccompanied to get raped or burglarized or get alcohol poisoning.

Yeah, that's me, alright.

The American beer companies had collaborated on a unified message as part of their ad campaigns 'know when to say no' when it came to drinking. I wish that someone had given me that same advice because it seemed like my mileage-scaling vision was getting impaired.

Chapter 14: Cocoa Loco

There were two competing narratives about the fate of Switzerland's troubled national airline. The public press releases gushed about a new era of Swiss Air as the newest merger partner of the burgeoning Lufthansa group, which had recently integrated Brussels Airlines, LOT Polish, and Austrian Airlines under its wings. Privately, Swiss Air did not share in this enthusiasm. The reality was, they were being forcibly absorbed by their traditional and fierce German rival north of the border. This new reality would include Swiss mileage program balances being converted on a 1:1 basis to Lufthansa's program, Miles & More.

The Swiss Air apparently decided to get their last licks in with a revenge promotion before they were integrated into Lufthansa in less than a month. And like Swiss chocolate and cheese, this farewell promotion was divine. Unless you were Lufthansa.

The promotion was simple, lucrative, and vengeful. Fly any connecting flight within Europe via Zurich on Swiss Air, and each flight would earn a five-thousand-point bonus in addition to the flown miles (one thousand minimum miles). The promotion was announced one month before the Lufthansa integration and would last only two weeks, leaving Lufthansa no time to squash it.

Yes, it was odd that I even sharpened my mileage alchemy pencil for this promotion. It involved numerous short-haul flights (up to eight) per day. And nearly all on those dreaded regional jets with cramped seats, low ceilings, and bare-bones service. The daily itinerary would be scheduled so tightly that one missed connection would create a cascade of expensive no-show cancellations. And even the on-time obsessed Swiss Air couldn't protect me from winter weather or air traffic control delays. The logistics were dicey.

With little advanced notice and with the flight window falling during Christmas break, I wouldn't be able to wrangle a crew of mileage-runners. It would have to be me flying a scaled-down version of the Baht Run—forty-eight flights in six days!

It would be a major time suck.

I would not only have to burn miles for a positioning flight to/from Europe but burn cash for five nights at an airport hotel. The payoff would be a measly four international Business Class awards for roughly $750 per award, assuming I did the math right (and spoiler alert, I didn't!); a serviceable price point, but I surely had no immediate need to boost my mileage balance with such a paltry mileage-take.

The value proposition of doing this "Swiss Revenge Run" was really plain stupid. The evidence was overwhelming. Yet, for irrational and egotistical reasons, this project was still a must-do.

On *FlyerTalk* and even the private forums, there was a fair bit of competition to keep-up-with-the-Joneses' … and I fancied myself as "Jones." I would have the bragging rights of being the only one to scale the Swiss Air 'Revenge' promotion because no one else could turnaround a decision to greenlight, conjure up a budget, and nail the flight and fare logistics required in less than three days as I could. When I announced the Revenge Run, I definitely surprised my mileage alchemy peers … just as I had hoped!

While basking in *FlyerTalk* kudos, my ego had overlooked one minor detail. I assumed I could find one-stop, intra-Europe roundtrip airfares for my targeted rate of $250. But, the majority of my travel was during the week, and all of my travel was within two weeks, which was considered last-minute by Swiss Air. And it would also be peak-season winter vacation break. I had *blithely assumed* I could just book a bunch of consecutive fixed-price airfares on the same route, just like the Baht Run. The Swiss Air fare structure turned out to be just as convoluted as U.S. airlines. Same-day roundtrips were pricing well beyond my target airfare. In retrospect I should not that have been surprised. This was Switzerland after all, where I still remember my daughter *not* being shell-shocked for buying an espresso for seven dollars!

Swiss Air flew to about twenty-five European airports, averaging three to four times per day. My fare research was becoming a disaster. Every possible European airport had twenty-four outbound and twenty-four inbound fare combinations, so it looked I would need to wade through 566 fare combinations. I had to figure out a way to whittle that daunting task down.

First, I knew I needed to ideally cram in eight flights per day. It turns out there was only one airport that had a short enough routing of thirty minutes to allow five flight frequencies a day to Zurich instead of three or four like all other cities. Stuttgart, Germany, had a super early 5:50 a.m. flight and super late 11:20 p.m. flight to allowed for eight flights a day. Otherwise, I would have been stuck with six daily flights that would have knocked down my mileage earning by twenty-five percent, making a stupid deal even stupider. Thankfully the Stuttgart fares were low and consistent all week. Stuttgart would be my base of operations.

Next, I needed airports close enough to Zurich that I could squeeze the other six flights segments in between 7:00 a.m. and 10:15 p.m. That scheduling restriction would exclude airports that were over ninety minutes away. Scandinavia, Eastern Europe, the Iberian Peninsula, and U.K. were crossed off the list. Which was a shame because there were amazing fares to London.

Also, I needed to ensure any remaining arrival cities had manageable airport logistics. I needed to deplane and re-enter security in less than thirty minutes for re-boarding. That restriction eliminated Frankfurt, Paris, Berlin, Amsterdam, and Munich.

Finally, I needed to nail that target airfare of $250. Numerous smaller and nearby airports had stubbornly high fares, even over the weekend. Dusseldorf, Marseille, Lyon, Prague, and Budapest could not make the cut.

Besides the mandatory Stuttgart, the only airports boasting the winning trifecta of low-cost, low-risk logistics and low-flight duration were Vienna and Brussels, but their low fares were only during four of the six days.

I would have to hold my breath with Milan. It was cheap, short, and the airport was manageable, so it was a natural candidate, *but* some wildcat labor strikes were rumored. I could get stuck or shut out of Milan, and both scenarios would have a devastating domino effect of making non-refundable no-shows for the rest of a given day's flying. But there was no way I was going to abort this project with so many voyeuristic mileage eyes on me. No, "Mr. Jones" would not disappoint. Milan would join the fray.

Unlike the Baht Run where the flyers were on the <u>same</u> aircraft for all eight flights per day, I had no such peace of mind with the Swiss Revenge Run. Every day—actually every flight—was high-stress.

I had to nail seven connections each day, and all were on separate tickets, so I was forced to exit into the arrivals area, then double back to the departure area, clear security, and hustle to the plane. No time to stop for airport meals, and the flights were too short to offer meal service. As a consolation for a meal, Swiss Air had a cute inflight ritual. Every flight included the flight crew instructing passengers to circulate a bowl filled with small Swiss Air-branded chocolate squares. There was apparently an implied Swiss social contract that dictated one or two squares per person, maybe three, if you missed a meal.

I flew with the same crew on my flight out of Stuttgart every morning and on the last flight returning to Stuttgart in the evenings. After the third day the crew had seen me six times, and I was easy to spot in my sweats versus all other suit-donning passengers.

By our sixth flight together, I sensed that I was being intently monitored by the Stuttgart flight crew. They seemed to be paying particular attention to the mesh pocket on my backpack.

The Stuttgart crew likely assumed I was a normal person simply flying back and forth from Zurich on their flight each day. So, their math was six flights x two chocolates = twelve chocolates were permissible.

Yet, my mesh bag looked like an unemptied garbage can that revealed many *dozens* of bright red Swiss Air candy wrappers. The actual truth was that I had been on twenty-four flights so far, so to me, the fifty or so wrappers made perfect mathematical and gastronomical sense.

As the passengers deplaned on the third evening, I was asked to stay on board by the crew. They had apparently prepared an impromptu "chocolate social graces" lesson. I was sternly advised that while there were no published or official rules about the allocation of chocolate, there were some informal guidelines about not being a glutton! They quickly commandeered my offending backpack. They disparagingly scooped all the empty wrappers out of my backpack mesh pocket. They looked at the pile of wrappers (well above the socially acceptable allocation) with disgust. Was I going to have to contact the U.S. Embassy to bail me out of an impending trip to chocolate jail?

Then, they derisively thrust the daily candy basket in front of me.

This must be a test. Did I understand the unspoken rule of one to two pieces? As I tentatively reached toward the basket amidst their deadly serious stares, I was assaulted.

With over one hundred chocolates dumped unceremoniously on my lap! And then the crews' sourpuss frowns turned delightful, almost giddy. And I realized that the dump was actually very ceremonious!

The flight crew had decided to research this curious-looking and chocolate-hoarding passenger and had discovered I was flying forty-eight Swiss flights in six days. For such loyalty, I had definitely earned a waiver out of the rigid chocolate rationing system. They had poured the chocolate on me to thank me for my business and to ensure I was well-fed, albeit not healthily fed. They were also kind enough to spread the word on my Vienna, Milan, and Brussels flights as I started receiving surreptitious napkins full of chocolates as I deplaned each flight.

And for the next three days, a similar "pouring" ceremony was performed at 11:57 p.m. as the last flight touched down in Stuttgart.

And speaking of rituals, the Swiss ritual for 'timeliness is godliness' was followed scrupulously for all forty-eight of my flights. Nary a delay.

I got a taste of how those Thai Flyers must have felt being on a plane for eight segments. Eight flights netted them sixteen dollars (not a bad take for rural Thailand) and netted me in Switzerland the equivalent of three-fourths of a US-Europe

Business Class award. Rest assured, we both put in the requisite time.

The Swiss Air Revenge promotion was proof that I wasn't afraid of proverbially getting my hands dirty in the dogged pursuit of miles.

But literally getting my hands dirty?

Could my fragile ego could live without being the biggest and the best…

… dumpster diver.

The movie chain Cinemark had a new promotion. Each specially marked peel-off code from a forty-four-ounce Coke cup would earn one hundred American miles. And there were no quantity caps. Movie concession stand prices treated a Coke like it was a glass of champagne—$3.50, that would otherwise cost about a buck at 7-11, not to mention the nine-dollar admission for each movie in order to buy the actual Coke cup.

bonus miles per cup	100	$3.50	cost per cup
number of cups	x 800	x 800	number of cups
intl. Business Class award	**= 80,000**	**= $2,800**	**Total award cost**
		vs. $6,000	cost of retail international Business Class airfare

Apparently, very few people outside of *FlyerTalk* were even aware of the deal. So, the vast majority of Cinemark filmgoers stuck to their normal routine, either leaving their cups on the floor or depositing them in the trash can at the end of their movie.

Ultimately, they would end up in the same place, consolidated into large dumpsters in the back area outside the theatre.

They say one man's trash is another man's treasure. After watching a film at a local Cinemark in Cleveland one night, I just couldn't resist. There was a decent crowd at the theatre, and just about everyone had purchased a beverage with the AA logo and one-hundred-mile sticker. And they all looked totally oblivious about the cups' mileage siren song.

The movie ended, but before I could scavenge cups left under other filmgoers' seats, the usher was ridiculously efficient and had already put them in a garbage bag. He looked at me suspiciously as I looked longingly at his garbage bag and shooed me out of the theatre.

There were maybe thirty cups to be harvested for a grand total of three-thousand AA miles that would be worth barely twenty-five percent of a one-way domestic Economy award! Was I really going to cool my heels in the desolate parking lot with terrible lighting, chilly wind, and soaking rain until the usher delivered the bounty into the dumpster? I guess I was intrigued how the bottom rung of the mileage earners ply their trade. So yes, I stuck around for the interminable eleven minutes until the usher deposited the mileage gold (plated!). I gingerly approached the dumpster, and the acrid smell hit me well before I even was close enough to open it.

But I soldiered and slowly opened the dumpster as the rain turned into more of a torrent. Every second that I waited, contemplating whether to join the ranks of mileage dumpster divers, the garbage bag got more soaked. Then, I realized that each gross, filthy, soggy cup AA sticker had to be practically surgically removed, and I had no rubber gloves. I took one cup home to dry and peeled off the one hundred-mile AA sticker.

It was official. I was in the hallowed dumpster diver club.

Did anyone hit that magic *eight hundred* cup threshold for a free international Business Class award going to the theatre dumpsters day after day, week after week, possibly even month after month??? If they did, they were too busy getting disinfected to post their bragging rights on *FlyerTalk*.

Although my brush with dumpster diving was just one time only and really only consumed about twenty minutes of my time, it represented a turning point. I had millions of miles due to my cutting-edge innovative mileage alchemy. And yet, I was scrounging for measly *three thousand* American miles in a garbage bin around midnight in the dark back alley of a movie theatre. And this was just days after I had returned from the triumphant Swiss Revenge Run and was lauded by my peers for executing it so lightning fast before the short promotion window closed.

But once the public adulation subsided, I realized the harsh reality. I had ditched my family over their winter break. The physical toll of a week's worth of being on a plane from 5:50 a.m.-11:57 p.m. being scrunched on regional jets with sugar as my primary sustenance took me another week just to recuperate from. And for what? By the time I factored in the mileage cost of the positioning flights to and from Europe, the airport hotel, and the time value of a week out of my life, it was a *terrible* value proposition. Maybe I had lost my bearings and my mojo. Was I allowing my mileage pursuits to distort my overall lifestyle decisions?

I could answer that question *affirmatively* with one word: Cancun.

I had been voraciously collecting hotel points to become top-tier elite and to partake in staying at their highest award category five-star properties. Maxing out hotel programs seemed to be consistent with my maxing out airline programs.

But during this moment of reflection about Cancun, I knew I needed to step back and take stock.

You see, I hated Cancun. And throw in Jamaica, Miami, Aruba, and Cabo, for that matter. The rowdy crowds, the commercialism, the marginalization of the locals, etc.

But that's where Hilton's five-star properties were. I had aspired for the elite access to free breakfasts, which I typically missed because I either slept in or had an early morning activity. I snagged free room upgrades, but barely spent any time in the room other than sleeping and showering. I was bequeathed the special key to the hotel lounges that had free happy hours and snacks. But the last place I wanted to be at 5:00 p.m. was cooped up with a bunch of other entitled elites in a hermetically sealed room on the twelfth floor. These types of hotels were clustered in hotel chain ghettoes, cut off from the authentic local towns. I went on vacation to escape the American vibe, yet these hotels were teeming with them.

I realized the vicious circle that the hotel programs fostered. During my Green Bay Packers trips, I would stay miles away in OshKosh where the nearest Hilton was and brave three hours of gameday traffic each way. When Hilton finally built a property in Green Bay, I would stay there and pay the extortionate gameday rates. I was so focused on the prize of top-tier status and the myth of Cancun as paradise that I compromised my time, my convenience, and my financial responsibility.

With *Kwik Witz* the pattern got worse because I sucked others into my vortex of earning hotel points at all costs. Instead of staying at a modest hotel walking distance from the downtown Chicago studio, I was insistent on staying at a Hilton. But the nearest affordable Hilton was forty-five miles away, and we were in rush-hour traffic both directions. And even that suburban Hilton forced me to cut more corners. I forced the crew into a cramped mini-van on the cheap instead of a proper bus for the two-hour traffic-snarled journey each way for a week. I really put the morale of my improv performers and production staff at risk as they dreaded that drive. And for what?

Cancun? My heart was telling me to travel to remote outposts in Indonesia, Vietnam, and Nepal, but my Hilton point balance and the heartache that it took me to amass that point balance was dictating to travel to American tourist ground-zero-Caribbean beach resorts.

Travel was so important to me, yet my independent thinking and decision-making about destinations had been subtly, but perniciously, hijacked by the demands of the Hilton program.

I put a hard stop to being hostage to Hilton. I tore up my card, canceled the Cancun trip, and basically used those Hilton points for their budget-brand Hampton Inns as a cash-saver when I would need routine domestic travel.

But more importantly, I realized that even with the airline programs, I needed to better manage how they impacted my overall lifestyle.

Instead of pouring over spreadsheets, obscure terms, and conditions and trying to squeeze every last mile out of a promotion down to the tenth of a penny, I would try and take a far more relaxed effort and attitude the next time a mileage opportunity bubbled up.

Instead of creating my own mileage alchemy from scratch and doing all the requisite R&D for the next scaling opportunity, I would just utilize the *off-the-shelf* formula of blindly following the patchwork of instructions that sprawled over a 150-page *FlyerTalk* thread, like most members with a normal life.

Chapter 15: Flying Blind

One of the consistent themes in every one of my mileage earning projects was my research and scrupulous adherence to program and promotion Terms and Conditions (T&C). That theme was also the source of heavy criticism leveled at me by some quarters.

The conundrum was that if I was really playing by the rules, why was I always so heavily reliant on scouring the fine print?

There was a key difference between being accused of doing something against the *law* versus something against the *rules*. If you are accused of doing something against the law, you have the right to defend yourself in a neutral court. While the plaintiff and defendant may have different interpretations of a legal precedent, the law itself is objective and transparent, and there is a third-party judge or arbitrator that ensures that.

When you are accused of doing something that goes against airline or hotel program policy, you are going against their in-house rules, not the law.

Airline programs have structured their T&Cs so that there is no legal basis for a member to seek redress in a dispute. Basically, any challenge that a program chooses to address from a member is conducted by *any* arbitrary decision-making methodology they want. In other words, in any customer dispute, the programs act as judge, jury, and executioner.

My critics would suggest a simple solution. "You know

what the risks are, you know the rules and internal processes are stacked against you, so just go find another sandbox to play in. Otherwise, if you continue to provoke these programs with mileage-earning conduct that they clearly don't like, don't be surprised, and don't count on any outpouring of sympathy if you have accounts shut down and mileage confiscated."

Therefore, the T&Cs had been my security blanket for more than a decade. I couldn't imagine just plunging head-first into a promotion by only reading the actual offer itself. Yet, that bare minimum of information seemed to be enough to implore the rank-and-file program members to participate in promotion after promotion without a whiff of trepidation. Maybe I could scale a promotion just as effectively by not overthinking it.

I had made that very promise to myself to not allow the mileage game to crowd out other more important lifestyle considerations. I was up for the experiment of eschewing the T&C deep-dive. Whenever the next promotion arose, I would nickname it "The Flying Blind" project—no independent research, just blindly follow whatever *FlyerTalk* thread was the source of a new promotion discovery and instructions to participate.

USAir's Dividend Miles mileage mall featured products could be paid for with miles that had outrageous redemption costs, or they could be paid for in cash at fully marked-up retail prices with lousy mileage bonus incentives.

Enter the Christmas holiday season. Inevitably, some companies would be looking to boost year-end numbers, so their sales team and management could boost their year-end sales bonuses. ValueMags and 1-800-FLOWERS were past holiday mileage mall earning opportunities.

The USAir mileage mall had structured some clever promotions in recent years where they incentivized shoppers to purchase a number of their vendors' products. Obviously, it was good for the vendors to have more sampling of their products and equally good for shoppers, as all those sampling purchases qualified them for a more lucrative mileage-earning promotion.

Most of these sampling purchases were relatively low-cost but were products that had perceived novelty value like cool gadgets aimed as gifts for co-workers and casual friends … and maybe even estranged family members!

There were two interlocking elements to their upcoming holiday promotion. (There will be an important reason why there are going to be a lot of caps and underlining and bolding!).

The first element was the sampling incentive. Purchase any five PRODUCTS, one each from a list of twenty or so vendors. For each different PRODUCT you purchased, your bonus miles would increase in fifty-percent increments all the way up to 250%.

The second element was once the fifth qualifying product was purchased, the sixth PRODUCT purchased would qualify for a 250% bonus, with no quantity caps. The promotion would be limited to the last two weeks of December.

At face value this seemed like a promotion that was so simple to understand and execute that I would be comfortable bypassing the time and effort on T&C vetting and just follow the crowd and use the burgeoning *FlyerTalk* thread as an instructional reference.

TrackItBack was a new company in the mileage mall. Their product was an RFID luggage tag which basically meant a trackable electronic chip to track lost luggage. Probably not the tops on anybody's holiday gift list, but this obscure product would become the most popular Christmas present that FlyerTalkers ever had! TrackItBack luggage tags could be purchased with cash, along with a mileage-earning incentive bonus of forty miles per dollar, which was nearly *five-hundred percent* more than any other product's mileage bonus. It had to be a typo. It was an obvious mistake that USAir would most certainly catch and correct once the *FlyerTalk* thread about TrackItBack's outlier mileage earning discrepancy would balloon out of control with excitement.

For two days there was no change in the TrackItBack offer nor any guidance from USAir's official lurker on *FlyerTalk*. The unspoken policy amongst the *FlyerTalk* crowd was never call any participating parties of a promotion. Why risk unwanted attention where a probable data entry mistake would not only be swiftly corrected, but the original offer would not have to be honored.

Someone broke the rule and contacted TrackItBack. They actually spoke to the president of the company who confirmed that the forty miles per dollar offer was absolutely legit and that they had plenty of stock on hand.

While forty miles per dollar was a far better earning rate than all the other vendors' single-digit mile offers, it was still not compelling on its own.

What made TrackItBack compelling was its positioning as "the sixth PRODUCT" that would earn a 250% bonus.

TRACKITBACK USAIR ANALYSIS

	all other products	TrackItBack
bonus miles per $1 spend	7*	40
6th product bonus	x 250%	x 250%
TOTAL bonus miles per $1 spend	= 25	= 140
		*average

The cost of TrackitBack luggage was irrelevant because the mileage bonus was based on cost per dollar, not cost per product. With confirmation from the company president, there was no quantity limit on the purchase of these luggage tags.

Before the math really sunk in, less-savvy people were asking what they would do with so many luggage tags? And the answer was, who cares! The mission was to buy as many of these luggage tags as possible to swell your USAir mileage account.

140	TrackItBack bonus per $1 spend
x $650	required spend for luggage tags per award
= 90,000	intl. Business Class award

There was no question that I was going to scale (and scale... and scale) some more this promotion. Especially since USAir was a program I had a grand total of four thousand miles in. It would be a terrific diversification project beyond United, QANTAS, and KLM/Air France.

There were two key considerations. First and foremost, once the deal had solidified on *FlyerTalk*, it was critical to move fast because the newfound level playing field had created much keener competition. For me moving fast meant within-the-first-eleven-minutes-fast! I anticipated a purchasing frenzy on these luggage tags, and I was not about to be locked out.

Secondly, I had to consider the optics. Although there were no quantity caps and this deal was squeaky clean, I was still questioning that whether there could possibly be blowback by USAir and *FlyerTalk* regulars if I purchased millions of points worth of luggage tags in my personal account. Perhaps, I should spread things out ... legally.

Over the next hour, I recruited cooperative family, friends, and my award-booking service staff to open USAir accounts that I would use to funnel TrackItBack mileage earning. They each opened their own USAir accounts in their own names and personal info. Then, they forwarded me their log-in info, and that was the beginning and end of their involvement. I changed their log-in info so I would have exclusive virtual access to their accounts, and I started loading all twenty accounts with $1,800-worth of TrackitBack luggage tags earning two hundred thousand miles per account. This earliest bird got four million miles worth of worms, good for about thirty-five international Business Class awards. This amount of mileage scaling was not addictive hoarding nor reckless greed. It was extremely well-thought-out ... for a change! I had made a multi-year commitment to several charities to supply miles for their fundraising raffles, so twenty-five percent of the miles were already spoken for. My daughter had reached travel-ready age and had close friends who had never left Ohio and were unlikely to do so anytime soon. So, she was allowed to invite two friends on our next few family trips to Asia, which consumed another twenty-five percent. And I had started a solar energy equipment start-up business based in India that required ongoing travel for me and a couple of staff, eating up another twenty-five percent. The last twenty-five percent would be for future, yet unplanned travel. The slush fund.

I quickly purchased the five PRODUCTS that cost seventy-five dollars for each of the twenty accounts to qualify for the 250% bonus for the sixth PRODUCT, TrackitBack luggage tags. I dutifully followed the *FlyerTalk* pack.

Three weeks later, 2,250 luggage tags arrived. They were too high-concept for my salt-of-the-earth hometown friends and family, so after begging people to take them for free, I still had 2,238 left!

There was one FlyerTalker who had donated a bunch to an organization supporting Israeli soldiers. If a soldier or their equipment got lost during a combat operation, they could be tracked and hopefully rescued. So, I followed suit.

Fine.

A month later, the miles started posting to the twenty accounts, but all had one hundred thousand instead of two hundred thousand miles. As the *FlyerTalk* thread had revealed that hundreds of members had their mileage bonuses post correctly, I was confident that it was a routine fat-finger data input hiccup. USAir routinely agreed to investigate the fifty percent shortfall, but they didn't seem concerned either.

After a few days, I received an email, and guess what words were in the very first sentence of their email response??!!

"Terms and Conditions" and "products."

I was advised that according to the Terms and Conditions, some of my purchases didn't qualify as eligible products. How could I have possibly screwed up such a straightforward promotion? No one else on *FlyerTalk* had any mileage-crediting issues.

Yet, USAir was claiming only two of my five purchases were qualifying, so TrackitBack wasn't my sixth purchase for a 250% bonus, it was my third purchase, so it only earned a 150% bonus.

I frantically contacted the USAir mileage-mall customer service center and asked to speak to a supervisor to clear up the obvious misunderstanding on their end. The agent denied the request, and it seemed like they were expecting my call. The agent accused me of misunderstanding the promotion … and that of all people, I should have known better to do more due diligence.

Ironic. The program's primary complaint about me was my being so persnickety about T&Cs, and here I was being singled out for *not* being persnickety at all.

And you wonder why I was so cynical about these programs?!

The agent impatiently explained my poor comprehension skills.

The other three of my purchases didn't qualify because they weren't PRODUCTS, they were **"ITEMS."**

Say what? I can't make this stuff up.

They emailed the specific T&C buried in the legalese that delineated between a product vs. an item. I asked if other people were tripped up by this hair-splitting detail. Nope, I was the only one. And apparently, they were right. On the *FlyerTalk* thread, everyone was in celebration mode. Not one member's qualifying purchases had gone sideways.

Ughh.

Every vendor had a product merchandise list, included were gift cards. There was nothing in the big print anywhere on the mileage mall site that alerted that gift cards were an item, *not* a product. Nor were there any home page alerts that gift cards weren't eligible for the promotion. Ironically, the gift card items were more expensive than some of the other qualifying products.

But rules were rules. And I had not followed them, and there was no redress.

So, I had purchased from the correct qualifying companies, but I had purchased incorrect items instead of correct products.

My 'Flying Blind' project lived up to its billing. Without the brightly-colored orange batons of the T&Cs, it was no wonder that project 'Flying Blind' came to a crash landing for me. While there was no appeal process with USAir, I did have one extrajudicial option—the irrepressible Randy Petersen. I hated to tap into his political capital, but he was my last resort to keep from losing two million miles. He scolded me for not following the *FlyerTalk* a little bit more carefully, but my oversight was still more than defensible. He assessed that no casual participant of the TrackItBack promotion who didn't have the *FlyerTalk* thread as a cheat sheet would ever think to master six pages of Terms and Conditions. They would rely on the straightforward promotion instructions on the mileage mall home page. For Randy, it was an open-and-shut issue of consumer protection and fairness.

He went to bat for me with USAir and ultimately succeeded in getting the full mileage earning reinstated. Without Randy, I would have been stuck with USAir's kangaroo court verdict.

Opening twenty US Air accounts would turn out to reverberate for years. USAir soon had semi-annual mileage transfers for one cent per mile with a one-hundred-percent bonus. If you had only one account and no friends/family that had miles they could part with, the transfer bonus was unworkable.

But with twenty accounts, I could do twenty sets of transfers of one cent pinging between all twenty accounts and earn an extra two million points—and another twenty international Business Class awards—every time this transfer offer surfaced!

Growing up the son of a concert promoter, I marveled at the seeming unattainable status of the rock stars that he produced. Imagine the shock both of father and son when I was contacted to headline the Lollapalooza of the mileage world.

Chapter 16: Paper or Plastic?

Frequent Traveler University and the Chicago Seminars were next-level *FlyerTalk* community gatherings. They were annual educational conferences attracting several hundred attendees. There were specific classes about every aspect of the mileage game for newbies to wannabe experts conducted by regulars like me.

I had been invited as a featured speaker at these events for four years straight. Topics ranged from scaling escapades to redeeming miles without ever having to use the extortionate Standard/Peak awards. Like every other speaker, I had implicitly presented a bullish perspective about the mileage game.

The upcoming conference in 2011 would be different. I had been asking myself many hard-hitting questions about the future of the mileage game. Was the mileage-game party faithful ready for a dose of seeming heresy from one of their own?

I was the final speaker of Chicago Seminars, and the subject was "'beaubo (my *FlyerTalk* handle named after my second son) — Go Big Or Go Home." Little did anyone know that I was actually ready to Go Home, and I wanted everyone to be braced for a similar path down the line.

While most of the pundits agreed that the programs had adapted a downward trajectory, they all felt that these negative changes were for the most part incremental: death by a thousand cuts, but there were still hundreds of cuts over many years still to come. Whereas I felt that the programs had cloaked daggers, ready for a far swifter kill.

The airlines had vastly improved their ability to protect their programs from what they perceived was a small, but persistent group of gamers, hackers, and my favorite word, abusers! They invested in far more sophisticated software to better profile customers earning and redeeming patterns. Additionally, they secured an antitrust exemption for their security and fraud departments in order to cooperate more effectively to catch people in the burgeoning mileage brokering business. Soon, we saw better structuring of promotions with quantity and/or time limit caps, or sometimes both. I don't begrudge the airlines for doing any of these things.

But the game-changing moment in the industry was missed by many who either didn't understand the canary in the coal mine, or they understood it and just didn't want to believe it.

The airlines finally realized (after twenty-five years!) that their most valuable customer was a *profitable* traveler, not a frequent traveler.

And it made total sense.

The frequent flyer would spend hours figuring out how to continue flying a lot for super cheap, and then redeeming the most valuable award, an international Business Class award, and often on an airline's partner, which had a hard cost for the airline program.

The profitable traveler usually booked airfares based on convenience, not cost. They were way far too busy to understand or care about the program. They would often redeem the domestic Economy award on the host airline as soon as they earned twenty-five thousand miles, which cost the program next to nothing. Or, if they really wanted the international Business Class award, they would have neither the time nor sophistication to redeem low-cost "Saver" awards. They would simply use the "Peak/Standard" award that could be 250 to 400 percent more.

I had perceived that was the airlines' new pivot: *toward* the rich and naive and *away* from the not rich, modest, and savvy. It was their gold, so they made the rules.

And I had proof to back up my hunch. But since the pivot I was about to describe was very incremental, I wasn't sure the audience would appreciate the future significance. But I gave it a go.

"My city, Cleveland, is a test locale for a seemingly innocuous pilot program. Continental will be offering a one-day, OnePass Elite status package for fifty dollars, including all the extras: preferred check-in, bigger baggage allowance, lounge access, preferred seating assignments, preferred boarding, and one hundred percent bonus miles for that flight. It seems like a lot of money for all of us used to getting this stuff for free as top-tier status members."

I saw in the crowd a lot of head-turning and eye-rolling. Nope, this crowd was not initially going to take my canary in the coal mine warning seriously. So, I figured I'd just rush through the rest of the analysis.

"Keep in mind, Continental will be selling something in a one-minute cash transaction that has taken most of you elite members a year of exerting supreme time, effort, and brainpower to earn."

Nothing like dredging up fairness and class warfare to bring the room back.

And then I extrapolated from there to predict what no one

else wanted to hear—that frequent flyers would be completely replaced by profitable flyers.

"If Continental could monetize access to elite benefits to anyone with cash-on-the-barrel, what would stop them from monetizing other products? Maybe they would start allowing for the purchase of upgrades?"

"Competition for upgrades was typically between the different levels of elite status. But what if the competition shifted to top-tier elites versus cash-on-hand by any random passengers with minimal or even zero loyalty? Who would Continental prefer? It wasn't a rhetorical question. Loyalty was intangible and money was tangible … and profitable."

The murmuring in the crowd was loud and agitated, and I had to pause for about thirty seconds until the din died down. I soldiered on.

"Currently, miles were only available for purchase in small batches and mainly as a courtesy to top off an award. The price was steep at three and a half to four cents per mile. What if the airlines were willing to sell bigger batches of miles at the same exorbitant price to people without a high mileage balance but had a big bank balance or their company's piggy bank? The rich and clueless would likely have no problem buying a lot of miles for cash on demand instead of having to wait for them to accumulate more cheaply by slogging through a bunch of flights, like us in the mileage game world."

"And to make sure that this new rich and clueless group didn't have to worry about the non-bankrolled but savvy group crowding them out, why wouldn't the airlines ultimately change the rules for elite qualification?

"Instead of the number of *how many flight segments* would be flown, why wouldn't the new metric be the amount *of revenue* would be generated for the airline. If a high fare was flown, the mileage earning bonuses should be significant, as high as 150 percent. But progressively lower fares should earn progressively less, as low as just twenty-five percent for the crazy cheap airfares we were used to earning one hundred percent or more bonuses.

Over time, why wouldn't the mileage runners, the gamers, and the travel hackers be eliminated from the ranks of the top-tier status?"

As a portent programs were already shifting their identities from "frequent flyer" programs to "loyalty" programs. And revenue, not flying frequency, would determine loyalty.

When I was finished with my bleak prognostications about the mileage game, the room of 450 attendees was shell-shocked. It was like *Invasion of the Mileage Snatchers*. The crowd was incredulous. "Who the hell stole Steve Belkin's soul?"

Everyone waited in hushed tones for me to circle back from the dark side and conclude with a hopeful and inspiring call to arms to defend against this impending mileage menace.

But I didn't.

I couldn't in good conscience implore the *FlyerTalk* troops to rise and fight these emerging trends. I did not cheerlead that we had strength in numbers. I did not reassure that Randy's bully pulpit would be our salvation. And I did not suggest that we could vote with our wallets to support compliant programs.

I felt strongly that the programs were ready to pounce on our mileage game cohort that they perceived had under-spent and over-redeemed for more than a decade, and now we were going to be marginalized. It would be a futile fight. I was simply the first to be so publicly brazen and fatalistic to declare that nothing would be able to stop it.

Randy hadn't written extensively about the coming era of monetization in his publication *Inside Flyer*. There were no major threads on *FlyerTalk* with thousands of posts predicting this apocalypse. Many thought my speech was just sour grapes because I couldn't earn a ba-jillion miles in one swoop anymore, but they assured themselves that for the normal FlyerTalkers, things would be OK.

Two months later, the next conference organizers asked if I intended to preach a similar perspective. I requested permission to do so, fully prepared to be disinvited. Instead, the event organizers just ensured their attendees knew the subject matter in advance. The topic was simply named- "beaubo: The Contrarian." And it was moved from the closing speech of the conference to a less anti-climactic slot.

I ended up attracting a main-ballroom crowd in the conference room and had to start ten minutes late because I couldn't be heard over the sound of metal clicking as attendees brought in chairs from the adjoining conference room to squeeze in.

Because of my newfound bearish approach, the conference did not want my perspective to go unanswered, so they planned a roundtable discussion where other experts could poke holes in my theories … and vice versa. It was a spirited session. My extrapolation about programs moving from frequency to profitability was based on simple rational economic theory for *any* industry. Corporate balance sheets are ultimately judged on profits, not revenue. My one hundred flights yielding $1,000 profit was far less attractive than another customer's twenty flights yielding $3,000 profit.

There just wasn't an argument that the value of volume trumps profitability.

I was right, but I was too early to convince the masses. After that conference, I was *persona non grata* at future conferences, although my relations with the other regulars remained strong.

Still, there was a lot of negativity on *FlyerTalk* accusing me of being a buzzkill. And a few sympathetic notes ... right message, wrong venue.

I have to admit, I was disappointed. I decided to take a short self-exile from *FlyerTalk.*

As a big devaluation had already taken place in the late 2000s, newbies after 2010 had no problem with a Business Class award requiring award redemptions for 125-140,000 miles to Europe to Europe instead of 75-90,000 miles; 160-180,000 miles to Asia, instead of 90-120,000 miles. What was the new devalued normal for grizzled veterans like me was simply normal for the new wave of believers.

While I was rushing around the world to squeeze the last bastion of value out of my United lies before their impending devaluation, the rest of my mileage peers seemed strangely unfazed. Instead of frantically looking for the next hidden scaling opportunity, they had found a steady and lucrative source of mileage replenishment: mileage-earning credit card sign-up bonuses.

This source had been around for awhile, but only recently had the competition between cards become so fierce. Sign-up bonus offers that were usually twenty thousand miles zoomed to as much as one hundred thousand miles. And every card company had multiple iterations of cards, all of which seemed to be available if your credit card score didn't suck.

Despite my sour attitude towards programs becoming revenue-focused and becoming untrustworthy with award devaluations, I was intrigued with this burgeoning credit card development. Most of these new cards had their own currencies like American Express Membership Rewards, Citicard Thank You points, and Chase points. These points were transferable to a bunch of airlines on an on-demand basis at an attractive 1:1 ratio. The flexibility of these points would allow me to compare multiple programs for a given award redemption. Based on the mileage amount, the airlines, the routing, and connection durations, I could cherry-pick the specific program to transfer my miles to. Instead of being captive to any one program, my miles would be like free agents.

And earning hefty introductory bonus points in these programs could be accomplished at the stroke of a pen for anybody with good credit.

It was time to get my three kids into the credit card sign-up game! The good news is that none of them had bad credit histories. The bad news was that they had *no* credit histories.

Credit card companies weren't interested in co-signers. The applicant themself had to be a good credit risk. The strategy to generate credit history for my kids was dependent on retailers.

Department stores like Macy's and retailers like Old Navy were happy to issue their branded credit cards to anyone (over 18) without any credit checks. They only extended token credit limits of several hundred dollars, which would ideally be spent at their stores, so there was minimal risk involved. I opened Banana Republic accounts for each kid, and maxed out their $250 limits with my own spending and immediately paid off their cards over the next six months to build a credible credit history.

Now it was time to scale.

Each company had a thicket of credit cards, but each sub-brand operated in splendid isolation.

So, in theory, you could sign up with six Amex cards.

Personal Gold
Business Gold
Personal Platinum
Business Platinum
Delta Amex

Hilton Amex

The same scenario was in place at the other large credit card issuers, Chase and Citicard.

If your credit score could pass muster, you could theoretically sign up and get approved for *twenty-plus* credit cards. Each one had sign-up bonuses ranging from forty to one hundred thousand miles with just a minimal spending requirement.

The credit cards had unknowingly positioned themselves as my next scaling project. It was one thing that the left hand didn't know what the right hand was doing. But each of the credit card companies had up to eight hands (sub-brands), and none of them knew what the other was doing.

I knew *exactly* what all twenty-plus sub-brands across three credit cards were doing.

My goal was twelve credit cards for each of our five family members. No high-maintenance labor pools, no cash in Starbucks bags, no deciphering arcane promotion Terms and Conditions. Just squeaky-clean credit that would activate huge mileage earning with the simple stroke of a pen on *sixty* Belkin credit card applications.

12	credit card apps per family member
x 5	family members
x 70,000	average sign-up bonus per card
= 4,200,000	Total family points
/ 100,000	international Business Class award (increased due to devaluations)
= 42	total awards

My kids only had a smattering of a clue that I was churning out all of these credit cards and earning all these miles under their names. Once in a while, I would call them to refresh my memory about their social security numbers or inquire if they had received any targeted credit card bonus offers in their mailbox. There was zero financial risk to their credit scores as the spending requirements were inconsequential, and I paid them off immediately.

While I admittedly kept the kids' sign-up bonuses under my control, their benefit was not meant to be expressed in miles earned or awards redeemed. Although they all were the beneficiaries of some cool travel adventures from the credit card points.

However, the long-term benefit was far more compelling. My scaling had generated *stellar* credit scores for all my kids, which would allow them to qualify for the lowest possible mortgage or car loan interest rates, saving them tens of thousands of dollars in interest.

For the next few years, more new iterations of bank cards were introduced, and we continued our sign-ups. A slower clip to be sure, maybe three cards and 175 to 200,000 points per person per year.

I even dipped my toes into a mega-scaling idea. I was going to advertise at local colleges. I would instruct the students to open up an account at a retail stores. For three months I would make purchases and pay them off on time to establish their credit history. Then, I would have them open mileage-earning cards. I would make purchases and pay off the modest spending requirement to earn the mileage bonus.

Next, I would transfer the point balances out of their credit card accounts into airline accounts I previously set up where I would control all log-in and mileage redemption. And I would pay them $150 for hopefully 200,000-300,000 points worth of earning. These students, like my kids, would have amazing credit scores to qualify for future low interest rates in exchange for my controlling their sign-up bonuses. Plus, their good credit history would grant them approvals for much higher credit limits that might otherwise take them years or decades to establish.

I would be like the Dr. Frankenstein of Credit, implanting innocent collegiates with turbocharged credit scores. What could possibly go wrong? Alas, my wife convinced this mad scientist that I had already had a nasty brush with the collegiate world in New Zealand. Did I really want to risk trashing my reputation in my own backyard as a sign-up bonus predator? She prevailed upon me.

Eventually, the credit card scaling era fizzled out as the banks and airlines finally realized these signing bonuses were not accomplishing their intended purpose to incentivize loyalty.

On the contrary the signing bonuses created a monster—a free agent frenzy, with everyone relentlessly hunting for the next big deal. Rules were eventually instituted to eliminate this phenomenon of 'churning.' Only a limited number of cards could be opened per year, or in some cases, every other year. New rules stated once you opened a card, you could no longer close the account and sign up again when a better sign-up bonus came along.

The credit card barn door was closing. But I got more than my share of mileage livestock, topping five million points.

My final mileage scaling project was so audacious that even today some of it is still cloaked under the secrecy of a Non-Disclosure Agreement.

Chapter 17: Who Is Minding the Store?

By the mid-2010s, mileage programs had caught on with the mainstream public, and the *FlyerTalk* online bulletin board benefited from a huge influx of new members. It was fantastic for our revered founder and all FlyerTalkers, as the newbies brought a fresh perspective, creativity, and expertise.

But it felt like some of the bonds of trust that united the community regulars were unravelling.

There seemed to be a bunker mentality emerging that future deals needed to be protected from *FlyerTalk*'s double-edged sword of popularity. Niche private forums were sprouting far-and-wide, sapping key sources of *FlyerTalk*'s creative juices. Once a close-knit community, *FlyerTalk* was seemingly devolving into isolated, paranoid, gated cliques.

Further squeezing the sense of trust out of the room was a forum called 'Coupon Connection.'

It was originally a matchmaking service for legally transferable coupons/vouchers.

For example, United used to include a 50% off hotel voucher and car rental voucher for every 25,000 miles earned. The 50% offer was based on high-cost rack rates, so the vouchers were of limited value. But it was still a nice giveback to offer them on Coupon Connection.

Over time other paper vouchers like domestic upgrade certificates were offered. Their value was better but limited, as they were often offered just prior to their expiration date. But offering them on Coupon Connection, was better than letting them go to waste.

The next evolution was domestic upgrades with long expiration dates, often up to a year. These vouchers had utility to practically anyone flying that given airline. These voucher offers were suddenly in great demand. So, to 'break the tie' of decisions as to which member should be given the voucher often depended on what the voucher's owner could possibly bring to the table. This was very informal, low-value bartering. Whereas the airline programs were focused on eradicating career brokers who would supplying high-value international Business Class awards. But it was technically bartering nonetheless, still against airline rules.

Until it became a 'gift,' which was not against airline rules. The new iteration on Coupon Connection was 'gifting.' Person A offered an item and interested parties would post their best offer. Once Person A chose their favorite offer, Person A gifted Item A to Person B. And Person B gifted Item B to Person A. Because it wasn't one reciprocal or concurrent transaction but two informal gestures, it still technically wasn't bartering.

People started offering international Systemwide Upgrade (SWU) certificates which had considerable value, even last minute. Even the most generous person would hesitate to gift SWU to a bunch of strangers. And then, a critical barrier was broken.

Instead of asking people others to make their best offer, SWU owners were requiring a very specific item of equivalent value in return for the SWU and in real-time. Coupon Connection began attracting actual full-time brokers who ratcheted up the value of trades even further, chasing after six-figure outright award trades. There was no mistaking these types of evolving transactions. The line between gifting and brokering had been crossed, and some folks started getting burned by trades gone bad. And they couldn't seek airline program assistance because they themselves were also in violation of program rules. And since trading wasn't officially permitted on Coupon Connection, the *FlyerTalk* management was unable to intercede. A lot of suspicion started permeating that forum.

The final breach of trust was actually within the programs themselves. Huge devaluations were painful enough, but even worse, they were often announced with little or no advance notice. Benefits were being clawed back. Fewer upgrade certificates were being issued, and it required much higher fares to use them. Lounge access was restricted. To qualify for Elite status meant meeting new airfare spending requirements to qualify for Elite status. Onerous fuel surcharges were further hollowing out the value proposition of the mileage game.

For me, it felt like the walls were closing in. The mileage game had ceased to be a game anymore. The challenge was gone. I was ready to stop playing this game and take my marbles (OK, miles) home.

As I was walking home…

I was recruited to join an uber-private group of just twenty people possessing different program expertise and proven skills in vetting deals. It was like the 'Greatest Hits' of *FlyerTalk* regulars. Signing a super strict non-disclosure agreement was mandatory to join. This was a painful requirement for me.

I had recently joined an award-booking service with a major blogger, and we had become as thick as thieves. In fact he shared a top-secret deal with me for which I would forever be grateful.

There was a glitch on the Hilton site. If you booked a room at the regular rate on December 31 at the San Juan Hilton, a five-star property, the rate would default to *one dollar* for every subsequent night for up to *364 nights* the following year. In theory, if you wanted to live at the San Juan Hilton for a year, you actually could for three hundred dollars on December 31, and $364 for the *entire* following year.

Knowing my scaling proclivities, my partner urged me not to do that. I complied. I simply booked a regular room for two-and-a-half weeks. My Dad booked a suite for $450 on December 31 and then three weeks for one dollar per day. And my father-in-law booked the Presidential Suite for $1,600 on December 31 and then stayed a month for one dollar a day. Why didn't I think of that!?

We booked this almost a year ahead, and Hilton had plenty of time to discover it. They didn't. At check-in they saw the mistake and tried to wiggle out of it. However, when it was escalated to the General Manager, he was quite impressed that we had discovered this glitch, and so he instructed his staff to treat us as special guests. And, of course, we did our share to enjoy the perks and tip generously. It was a magical stay.

The best way to repay my gratitude was to invite my blogger partner to my newly-formed uber-private group. My ask to the group was answered with a unanimous "no." How could a blogger withhold the private group's plots and schemes from his readership? They concluded he wouldn't and couldn't. It was a ridiculous supposition that I vigorously protested, but I was outgunned. In fact I was told that the private group had actually questioned *my* initial recruitment due to the public attention I had attracted with past deals.

I was advised that I was lucky to be accepted and that the discussion about my partner was closed.

I had to give my solemn word that I would never divulge the existence of our private forum to my partner, nor could I even do anything on his behalf as a surrogate. Not being able to reciprocate to my partner on top-secret deals that I might be privy to was a very tough pill for me to swallow. After a lot of soul-searching, I agreed and would not break my word.

The private group which hovered around twenty members, I dubbed the "Tenacious Twenty." They were just beginning to dissect a mileage-earning opportunity that involved a mileage mall. But there was apparently a separate thread that contained the actual specifics that *only* the administrators of the site were privy to at this point. The focus of their preliminary efforts was not on playing offense —how to *research* scaling *before* the fact, but rather playing defense—how to *defend* the scale *after* the fact.

In other words, while the methodology for this project was apparently T&C compliance to the letter of the law, the group was deeply concerned that it would still provoke the "didn't like it" reactions that haunted my early brushes with airline legal and fraud departments. And they wanted to be ready for a fight, and be ready to win it … in federal court, not the airline programs' kangaroo courts.

Whoa.

The only faint rumor that I heard about the secret project was that it would earn enough miles for international Business Class awards at about seven hundred dollars a pop. With the recent airline program devaluations, the new normal sweet spot for mileage scalers was closer to about twelve to fourteen hundred dollars. So, this project looked to be a doozy! Even though the rest of the group wasn't in the secret research loop yet, we were given a week to decide how many miles each of us would want to earn once the details were revealed.

So, we had to make commitments before having a clue what or how the miles would be earned. The Tenacious Twenty were not intimidated. We trusted the people and the process. Collectively, we committed to 108-million miles worth of whatever the hell was brewing in the administrator-only thread!

We were finally told that the stakes of this project were so high, there was no margin for error. The project was finally released to the whole group in small doses. The group had two lawyers who received the first assignment to do a line-by-line analysis of the Terms and Conditions and then find legal precedents that could actually be used to support our position in any dispute with any airline program in a court of law.

As a lay person I had no idea that the airline T&Cs could ever be challenged. This group was far more fastidious and thorough than me! They even scoured the T&C of any third-party involvement like vendors or mileage-mall management companies.

The rest of the group was finally given their details of the secret project. It would involve US Air's and Hawaiian Airlines' mileage malls. We were tasked with mastering the chain of command of the mileage-mall structure and process.

I learned that these mileage malls subcontracted out the management of these malls to third-party vendors who specialized in fusing mileage programs with e-commerce. These management companies actually operated the mileage malls—the airlines simply lent their company brand names for credibility and supplied any miles that vendors wanted to purchase to incentivize shoppers to buy their products.

Despite our best sleuthing, our group could not readily determine which party would have primary accountability in the event of a dispute: the airline program, the mileage mall manager, or the vendor?

Whereas I had always sought to avoid or mitigate any interaction with airline program brass, this group was 92% convinced that there was going to be a fight, and they were armed and ready!

They were in it for the win. It was an exhilarating feeling to be involved with this irresistible force confronting the immovable object that I always thought the airline programs were.

After a solid two weeks of legal and mileage mall vetting, the consensus was that our scaling conduct was absolutely bulletproof. The administrators were finally ready to unveil the proposed scaling goldmine.

USAir mileage mall was offering 4,757 miles for the purchase of annual internet storage space from a company called easyCGI. Storage space cost eleven dollars for the first month and one dollar fifty for each additional month. The Terms and Conditions were crystal clear. Listed under Restrictions, it said, "There are no restrictions at this time," and the Frequently Asked Questions stated, "Q. Is there a limit to the amount of miles I can earn?" "A. NO, you can earn as many miles as you like. There is no cap." The admins had taken screen shots with date stamps of every single, potentially relevant web page from the vendor, mileage mall, and airline, in case they tried to surreptitiously change them down the line. This was next-level due diligence.

The vetting didn't stop there. To make sure the 4,757-mile offer wasn't a mistake, we were tasked to check every other mileage mall. We were able to determine that easyCGI had a parent company called Endurance that had other subsidiaries with mileage mall offers. While not as generous as the USAir or Hawaiian offers, Endurance's other products still offered very generous mileage bonuses, all outliers. One of the group members figured out how to pull up screen shots of the easyCGI offer from a previous month to further reinforce that this was an ongoing offer, not a recent mistake.

I was raring to go. But frustratingly, the Tenacious Twenty kept on insisting on yet *even more* layers of vetting. Didn't these smart guys understand the need for alacrity to act before this revolutionary deal was discovered and pulled? But my old school approach, of "buy now, think later," had been replaced "think now, buy later." They weren't worried about the deal being pulled as it had already stuck around for close to three months in total obscurity.

The most painstaking vetting was the group's insistence on testing the deal with a small purchase and then waiting for the miles to post so that they would have a verified paper trail as evidence that the deal wasn't a mistake. And they weren't worried about the deal being exposed by *FlyerTalk*. FlyerTalkers were only focused on new deals. The easyCGI offer had escaped unscathed from the discerning eyes of *FlyerTalk* scouts and had stuck around going on three months.

Waiting another month for the test purchase to process and miles to be credited was a torturous wait for me, but I admired the group's sense of calm deliberation and singular focus on accomplishing this mileage mission.

The test purchase was a success and actually posted in just one week. The products were qualified for the mileage bonus and were credited correctly. The mileage stars had aligned.

internet storage packages	21	21	internet storage packages
bonus points	x 4,757	x $28	cost
intl. Business Class award	**= 102,000**	**= $588**	mileage and cost of intl. Business award (increased due to devaluation)
		vs. $6,000	cost to purchase retail international Business Class airfare

In the interim of our fine-tuning, the easyCGI/USAir project, USAir had introduced a limited time offer, a three-month trial basis of their top-tier Chairman's elite status for six hundred dollars. Under normal circumstances, the offer was a laughably awful value that no mileage junkie would consider purchasing.

However, Chairman's status included a *seventy-five percent* bonus for **any** miles earned during the trial period.

Game changer.

For the same money we had committed to earn 108 million miles, the earning potential now zoomed to 187 million miles while our cost per award plummeted.

internet storage packages	12	12	internet storage packages
bonus points	x 4,757	x $28	cost
intl. Business Class award	**= 102,000**	**= $336**	mileage and cost of intl. Business award (increased due to devaluation)
		vs. $6,000	cost to purchase retail international Business Class airfare

USAir had already seen the purchasing impact their no quantity caps had generated with the TrackItBack deal. So, we came to two conclusions about the lucrative easyCGI deal. One—these airline programs, mileage malls, and vendors obviously had the staff, resources, and past intel about how to properly structure a promotion to prevent or mitigate scaling that might have unwanted financial consequences.

Or two—as usual, these folks were just clueless.

The vetting was finally over, but another delay had surfaced. The group had a major internal political challenge to wrestle with. How should the purchases be paced?

There were two schools. The first was to earn slowly and steadily over several months. Stay under the radar. One problem with this perspective was that it could play into the airlines' defense that we knew that there was a glitch with the promotion and that we were trying to avoid detection. The second problem was that internet storage was normally a one-and-done purchase. If we were purchasing reasonable but ongoing quantities for consecutive weeks, it would create an unusual purchase pattern that could alert the other parties and likely kill the deal.

The second school of thought (of which I was the principal!) was to engage in a purchasing frenzy over a day or two days so that it would be a *fait accompli* before all the other parties could rally and change the terms or shut it down. This would be done so transparently and brazenly because we would be buying with confidence. We were doing everything absolutely right with nothing to hide. Each person would only open one account, not multiple accounts, which might be perceived as obfuscating our identities and intent. And everyone would use one credit card in their own name for the same reason. But that strategy would definitely trigger an intense, likely hostile reaction from other parties. Someone was going to be stuck with paying for miles well above what we would be paying.

Interestingly, a few years earlier, airline programs had been forced by the government to treat miles as a liability on their books, so they had to come up with an actual cost. Obviously, the airlines wanted a low valuation so their trillions of miles worth of liabilities wouldn't overwhelm their balance sheets and spook investors. So, they settled on a *two-tenths of a cent* valuation of a mile. Our targeted earning of 108 million miles had a hard-cost accounting liability of about $370,000. If there was a dispute, the airline, mileage mall manager, and vendor could share the pain of covering their mileage liability for $120,000 per party.

We battled back and forth for a week, but doing the "fast and furious" purchase strategy carried the day.

Maybe I should have thought of this earlier, but it was now my turn to actually suggest a further delay in the proceedings. I had a strategic suggestion that created a second internal political struggle.

I implored the group to let Randy Petersen, *FlyerTalk* founder, join the project. Randy was the reason we all knew each other. This project would be an incredible way to show appreciation for his shepherding of the *FlyerTalk* community for almost two decades. It was a sincere plea. The group was split on the idea. Everyone agreed he was a great guy and mentor, but could he be trusted not to expose our bombshell opportunity? Or even worse, if the easyCGI scaling deal didn't pass his smell test, was it possible that he might rat us out to the other parties? Just like their absurd and delusions about my award-booking partner, Randy was now subject to their paranoia. I was disappointed that I could not corral a consensus on Randy's behalf.

It was time for me to bring out the heavy artillery.

If Randy was in on the deal, then we would have his commanding reputation as credibility if there was trouble down the line. And based on the group's incredibly intricate defensive legal strategy, trouble down the line was going to be a when, not an if.

Still, there was concern about letting him in the private forum as other projects were being developed that weren't yet ready to pass anyone's smell test! So, we agreed to send him the easyCGI deal without letting him into the private forum. If he greenlighted the deal and wanted in, we would make the easyCGI purchases and input his USAir account info on his behalf.

We waited in suspense while Randy raked the project over the coals. We were poised with an array of responses to counter all of his expected objections.

To our amazement, Randy was in, unconditionally.

There was one last vetting that roadblocked our ability to finally pull the trigger on this deal.

Once we decided to go big, we had to confirm that our purchasing pacing and volume wouldn't overwhelm and crash the mileage mall software system. We posed the troubling concern to our e-commerce specialist in our group. We figured she would need a few days of expected research and testing before she could answer the looming and burning question.

It would require 120 transactions for each one million miles generated. So our final 187-million-mile target, would require about twenty-two thousand transactions.

In less than forty-five seconds, she posted … "spit in the ocean. Case closed."

Any guesses on my personal mileage??

Fifty-seven million miles.

It was go-time! It was gonna be epic. Both our pushing the limits of scaling history … and the likely fierce pushback from the unsuspecting participants in our historical narrative.

For three days our purchases were routinely processed, mileage numbers inputted, receipts generated, credit card statements posted. Nary a hiccup.

For the next week, things were eerily quiet. Wow, maybe USAir, easyCGI, and Freecause had huddled in earnest and found no reason to protest, so they surrendered without a shot. Not even an email or phone call to initiate a fishing expedition.

We knew we were good, but not that damn good.

And then…

Chapter 18: Abusers Or Abused?

A week after our easyCGI purchases, the Tenacious Twenty had smugly taken stock—twenty-two thousand online orders paid for, processed, and confirmed with e-receipts from the US Air mileage mall, easyCGI email confirmations, and our online credit card statements. With the audit trail executed exactly as we had expected, the miles posting in our accounts in the next seven to thirty days seemed a foregone conclusion.

Then something totally perplexing happened.

One of our group members, who had made a comparatively small purchase, just a couple of million miles worth, received an odd online alert from his credit card company. Some of his easyCGI purchases were being credited as refunds.

As the day passed, one by one, each member started getting the same alerts. Obviously, none of us had requested any refunds, yet *someone* was processing unilateral refunds, and fast.

We contacted our credit card companies, and they all confirmed the purchases had been reversed as refunds. But there was no record as to which company, USAir or easyCGI, had initiated the refunds, nor any notations as to *why*.

One of our group members was from Boston, home of easyCGI, and he volunteered to make a friendly inquiry to discreetly smoke out the situation for the rest of the group. Our collective gut was to never directly contact a travel program or vendor in the midst of a promotion, but we felt we needed to act quickly before things spun any more out of control.

He was told his purchases were refunded due to "suspected fraud." He assured the company that his purchases were indeed legitimate and authorized by him. He asked what was required to verify his identity and reverse the refunds. He was advised the company would contact him in the next couple of days with identity verification instructions. He reported the suspected fraud claim conversation back to the group.

We all agreed that the "suspected fraud" refund explanation was perplexing. First off, if such high purchase volumes were suspected of fraud, they would have been caught within twenty-four hours, not seven days later. Secondly, even giving easyCGI the benefit of the doubt that they needed seven days to figure out the suspected fraud, why didn't they simply contact each of us firsthand to inquire about the veracity of the purchases *before* refunding such a huge purchase? That logical approach would have saved easyCGI the man-hours to reverse twenty-two thousand transactions, not to mention the $450,000 that we had legitimately spent with them.

Bottom line, easyCGI had refunded our purchases on the basis of suspected fraud without ever having made the effort to confirm that it was fraud. And now they claimed they needed two days just to figure out which ID's they needed from us to be able to reinstate the purchases? It seemed simple to us; just provide them a copy of drivers' licenses, passports, or credit card statements. Whatever the hell they wanted, we would surely comply.

Our Boston contact reported easyCGI had finally reached back out to him.

easyCGI now advised that they had never actually made any mileage mall offers. Rather, an unnamed "rogue affiliate" had posted the mileage offer without easyCGI's knowledge or permission.

We quickly fed the Boston member follow-up questions to ask easyCGI.

Why did easyCGI even bother with the credit card fraud explanation about the pretext for refunds when they could have immediately used the unauthorized rogue offer defense?

We were trying to understand how come easyCGI was not aware of the "rogue affiliate" until now, even though the company's mileage mall presence and bonus offer were over three months old?

These seemed like fair questions, and we were poised to have a constructive dialogue with easyCGI. Instead, they simply concluded that "whatever the problem was," there was no mileage bonus owed since our purchases had been refunded. So, there was really nothing to dispute. And with that easyCGI promptly cut off contact with us.

We had anticipated many worst-case scenarios. But not arbitrary refunds. easyCGI was not challenging the eligibility or even the intent of our purchases; they simply denied the purchases, which were required to trigger the mileage-mall to process the order and generate mileage bonuses into our accounts.

Was a company allowed to unilaterally refuse a good faith purchase?! We weren't sure.

We reached out to the USAir mileage mall customer service about our conundrum. They seemed sympathetic but passed our grievances, like hot potatoes, to the mileage mall management company, Freecause.

Freecause apparently was the primary party responsible for administering and posting all vendor pricing, mileage bonuses, and related terms and conditions on the shopping portal site. We figured that Freecause would be able to coax their client, easyCGI, into reinstating the purchases so the miles could be earned. Plus, we were encouraged that Randy knew the President of Freecause, so we were relieved to have an active ally to expedite resolution with easyCGI.

While easyCGI had processed the original purchases in just a couple of days, weeks passed without any contact let alone progress from Freecause about easyCGI re-processing our purchases. Randy's gentle email and phone follow-ups were surprisingly not responded to by the Freecause president. That was a particularly foreboding setback.

After about eight weeks of waiting, it appeared that none of the three parties on the opposite side of our financial transactions were accepting any accountability.

If nobody was going to investigate what happened, then the Tenacious Twenty would start investigating them as we had an inkling of what might have happened.

There were no bad actors with ulterior motives at the outset but rather an unfortunate confluence of lack of coordination, communication, and oversight.

easyCGI probably intended to offer the 4,757 bonus mile offer for their company. But, it was meant to be targeted to one of their higher-cost products and certainly not the barebones priced items we zeroed in on. But the published offer clearly stated "*any* product was eligible." Or maybe it was meant to be *one* product purchase per customer. But the published offer clearly stated "no quantity caps". Apparently, no one at easyCGI vetted the offer details *before* they provided it to Freecause, nor did they do quality control vet of the offer *after* it was published online by Freecause.

Or was it possible that Freecause incorrectly posted one (or some) of easyCGI's mileage mall offer details onto the shopping portal site without having an internal process in place to double-check their accuracy?

USAir seemingly could care less about either party. They simply sold the licensing of their mileage mall name for Freecause to leverage as a credibility in order to induce USAir members to shop at the mileage mall. USAir was simply obligated to sell Freecause miles at a wholesale cost to supply all Freecause vendors' mileage bonus offers. But US Air claimed to have a hands-off policy to the mileage mall, so they were certainly not involved in micromanaging the vetting of transactions between Freecause and their vendors.

Our purchasing volume had likely exposed the sloppy vetting that had been overlooked for months … probably because internet storage space was an obscure product to be purchased on an equally unappealing shopping platform with anemic sales at best. easyCGI and Freecause could not care less about how accurately the deal details were articulated and published; nothing was really at stake for either party … until our unanticipated scaling.

Beyond our speculation, the indisputable reality was that our purchases reflected what *was* published on the mileage mall—not what EasyCGI or Freecause felt *was supposed* to be published due to poor or negligent vetting for accuracy by either party.

Freecause and easyCGI must have discovered the error of their ways *after* we had made our purchases. They were presumably fighting about who made the vetting error, who should have found it, and who would be responsible for paying for our mileage earning liability. That might explain why we were being ignored for so long and the resolution process was so drawn out.

We wanted to give all the companies the absolute benefit of the doubt. There were some honest but unanticipated mistakes made by the other companies. And we appreciated the fact that they needed time to internally hash out how to solve such a unique and unanticipated problem. We were hopeful that the expertise of three large companies' legal, financial, and marketing departments would have the creativity and resourcefulness to craft a workable solution.

We had conducted ourselves in an ongoing patient, respectful, and pleasant manner for three months. All of our correspondences were conciliatory and upbeat. We sympathetically acknowledged our need to be patient because the three companies in the mix were dealing with an unfamiliar situation.

After three months of steadfast waiting and hoping since the unilateral refunds, we began to despair. How could we impress upon the other parties about our seriousness?

We decided on a mini-public relations blitz. We marshalled our in-house resources, including a cover article in Randy's influential *Inside Flyer* magazine and posts by influential frequent flyer bloggers we knew. These articles were not meant to be inflammatory or derogatory; they were simply meant to factually explain our problem and respectfully express puzzlement about the absence of a seemingly obvious and easy solution—reinstatement of our purchases to earn our miles. Despite Randy's active advocacy, which usually was an effective bully pulpit, neither USAir nor Freecause, seemed intimidated, and they maintained their ongoing silence.

We were running out of bullets to get their attention. We didn't want to be adversarial or negative, and we didn't want to question their intentions. We wanted to focus on resolution, not blame assessment. We weren't interested in pointing fingers, just pointing miles into our accounts. We decided that requesting binding arbitration might be a quick, cheap, and easy means for both sides to address the impasse. And that the whiff of a legal process would telegraph our renewed seriousness.

No response again.

We had prepared for months about the possibility of the need for a legal remedy. But deep down, no one really fathomed that we would ever need to press the nuclear button. It was a daunting prospect.

While we might have the advantage of a case that had not been refuted, just ignored, the other parties had the definite advantage of deep corporate pockets to bleed us financially with a protracted legal proceeding.

By suggesting binding arbitration in the first place, we had inadvertently implied that we didn't have the financial stomach for an actual lawsuit. So, they really had no incentive to re-engage with us since we had no leverage or nerve. And it seemed they were right.

We started pricing out lawyers and getting their opinion about our chances. The lawyers we interviewed fell into two schools of thought.

The pessimists advised that easyCGI had refunded all of our money, even though it was against our will and without cause. Since we were made whole with the refunds, the defendants could claim there was no ongoing liability.

The optimists looked at our purchases as part of an inter-connected package—internet storage as a means of earning mileage—which was explicitly offered on the mileage mall. The defendants could not arbitrarily cancel one part of the package, making the rest null and void.

We initially did not want to make USAir a party to the suit. They stood to make a lot of money if easyCGI and/or Freecause would be compelled to pay for our mileage earning at their wholesale rate, which we estimated to be nearly 1.2 cents per mile. So, with north of *two million dollars* of revenue at stake, we felt USAir seemed to have an incentive to coax the mileage mall and vendor to cooperate and avoid a suit. But USAir remained resolute of not getting involved at all, believing that their T&Cs absolved them of any responsibility. Plus, unbeknownst to us, USAir was being courted by American Airlines as a merger partner. Being dragged into a lawsuit that exposed the lack of accountability of the mileage mall system wasn't something that USAir likely wanted to gum up their deal.

With great disappointment and trepidation, we all agreed that USAir would have to be named as a co-defendant.

Randy directed us to a unicorn attorney, someone who might accept a contingency case and accept the proceeds of a settlement in miles instead of cash. With 187 million miles at stake, this attorney was happy to sign on for a nominal hard cost for expenses.

As such, we could confidently initiate a lawsuit and not fear being financially bled to death from the inevitable delays from incessant pre-trial legal maneuverings and technicalities that he advised we would be subject to before we could get to trial. He had won a major class-action suit against American Express and was compensated in hundreds of millions of (nontaxable!) points.

His first move was brilliant. He titled our lawsuit "*Randy Petersen* vs. USAir / Freecause / easyCGI."

While the defendants would be poised to tarnish our group as a bunch of gamers, hackers, and abusers, they would be far more reticent to question the impeccable integrity and reputation of America's mileage guru.

Having the impeccable credibility of Randy atop of the lawsuit filing masthead was a real confidence-builder for the group.

It took months just to figure out the venue as easyCGI,

Freecause and USAIR were all located in different states. Then USAir churned out more months fighting to be taken off the defendant list, claiming their T&Cs precluded any legal action against them. Then there were multiple attempts to get summary judgements that would disqualify our case for a trial. Furthermore, they spent additional time trying to force in-person depositions rather than remote depositions from our group. And they cleverly focused on our group's few Europeans, to whom in-person meetings would mean tangible costs and employment hardship.

It was their first exposure to the legal system for most of our group, particularly to the especially slow wheels of the Federal courts. It was a terribly demoralizing and dispiriting shock that the first two years were just trying to get to the starting line of the lawsuit. But while it was emotionally draining, unbeknownst to the opposition, their efforts were not financially draining for us. They were totally in the dark about our contingency arrangement, the secret sauce to our unanticipated staying power.

At some point, it was probably more rational for the defendants to settle with us than burn through continued exorbitant legal costs that we were shielded from. But maybe they were intent on making an example out of us. They were committed to foiling any legal precedent that would allow future aggrieved parties to use the legal system, rather than their rigged in-house kangaroo courts, to remedy disputes.

Our endurance was finally rewarded after almost three years. We had a firm court date and a jury trial.

We should have been ecstatic, but we were perplexed more than anything. We initiated the lawsuit to get their attention to settle peacefully and collaboratively, not to provoke a prolonged fight.

But our idealism wasn't meant to be. Our lawyer explained

that while we had watched the seemingly arcane legal wranglings from afar to this point, we were about to be thrust into the belly of the legal beast.

Depositions.

Our attorney advised us that the actual process was a lot more go-for-the-jugular questioning than the benign definition implied. I was the first witness called because my fifty-seven-million-mile claim represented roughly thirty percent of the total miles. We assumed the defendants' thinking was that by totally rattling me, I would then persuade the group that we should cave, by settling or even dropping the lawsuit altogether.

My deposition was in an airy conference room in Boston. Despite being well-prepped about what to expect by opposing counsel, I was truly in fear when I saw nine lawyers—three from each company—enter the conference room. Not one verbal greeting, just nods, grunts, and unfriendly faces. Each company was represented by three lawyers. My attorney was annoyed at the seeming overkill, and he chalked it up as most likely a ploy meant to intimidate and urged me to ignore the theatrics.

My lawyer started the meeting with a brilliant observation that he felt might knock the opposing counsel off-balance and would help shore up my confidence.

He explained that although I was the common enemy to all the defendants, there were other enemies at the table—the co-defendants themselves. His proof was that instead of one set of attorneys to represent the three companies, each company had their own counsel … to protect themselves from the unspoken enemies—each other.

He surmised that easyCGI and Freecause couldn't agree on who was culpable for the poor offer vetting.

USAir and Freecause couldn't agree if their contract precluded dragging USAir into the lawsuit.

And easyCGI and USAir couldn't agree if Freecause was a "rogue affiliate" that had fraudulently posted easyCGI as a mileage mall vendor. He concluded that for every dagger aimed at me in public, each lawyer likely had two more daggers lying in wait for the other two defendants.

That revelation didn't deter the three separate sets of attorneys from subjecting me to a withering barrage of questions. The deposition felt like a complete character assassination. I was called unethical, greedy, parasitic, despicable, abusive, a hoarder, a schemer. It was hard not to feel rattled. And before I answered each provocative and personally painful question, I would look over at my lawyer, waiting for him to weigh in with a passionate objection. But, over the course of the day, I was left puzzled as my lawyer continued to let the defendants borderline defame me without any objections.

They chronicled my two decades of mileage earning history as a shameful exercise in greed run amok. At one point, during a particularly vicious round of condemning my value system as utterly irredeemable, I thought I detected a slight smirk from my own attorney.

Was he really letting me hang out to dry, or was there some kind of diabolical strategy that he was letting unfold? During the break, before I could register my sense of protest and humiliation, my attorney's smirk turned to a beaming smile as he clued me in about *the trap* that he had laid while being so silent during opposing counsels' awful questions.

When we resumed, it was my turn to activate the trap.

I conceded every single accusation, character flaw, and moral bankruptcy claim that the opposing counsel unleashed on the rest of my group and me. *Yes* indeed, the Tenacious Twenty was *obviously* the motley crew of lowlifes, scumbags, and greedy bastards the defendants had accused us of being.

So what! Clearly, the defendants were well aware of our reputation as scoundrels, so they had plenty of opportunity and resources to *preemptively* protect themselves against our kind. Why didn't these sizeable and shrewd companies have the simple quality-control protocols in place to keep mileage predators like us at bay? Or better yet, why didn't these programs actually hire guys like us to help them vet their promotion programs to avoid situations like this in the first place?

My lawyer's gambit was astounding. The opposition had damning and detailed dossiers on all of us, and our lawyer had *transformed* our biggest liability into our biggest asset.

They had a lot more nasty things to say about me, but since it was futile at this point, they moved onto the subject matter of how financially ruinous our 187 million-mile liability would be. The defendants harped on the "virtual mileage heist" that would rob them of over seven million dollars. I couldn't believe that they were hauling out an argument that was so incredibly refutable.

First off, their calculations were based on the retail cost of a mile, three-and-a-half cents, what USAir sells to their members. The wholesale cost was closer to one to one-and-a-half cents, which was what USAir charged high-volume purchasers like credit card companies and mileage malls. So, in one fell swoop, I chopped down their outsized liability damage claims from seven million dollars million to nearly two million dollars. Were they testing my understanding of retail vs. wholesale pricing, or were they collectively clueless?

Before they could change the subject, I barreled on.

The airlines submitted their own 10-K tax statements as valuing the hard cost of their miles for accounting purposes at *two-tenths of a cent,* which diminished the liability of our mileage down to $376,000. With three sets of defendants, each paying an equal share, the "financially ruinous" total would be close to *$125,000* per party.

In less than three minutes, I had knocked their seven-million-dollar liability claim down by *ninety-five percent.* It seemed like a severe blow to the credibility of the defendants by not understanding the basic math behind *their* monetary injury claim. And that on-the-record evidence of such ignorance at best and misleading at worst could haunt them as future evidence against them in court.

And I still wasn't finished yet, despite the opposing attorneys' vehement attempts to change the subject. My lawyer was equally resolute that I be allowed to fully answer the question as long it was unquestionably relevant as to how our group conduct had negative financial consequences. I was permitted to continue.

Finally, I concluded that USAir had claimed throughout the proceedings that they should not be included as an accused party. If they had been part of the solution, instead of ignoring the problem, they would be *earning* anywhere between two million dollars and seven million dollars in mileage sales. USAir stood to make a windfall, as opposed to the other defendants, who were contracted to purchase the miles. Yet USAir knowingly forfeited their mileage earnings by refusing to help us resolve the impasse, which forced us to include them in the lawsuit.

Further, the defendants didn't seem to find that employing three separate sets of outside counsel whose two years' worth of billable hours didn't seem to faze them as being "financially ruinous."

At the end of my deposition, my lawyer joked that the upcoming jury would ultimately rule for the party *that least disgusted* them. To be honest, neither party painted an overly pretty picture. Greedy David vs. Arrogant Goliath.

The trial was rapidly approaching, and while our contingency agreement covered most of the pre-trial costs, we were going to be on the hook for a significant five-figure out-of-pocket cost for going to trial. We had come so far with minimal financial risk. A trial was vindication that our case had merit. But merit did not guarantee victory. And the depositions that were currently behind closed doors, the ones that besmirched our characters, would soon be on display in the public record, and possibly even media coverage.

Our lawyer explained that we would be painted as despicable lowlife schemers, whether it was true or not. The jury would then decide if the companies were reasonably responsible in protecting themselves from our unreasonable, but within the rules, scaling conduct. Our attorney thought it could go either way.

If any of the plaintiffs in our group dropped out because of the fear of the inevitable negative public exposure, we would have to refile the suit from scratch. There were several plaintiffs from our group who had legitimate fears that the publicity of a high-profile lawsuit could hurt their job status or their client relationships. For me, most people I knew who had a fuzzy, but benign understanding of my mileage exploits, would soon have an unpleasantly crystal-clear lens. For some reason, this did not faze me. But the rest of my family might not be so excited to have a guilt-by-association stigma from having their son's name dragged through the mud.

The other issue that threatened our ability to keep everyone on board was financial. Despite the contingency arrangement, going to trial would entail a lot of hard costs that the group would have to pony up. And our attorney glumly warned that there was no financial cap to the possible spending depending on how long the trial dragged on. Financial hardship was a real consideration for a couple of the group members whose mileage orders were small to begin with.

So, there were three wildcat situations: getting tarred and feathered in court, actually having to pay for it, and the uncertainty of our chances to win.

Our feeling was that the defendants were blissfully unaware of our emerging internal fault lines. They likely assumed we were raring to go to trial with no financial encumbrances as they had *finally* determined that our legal arrangement was on a contingency basis.

We were confident the three companies had their own internal issues to grapple with. Was it worth the risk that we could expose proprietary information about miles pricing and create some new consumer-friendly legal precedents that could destroy their airline kangaroo court system?

The reality of a jury trial was likely spooking both parties for different reasons.

Days before the looming court date, the defendants blinked!

But they didn't surrender. They requested binding arbitration. It was the cheap, easy, and short resolution that they had *rejected* two-and-a-half years ago. Binding arbitration would ensure a settlement, but again, there was no predicting whether our assigned arbitrator would perceive us as victim or victimizer.

Our group was allowed three representatives at the arbitration. We really wanted Randy to be a commanding and credible presence, immune to the ad hominem attacks, but unfortunately, his schedule wouldn't permit it. I really didn't want to be the subject of another firing line either, but as "Mr. Fifty-Seven Million," the arbitrator would certainly want to see the head of the snake that the defendants had painted. Hopefully, I could shift the perception to a more docile reptile, perhaps, a likable gecko!

In preparation for the settlement talks, my attorney conducted a mock settlement session to help me best understand what to likely expect during the real thing. He conjured up uncomfortable and provocative questions.

How could I not reasonably be tempted to illegally broker my miles for cash with fifty-seven million in my coffers?

What possible ethical justification beyond just pure greed was I using to rationalize such a monstrous purchase amount?

Our attorney gave us a few doses of reality to manage our expectations. He felt that since neither party really had a clear-cut advantage, it would be important not to be perceived by the arbitrator as uncooperative or arrogant. So, he was insistent that we preemptively abandon all hope that anything close to 187 million miles would be the settlement. But he felt equally confident that the arbitrator would coerce the defendants to abandon all their hope that anything close to zero would be their mileage payout.

He advised us that the ultimate goal of the arbitrator would be to extract a mutually-agreed upon settlement that ensured that *both* parties were prepared to *suffer serious pain*.

He reflected that it turned out the best decision our group made was to scale on such a historic basis, since settling for *any reasonable* percentage of 187 million miles, would still be a solid number. If we had only collectively earned a few million miles, it was unlikely the contingency lawyer would have even represented us. He lauded us for our foresight in Going Big. It had given us much-needed leverage to level the playing field with the big corporate players.

He also soothed us about the blessing-in-disguise that the two-and-a-half years of litigation had yielded. In that time USAir was merged with American Airlines, so any settlement would be supplied in American, not USAir miles. That was a big advantage because the AA program had better partners in

Etihad, Qatar, and Cathay Pacific and award redemption levels that were 25-30% less.

Finally, he cautioned us that no matter how the arbitration hearing was ultimately resolved, that the defendants would try and slap an NDA on it. We vehemently objected to having to agree to the prospect of such a muzzle of our ability to trumpet our hoped-for bragging rights. Our attorney soberly reminded us that our case was still wobbly and had some tangible vulnerabilities. If the predicted NDA actually was part of the settlement, it would be a double-edged sword. If we won, there could be no public victory lap. The eerie silence of a secret sense of justice would have to suffice and would forever only be known by the Tenacious Twenty. But if it ended up that we got our asses kicked, we would be protected from the public humiliation of three years of a legal slog and nothing to show for it. So, we acquiesced that our attorney would agree to a proposed NDA without a fight.

And as predicted by our lawyer, those NDA provisions were indeed enacted during the proceedings ... and your only glimpse into the final resolution between "Randy Petersen vs. easyCGI/Freecause/USAir/Hawaiian Air" is the mandated language from Point 4. General Provisions; Section e- Confidentiality, Disclosure, and Non-Disparagement:

"The matter has been resolved." The Tenacious Twenty never really recovered from that legal morass. We lost our swagger. Our risk tolerance was dialed down quite a few notches. Our trust in the mileage game system was close to shattered. The group never officially disbanded, but a bunch of in-progress research projects quietly withered from benign neglect. And we all lost touch less than two weeks after the arbitration hearing.

In retrospect, the lawsuit was so incredibly bittersweet that we all blocked it out ... and in the process, we blocked each other out as well. Settling should have felt like winning, but in truth, settling truly felt like … settling. It was not a bad feeling, but it certainly wasn't a good feeling. I guess that's what settling feels like.

Just like the arbitrator had hoped!

It was official. I was DONE with the mileage world.

Until.

EPILOGUE

Unrest in the Middle East had decimated the tourist trade, and Hilton was not spared. To try and jump-start demand, Hilton changed two of its Red Sea resort properties in Hurghada, Egypt, and Salalah, Oman, from Category 5 redemption amount to Category 1. Meaning a top-tier beach resort could be redeemed for the award price of their budget chain Hampton Inns. Hawaiian Airlines had an unusually generous transfer ratio to Hilton points, and some of the Tenacious Twenty chose to receive Hawaiian Miles instead of American for their settlement, so I could easily arrange a swap.

I had a wild idea. I could actually *live* at one of these five-star resorts for a *whole year* for just a small portion of my settlement.

These properties offered free breakfasts that were purportedly so lavish that they could straddle both breakfast and lunch meals. After staying thirty days, I would earn Hilton Gold elite status and then be upgraded to a huge suite for the rest of the year. Neither property attracted Americans, so I would be *cause célèbre* at the hotel pool, beach, and lounge.

I was so serious about this Mideast Mission that I had my wife send out a discreet inquiry about a one-year sabbatical from her medical practice. And I hopped on the next plane to personally research my planned second home. Surely, they would both be paradise, but a bit of due diligence was in order.

The Hurghada Hilton was a six-hundred room sprawling monstrosity located in a resort town that was chock full of other six-hundred room sprawling monstrosities! Where a hotel wasn't hogging its private beachfront view, tacky souvenir shops and shopping malls that featured predictable brand name stores, stepped in the breach. There were a lot of signs translated into Russian. And a lot of Russian women of the evening trolling the boardwalk. Hurghada was basically a very downscale version of Cancun.

Hard pass.

Salalah was magical. It was the home of frankincense, and the aroma permeated the hotel. Salalah was the polar opposite of Hurghada. The hotel was petite, just a hundred or so rooms, and the town was rustic and quaint. No other hotel was within walking distance. It was empty due to tensions in the Middle East, but it was fully staffed. Very fully staffed! Every minute of the day during my short research stay, I would be under the watchful eye of some overly-eager-to-please waiter, lifeguard, bellhop, or assistant manager. While I could get used to a staff focused on attentive service, I was actually feeling more of a slavish devotion. And it felt kind of suffocating.

In the end my last scaling opportunity of spending a year ensconced in Hilton's top properties at a bottom-feeder award rate for a full year was a bust. I'm pretty sure Julie was very relieved.

I remember my former client, Green Bay Packers Head Coach Mike Holmgren admonishing his players for any type of celebration in the endzone after a touchdown.

He would snap "*Hey, act like you've been there before.*"

I have flown on well over a hundred Business Class flights thanks to my mileage stash, so yeah, I've "been there before". But even today, whenever I board a flight on a huge 777 or A380, I get a huge rush when the flight attendant directs me to turn left and enter the curtained-off area. I enjoy intently studying the five-page gourmet and wine list; pushing every button on the seat console; inventorying every little knick-knack in the amenity kit; excitedly accepting a glass of bubbly. Invariably, a flight attendant will saunter over to witness my childlike wonderment and kinetic energy. In a very faintly condescending but amused manner, they inquire "Have you ever been here before?"

With wide-eyed jubilance and exuberance, I always reply "Yes, I've been here before and I ABSOLUTELY LOVE IT!" Cue the air-spiking the football and the Ickey Shuffle.

Sorry, Coach Holmgren.

Lightning Source UK Ltd.
Milton Keynes UK
UKHW020816260721
387781UK00004B/714